COVERING CASTRO

RISE AND DECLINE OF CUBA'S COMMUNIST DICTATOR

Books by Jay Mallin Sr.

Fortress Cuba
Caribbean Crisis
Terror in Viet Nam
"Che" Guevara on Revolution
Strategy for Conquest
Terror and Urban Guerrillas
Spy for Fidel (ghost-written)
Merc: American Soldiers of Fortune (co-written)

COVERING CASTRO

RISE AND DECLINE OF CUBA'S COMMUNIST DICTATOR

JAY MALLIN SR.

Co-Published by
U.S.☆Cuba Institute Press
Washington, D.C.
and
Transaction Publishers
New Brunswick, New Jersey and London, England

P G PM

pp. 15-36 — Copyright by Henry Regnery Company. Reprinted by permission.

pp. 37-41 — Copyright by University of Miami Press. Reprinted by permission.

pp. 57-65 — "The Communists," from *Caribbean Crisis* by Jay Mallin, copyright by Jay Mallin. Used by permission of Doubleday, a division of Bantam Doubleday Dell Publishing Group, Inc.

pp. 67-84 — Copyright by University of Miami Press. Reprinted by permission.

pp. 97-111 — Reprinted by permission of the Research Institute for Cuban Studies, University of Miami.

pp. 113-131 — Copyright by E.A. Seemann Publishing, Inc.. Reprinted by permission.

pp. 133-146 — "Castro's Spies," five part series from *The Washington Times*. Reprinted by permission.

pp. 147-150 — Copyright 1982 by The Reader's Digest Assn., Inc.. Reprinted from the August 1982 *Reader's Digest* by permission.

FIRST EDITION

LIBRARY OF CONGRESS CATALOGING-IN-PUBLICATION DATA
Mallin, Jay.
    Covering Castro: rise and decline of Cuba's communist dictator / Jay Mallin Sr. -- 1st ed.
        p. cm.
    Includes index.
    ISBN 1-884750-00-1
        1. Castro, Fidel, 1927- . 2. Cuba--History--1959-   3. Cuba -Foreign relations--1959- I. Title.
    F1788.22.C3M25 1994
    972.9106'4--dc20   93-46178
                                                        CIP

Cover design by William R. Wright
Printed in the United States of America

To Kelsey and Brennan,
who will see a free Cuba

*ack*ACKNOWLEDGMENTS*ledgments*

Ralph J. Galliano helped to develop the concept of this book and encouraged the author and assisted the editor in putting it together.

table of contents

preface PREFACE

I have seen the Sphinx, the Berlin Wall, the endless plains of Africa, the dense jungles of Panama, the magnificent mountains of Bolivia. I have gazed upon the My Tho in Viet Nam, the Nile in Egypt, the Amazon in Brazil. I have flown over the Alps and the Andes, witnessed the terrible devastation of the last Managua earthquake and seen Paris' epic celebration of the bicentennial of the French Revolution. I have been tear-gassed in Montevideo and ambushed in Santo Domingo and I introduced Ernest Hemingway and Graham Greene to each other at Sloppy Joe's in Havana (it was perfunctory; they didn't like each other). I have covered some eight wars and many other violent manifestations of the human condition.

Over the long run, however, none of these compares with the fascination of watching and reporting the deeds and misdeeds, declarations and declamations of Fidel Castro Ruz. I have done this for more than 35 years. Voluble, charismatic and utterly ruthless, Castro has sometimes veered close to the antic, but he has also on occasion achieved center stage alongside leaders of world powers. The late dictator of the Dominican Republic, Rafael Leonidas Trujillo, is said to have commented, "It is my tragedy to have been born to lead a small nation." Leading a small country has not kept Castro from placing himself in the international spotlight, nor from extending his power into other nations, some of them far distant.

Nikita Khrushchev said Castro was "a very hot-tempered person." TV producer Bill Cran called Castro "a silly, impractical man." Academician Jaime Suchlicki saw him as "a profoundly anti-American, megalomaniac and cunning leader." To academician Gillian Gunn, Castro was "a man trying to survive in a radically changed world." Author Robert Stone said of him:

> *He ... was a soldier, a knight of faith. He may have been the only Marxist head of state on earth who actually believed in the doctrine. For that he probably deserves to be left holding the bag.*

Castro is multi-faceted; all these descriptions are accurate.

Castro came to fame when he unsuccessfully attacked Moncada Fortress in 1953. I had started my journalism career, working on the *Havana Herald*. The last time I saw the *Maximo Líder* I was aboard Jesse Jackson's campaign plane in 1984 during a stop in Havana. Castro came aboard, we chatted and—good heavens!—he put an arm around me.

In 1993, Castro is still in power. For this reporter, covering him has been exciting, frustrating, challenging, hazardous and, in professional terms, highly satisfying. This book has some of the material written over a span of a good many years about one of the most colorful and dangerous persons of our time.

Jay Mallin Sr.
Washington, D.C.
November 10, 1993

COVERING CASTRO

RISE AND DECLINE OF CUBA'S COMMUNIST DICTATOR

chapter one

In late 1956, Fidel Castro sailed for Cuba from Mexico with 81 other expeditionaries. Their landing was supposed to coincide with an uprising by the 26th of July Movement in Santiago de Cuba, the country's second city. But the rebellion occurred before Castro could land, and it was crushed by the Army. When the expedition debarked near the town of Manzanillo, it was quickly decimated by government troops. Castro and his tiny remaining band fled into the nearby Sierra Maestra Mountains. This article, published in the *Marine Corps Gazette*, describes the 2-year campaign that followed.

On the morning of 27 November 1956, a cable from Mexico was received in Santiago de Cuba. Decoded, the message read simply, "Requested edition sold out."

Fidel Castro Ruz and 81 other expeditionaries had sailed from the port of Tuxpán in Mexico aboard the 43-foot yacht *Granma*, and the Cuban Revolution was about to begin. Its repercussions would one day shake the world.

The cable from Mexico was directed to the underground organization of Castro's 26th of July Movement in Santiago. It notified the underground that Castro had sailed, and an action plan was to be set in motion.

Just before dawn on the morning of 30 November, the rebel underground rose up in Santiago and attempted to seize control of the city, second in importance only to Havana. Two rebel cars pulled up in front of the wooden police headquarters in Santiago, and young rebels piled out of the vehicles and began firing at the building and at the police guarding it. Simultaneously other rebels fired at the station from the roof of an adjoining building. The rebels threw grenades and Molotov cocktails, and soon the structure was blazing and ammunition inside was exploding. The police fired back at the rebels, but after an hour the battle was over. The police headquarters was destroyed.

Throughout the city rebels wearing olive-green uniforms and 26th of July arm bands attacked other government buildings. They moved boldly around the city, commandeering cars and trucks, ordering commercial establishments to close, seizing weapons in hardware stores. They attacked Boniato Prison and released prisoners.

The rebels, however, were unable to maintain control of the city. Troops began to move in from Moncada Barracks, and they skirmished with the rebels, killing, capturing, and dispersing them. By afternoon the troops had regained control of Santiago. Rebel snipers continued sporadic firing for several days, but the uprising had been crushed. Four hundred troops were rushed from Havana to reinforce the Santiago garrison.

The rebel plan had envisioned the Santiago uprising as coinciding with the landing of Castro and his expeditionaries on the southwest coast of Oriente Province. Bad weather, however, delayed *Granma*. One of the expeditionaries, Faustino Perez, later wrote:

> *It was one of those so-called northers, so frequent during that season. As we moved along, the storm became worse and the enormous waves, like animated mountains, played with the small but tenacious vessel....*

Granma was close to capsizing:

> *The pumps were ordered put into use, but the water, instead of receding, increased slowly but visibly. With rapid and nervous movements we seized two pails as one takes refuge in the last saving resource. The results appeared self-defeating. The water continued rising to our feet, and uneasiness mounted in everyone. Hiding my anxiety, I addressed those in charge of navigation: I asked them the distance to the Yucatan coast. One of them answered: Very far. This is lost.*
>
> *Without giving up all hope, I returned to look for Fidel, who worriedly assisted at the incessant and almost useless movement of the pails. I intended to suggest turning toward the coast. But I saw that the water was diminishing. Once again the floor boards were appearing....*

Finally, Cuba: "Our vessel advanced, until it could no more, less than 100 meters from the shore. There was no time to be lost...."

Ernesto Guevara, an Argentine doctor who had joined Castro's group, has described the landing in his book, *Pasajes de la Guerra Revolucionaria* (Passages of the Revolutionary War):

> *We had landed 2 December at a place known as Playa de las Coloradas (Coloradas Beach), losing almost all of our equipment and walking for interminable hours through sea-water marshes with new boots. These had caused ulcerations on the feet of almost all the troops. But the footwear and the fungus infections were not our only enemy. We had reached Cuba after 7 days of journey over the Gulf of Mexico and the Caribbean Sea, without food, with the vessel in poor condition, with almost everyone seasick, being unaccustomed to sea travel.... All this had left its mark on the troops made up of novices who had never been in combat. Nothing remained of our war equipment except rifles, cartridge belts, and some wet bullets. Our medical stores had disappeared, our knapsacks, for the most part, had remained in the swamps. We walked ... along the paths among the sugar cane of the Niquero sugar mill.... Due to our inexperience, we satiated our hunger and our*

thirst by eating cane at the edge of the path and leaving the bagasse there [where it could be seen by pursuers].

The expeditionaries were pursued by the planes and troops of Dictator Fulgencio Batista, whose regime they had come to overthrow. At a place called Alegría del Pío the troops caught up with the rebels. Wrote Guevara:

Compañero Montané and I were resting against a tree trunk, discussing our respective children. We were eating the meager ration—half a sausage and two crackers—when a shot sounded; a space of only seconds and a hurricane of bullets—or so it seemed to our anguished spirits during that trial by fire—fell on the group of 82 men.... Fidel tried in vain to regroup the men in the nearby canefield ... (but) the surprise had been too great, the bullets too numerous.

The rebel force was nearly wiped out. Those not killed or captured fled as best they could. A fortnight later, when Castro managed to gather the remnants of his group, he had in addition to himself and his brother Raúl (who had also come on *Granma*), only 13 other men. They recuperated at the home of a friendly citizen, and when they left him after 8 days, they signed a note thanking him and stating, "We will continue battling until we win or die."

The defeat suffered by the rebels became their greatest boon. The government figured that the few men who had escaped into the Sierra Maestra Mountains posed no threat. A dispatch filed by the author from Havana at that time reported:

The army operation was hardly a model of success. Troops who had spent their lives in the easy life of barracks were unhappy at being thrown into an outdoor campaign. They were particularly unhappy when the campaign carried them into the rugged, unfriendly Sierra Maestra. There were reports of army units mistakenly firing at each other. Food supplies were slow in arriving.

After a few weeks, it became apparent to the government that the campaign had largely petered out. Only an occasional rebel straggled in to surrender. The troops were getting nowhere in the attempt to pursue the Castro group. Finally, after conferring with his military chiefs, Strongman Batista decided to order most of the troops back to their barracks, leaving enough around the mountains to form a cordon sanitaire. Batista's decision was a major mistake.

On 17 January 1957, Castro's small band of men staged their first attack. They successfully overran a minor army post at the mouth of the Plata River. The rebels suffered no losses, but two soldiers died, five were wounded, and three were captured. The rebels seized supplies, including food, clothes, ammunition, eight Springfield rifles, and a machine gun.

Castro followed classic guerrilla tactics and staged other hit-and-run attacks. Worried by the rebel activity, Batista suspended civil rights and clamped censorship on the press. The government borrowed 5 commercial planes and airlifted some 800 troops from Havana to troubled Oriente Province. The army, however, ill-trained for a mountain campaign, had little heart for pursuing the now tough and blooded guerrillas.

Castro's forces grew slowly but steadily. Recruits from the cities made their way into the mountains, and youths from rural and mountain areas also joined up. Despite this, there was little change in the basic position of the guerrillas and the army. The guerrillas staged their raids in isolated areas, and the army, except for occasional probes, stayed mainly along the rim of the mountains.

But although the guerrillas were contained within the Sierra Maestra, the rebel movement as a whole across the island was gaining in strength and impetus. The underground was carrying out an island-wide campaign of terrorism and sabotage. Bombs exploded, fires were set, trains were derailed. Desperately trying to crush the rebels, Batista's ruthless police countered terrorism with terrorism, wantonly torturing and killing suspects. As the population turned increasingly against the Batista regime, the rebel movement garnered more support, more recruits, more funds.

The rebels were adept in the use of publicity as a weapon. Castro had not been in the Sierra 3 months when the underground arranged to have him interviewed by Herbert L. Matthews of *The New York Times*. The *Times* had published in December an erroneous United Press report to the effect that Castro had been killed during the original landing, but now Matthews, after speaking with Castro, happily wrote three laudatory articles about him. Declared Matthews:

> *Fidel Castro, the rebel leader of Cuba's youth, is alive and fighting hard and successfully in the rugged, almost impenetrable fastnesses of the Sierra Maestra…. "We have been fighting for 79 days now and are stronger than ever," Señor Castro said. "The soldiers are fighting badly; their morale is low and ours could not be higher. We are killing many…. The Cuban people hear on the radio all about Algeria, but they never hear a word about us or read a word, thanks to the censorship. You will be the first to tell them…."*

In the months to come, other American correspondents followed Matthews to the Sierra, and they were always welcomed by Castro. They kept his name before the people not only of Cuba, but also of the United States and of the world. The rebels also utilized other tactics in order to achieve public attention. On one occasion they kidnapped Auto Racing Champion Juan Manuel Fangio, who was in Havana in February 1958. On another occasion the underground set off some 60 bombs in Havana in a single night. The rebels were not only seeking publicity; they were also trying to show that the Batista regime was weak. The Cuban rebels showed the way, and now these same tactics are used by militant communist organizations throughout the hemisphere.

In his mountain domain, Castro continued to build up his guerrilla forces. Andrew St. George, a photo-journalist who made five trips into the Sierra to cover the rebels, reported [in the February 1958 issue of *Coronet*]:

> *Of all wars, civil wars are the cruelest, guerrilla wars are the toughest, mountain wars are the most exhausting, and jungle wars are the most dangerous. Castro's rebel army is fighting all four at once. Since their trackless forest routes will admit no transport, sometimes not even a mule, the men endure tremendous hardships; they have no tents, no regular changes of clothing, no supplies of any kind which they cannot carry themselves. They*

sleep in hammocks strung precariously from steep hillsides, eat rice, beans, and an occasional chunk of pork from black horsebuckets.... The Cuban Army has prudently withdrawn from the vast Sierra Maestra Range, leaving the rebels wholly to themselves. The rebels, for their part, make sorties far out into the plains around the towns.

It is one of the principle axioms of guerrilla warfare that guerrillas must win over the rural folk in the areas in which they want to operate. The Castro rebels were careful to pay for all food they received from *guajiros* [peasants], and they helped them in such ways as they could, providing medical assistance and dispensing rudimentary justice. The rural people served as couriers and guides, they transported supplies contributed by the underground movement in the cities, and they provided Castro with information on the movement of Army troops. A number of *guajiros* took up arms alongside the rebels.

In March 1958, the rebels made a major move to extend guerrilla warfare beyond the limits of the Sierra Maestra. Leading about 10 men, Raúl Castro moved out of the Sierra and across the lowlands. The band reached a small mountain range in the northern portion of the province, stayed there awhile, and then headed to the mountainous eastern section of Oriente. An Army drive aimed at recapturing the area was harried and ambushed, and finally the government troops withdrew and left Raúl Castro in firm control of an area larger than that held by his brother Fidel.

In a desperate effort to wipe out the focal point of the spreading rebellion, Batista determined to launch an all-out offensive against Castro's Sierra Maestra stronghold. The size of the Army was increased from 21,000 to 28,000 men, troops were concentrated in Oriente and quantities of weapons were purchased in foreign countries (by now the United States had banned arms shipments to Cuba).

In mid-May the offensive began, and the government troops moved into the Sierra. Following classic guerrilla tactics the rebels avoided direct confrontations. They fell back, harassing the troops with sniper fire as they retreated. The further the troops advanced, the longer and more vulnerable their supply lines became. The rainy season was in full swing, and the advance was slowed by water and mud. The rebels managed to surround and decimate two forward Army battalions, and the offensive slowed down and came to a stop. A third battalion was surrounded and forced to surrender.

The offensive was a failure. The Army withdrew its troops, and Castro was now securely in control of the Sierra fastness. The government's position would thereafter rapidly weaken.

In August 1958, Castro again extended his guerrilla activities. This time the rebels moved closer to the capital at Havana. Two top commanders, Ernesto Guevara and Camilo Cienfuegos, left the Sierra and marched westward to the center of the island. There were about 180 men in Guevara's group, and half that many in Cienfuegos'.

The two groups of men—the guerrillas were now divided into what they called "columns"—met some resistance, but the Army did not stop them. One reason for this was that corrupt officers had been bribed to let Guevara and Cienfuegos cross their territory. Nevertheless, the rebel columns did endure hardships in the course of their long march. Guevara suffered from severe asthma, and he was able to keep going only by using a pocket inhalator. Cienfuegos reported to Castro:

> ... For 15 days we marched with the mud and water up to our knees, each night evading ambushes and troops situated on the crossings that we had to make. In the 31 days that the trip through Camagüey dragged on, we ate only 11 times....

At one point Guevara noted in his diary:

> We advance into the swamp about two kilometers, parallel with the railroad, and camp with the water up to our knees. We endure 2 days without food and shivering with cold, drinking this pestilential water that is our only nourishment. The tortures that we are suffering are terrible.

The Cienfuegos group made it into the mountains of northern Las Villas Province, and Guevara arrived in the cave-pocked Sierra del Escambray in the southern portion of the province. The rebels were now in position on either side of the vital Central Highway. There were two additional independent guerrilla groups in the Escambray. One was the *Directorio Estudiantil Revolucionario* (Revolutionary Student Directorate), led by Faure Chomon, who later held high positions in the Castro government. The other group was the *Segundo Frente Nacional del Escambray* (National Second Front of the Escambray), headed by Eloy Gutiérrez Menoyo and an American, William Morgan, both of whom later became active enemies of Castro.

During the last quarter of 1958 the civil war flamed with increasing intensity. The rebels rapidly became stronger; the government's control deteriorated. The Cuban economy was in peril, and the government's finances were fast ebbing due to the cost of the war. At command levels, conspiracies plagued the Army, and in the ranks soldiers were unwilling to battle the rebels. Guerrillas moved out of the mountains and operated boldly in the lowlands. Army garrisons were overrun, and the government desperately held on to the major cities of eastern and central Cuba, most of which were virtually encircled by the rebel forces.

Late in October, after a flight from Havana to Santiago, the author wrote a dispatch reporting as follows:

> Upon flying eastward, the intensity of Cuba's strife becomes every [day] more apparent. At Havana Airport, passengers about to board a plane are searched. At Camagüey Airport, five B-26s are grouped at one end of the field and two more fly in escorted by two F-47s.
>
> Manzanillo's tiny airport building is bullet-pocked, and sandbagged trenches protect it. Heavily armed troops stand guard by the plane until it leaves, and other troops stop and search every vehicle on the road running by the airport.
>
> A sizeable detachment of troops guards Santiago Airport, and the Army searches all incoming baggage. Santiago is a semi-blockaded city almost cut off from the rest of the country. Rebel troops encircle it, and the only means of communication and transportation are via radio, plane, and boat. Phone and telegraph lines are down, and vehi-

cles infrequently move on the roads. The rebels previously burned all the cars they caught, but now they simply make off with them for their own use. The city's food stocks are fast decreasing, and prices are rapidly rising.

The Santiago garrison has been extended to about 3,000 men. The unfinished Provincial Hospital has been taken over as an emergency barracks. Army patrols hardly venture from Santiago. The towns around Santiago are a no-man's-land.

The rebels have made forays into the outskirts of Santiago.

The government forces were now entirely on the defensive. Two years after Castro's small expeditionary force was routed at Alegría del Pío, the rebels had grown strong enough to take the offensive, and across half of Cuba they had the government troops boxed into the cities.

By December 1958, the rebels were capturing towns and launching attacks on cities. Guevara took Sancti Spiritus, the first major city to fall to the guerrillas, and other cities in Las Villas and Oriente were soon captured.

The war was over. The rebels were victorious. Batista, his family, and his top officials fled the country, and the Batista regime was no more. A revolutionary government, quickly dominated by Fidel Castro, took control of the country.

Against very great odds, Castro had won his campaign. Starting with a tiny, bedraggled, fleeing band of men, in 2 years' time he defeated a professional army far larger and far better equipped than his own guerrillas. Always a bit of an egomaniac, his victory served to inflate his ego beyond reasonable limits and well into psychopathy.

He betrayed his people and set up an absolute totalitarian state. He disavowed electoral processes and introduced communism. He broke with the United States and took Cuba behind the Iron Curtain. He abandoned the ways of peaceful neighborliness and launched a campaign of subversion throughout the hemisphere. And the day would come when he would have a hand in almost precipitating the world's first nuclear conflict.

Few guerrilla campaigns in recent times have led to such striking and terrible results.

chapter two

ON THE ROAD TO HAVANA

The civil war having come to an end when Fulgencio Batista with family and close associates fled Cuba in the early hours of New Year's Day, 1959, the clandestine movement took control of Havana. Two of the top guerrilla captains, Ernesto Guevara and Camilo Cienfuegos, raced to Havana with troops and seized the capital's primary military points, Camp Columbia and La Cabaña Fortress. Castro, still out in easternmost Oriente Province, began a slower trip to Havana. Mallin, with another *Time* reporter, Jerry Hannifin, and a *Life* photographer, Grey Villet, flew in a small aircraft to meet Castro. They commandeered a former Military Intelligence car and a Red Cross driver. Mallin later filed this report to *Time*.

In an endless, irregular line the rebel army is pouring across Cuba from Oriente toward Havana. The troops are moving in cars, jeeps, trucks, armored cars, light tanks, medium tanks. Smooth-cheeked teenagers and grizzled oldtimers wearing discolored, shapeless khaki and blue-gray fatigues in various combinations grin and wave at citizens gathered along main streets and even highways.

The great majority of the rebels are from Oriente Province ("Cradle of Heroes"), most are peasants (many gawking at big cities for the first time), and all have long hair. All those who can have grown beards, which have become a symbol of Cuba's newly-won freedom. Citizens toss oranges at the soldiers and serve them hot coffee. Some soldiers sport flowers on their hats, jeeps, rifles.

A small number of female guerrillas are also participating in the parade, as are a good many citizens who have joined it in their own cars. Probably over 5,000 people are in the victory march, an event unique in Cuban history. The number will undoubtedly swell as the column approaches Havana. In Havana, advance rebel troops have already moved into swank hotels.

The column has been moving day and night almost from the moment Fulgencio Batista fell. Hammocks have been swung in some trucks, soldiers in other vehicles sleep as best they can leaning against each other. The tired but happy army winds along the Central Highway detouring only where bridges have been knocked down.

The *Time-Life* team and a Venezuelan journalist, traveling late at night over a backwoods road, came upon a large, bogged-down segment of the column. The Venezuelan hopped out and woke up enough drivers to get the column moving again. When one car stops on the narrow road, the other vehicles behind must also halt, and weary drivers start falling asleep.

At scores of Army and Rural Guard posts along the route rebel and regular Army troops mingle freely and are even living together under rebel commanders. Asked what he thought about this situation, a sergeant at a Ciego de Avila post answered, "It is best this way."

Although the people are proud of the first victorious army since Cuba won its independence, they are most proud of Fidel Castro Ruz, now a legendary figure who started with a handful of followers and within 2 years brought a dictator's mighty army to its knees. At Ciego de Avila citizens crowded the sidewalks for 2 days hoping for a glimpse of Castro. Castro started out from Santiago de Cuba, rode to Bayamo, then went north to get to Havana, but adulating crowds have slowed his victory parade to a snail's pace. So Castro decided to give speeches only at provincial capitals. He boarded a helicopter in Camagüey and headed west. A storm forced the 'copter down at the town of Florida.

Castro told us:

> *I was terrified of the crowd that formed. They saw the helicopter land and they came running to see what had happened. Now I know what it feels like to be a chivato [stool pigeon] caught by a mob. People do not really have consideration. The [same] man who tells you to take care of yourself grabs your arm and doesn't let go. One day I expect that so many people will grab me that one-half of me will go one way and the other half will go another way.*

Castro managed to escape from the crowd, got into a car, and was driven unnoticed through Ciego de Avila, stopping only to talk with local Captain Jaime Vega. The small Castro cavalcade tried to slip through Sancti Spiritus shortly after midnight but waiting throngs spotted him and almost overwhelmed his car. Church bells peeled.

With rifle-toting Sierra Maestra veterans sitting atop Castro's car to keep hysterical people off, Castro made it to the white El Progreso Club building facing the city square. A speaker's stand had been prepared on the second-floor balcony with a large Cuban flag draped over the railing. Smaller July 26th red and black flags had been placed less conspicuously at either side of the building.

While his men kept the crowd back, Castro went into the building. He chatted with dignitaries, patiently posed for photographs. He was accompanied, as he always is, by his chief aide, Celia Sanchez.

Approximately 7,000 people waited in the plaza. Castro did not begin speaking until a little before 1 a.m. Most of the crowd was still there when he finished speaking 2 hours later. Before he made his speech Castro commented to people chatting with him: "There is always a long list of speakers at political meetings. But no one wants to speak at revolutionary meetings."

A youth asked Castro for one of his bullets. He took a clip out of a pocket. He had entered the building carrying a Belgian submachine gun and wearing a revolver. Castro laughed and said to the young man, "No, I would be left without bullets." He gave one anyway.

In a speech in Camagüey the previous night Castro had lambasted graft in Cuban public life ("There is dirty business everywhere") but in his Sancti Spiritus speech he touched on many topics. Of the previous regime he said, "You almost had to thank them when they did not kill you in the streets." What had happened to some of the Batista government killers that had been captured? "Ask the blessed devil." Of his victory he said:

> For the first time since Columbus discovered America there has been a true revolution in Cuba. For the first time it is the people who command. For the first time the men with the guns in their hands bow reverently before the people. Now you will see what a people that progresses are.

Speaking with lights behind him, Castro appeared as a tall, dramatic shadow before the upturned eyes of the crowd. He gesticulated frequently, sometimes almost doubling forward in order to make a point. He knows how to keep a crowd's attention, deftly combining humor, sarcasm, anecdotes about his days in the Sierra, current slang, and lawyer's eloquence—all at a level of simplicity readily understood by the average citizen. He referred to "the valiant dictator who fled" and to an offer of amnesty by the former government ("They offered amnesty as if they were pardoning us"). He referred to General Eulogio Cantillo's permitting Batista and his cohorts to flee and said, "From him [Cantillo] we will demand an accounting." In regard to General Francisco Tabernilla's family's reported embezzlement of $40 million from the Army's retirement fund, Castro said, "We will keep a record of this and it will be paid even if we have to wait 50 years."

Castro declared that when he got to Havana he would hold a mass meeting at Camp Columbia, the Army's headquarters, and would open the gates to the public "because Columbia today belongs to the people." Of his future plans Castro said:

> I do not intend merely to review troops, tanks, and guns. I will do my duty but I also intend to undertake things in the civil field. My first work will be in the Sierra Maestra. Small hydroelectric plants can be built to supply peasants with electricity. There is a need for more education.

He added:

> We don't know everything. We are young. We know nothing, but we will learn. The nation can forgive mistakes but never shamelessness. Only one desire impels us: to work.

Castro establishes two-way communications with his audiences. He makes comments on matters of interest and he answers questions from the audience. One woman asked why she wasn't allowed up on the balcony with Castro. Replied lawyer

Castro:

> If some people were allowed up here and not others, that would constitute special privi-
> lege. We are against privileges. Not everyone can come up here because we could not all
> fit, but I do fit down there, so I'll come down.

Before concluding his speech Castro introduced several of his captains to the audience.

After leaving El Progreso, Castro drove with a small group of his men to a nearby cantina. With Celia Sanchez nearby, Castro sat on a bar stool, nibbled crackers and pieces of ham, and sipped beer. Although he had hardly slept since Batista fell, Castro's great store of energy was indicated by his exuberance and his loquacity. So talkative was he that it was difficult to introduce questions. He spoke of his plans for the armed forces. "I'm going to create three model forces. Criminals and incompetents must be eliminated from the armed forces." What was he going to do about the defeated regular Army?

> I cannot disarm them all. The country's defenses must be maintained. We need the good
> professional officers and the technicians. Some of the officers were honorable [in the con-
> flict]. Some whom we captured helped us.

Sierra veterans will be incorporated into the Army and the Army will be reduced in size.

> The veterans must now learn military discipline and ways. When I was at Camagüey
> air base, I had but to give an order, a plane here, a plane to be sent there, and the order
> was carried out. This is military discipline.

What about his *escopeteros* (riflemen—field militia)?

> They were useless. They did not help us at all. We could not depend on them. But many
> of my soldiers were trained at a hard school I set up. They learned how to fight, how to
> walk barefoot through the Sierra.

Castro said *Comandante* Juan Almeida would boss an armored force composed of Sierra veterans.

Much has been made of the Batista government's aerial bombings. Said Castro:

> At first they terrified us. But we learned that they did not hurt us much. As for towns
> that were bombed, most were not badly damaged. Some shots here, some there.

One of his men asked him about the bombing of Santa Clara, where possibly as many as 200 civilians were killed. Castro responded: "Where was the rebel army? Was it within the city limits?" The soldier replied, "Yes." Said Castro:

> Then they had a right to bomb. Could we ask them not to fire on us? In the cases of attacks
> on guajiros, weren't the guajiros feeding us and giving us supplies? Then they were help-
> ing our forces. Let us be fair about this.[1]

---

[1]*Castro's fairness toward the aviators, as in many other cases, did not last long. A show trial was
staged and a number of flyers were sentenced to prison.*

Castro said that his main problem with the air force now was that he had more planes than men. Most of the latter have fled.

Someone asked Castro if he wasn't concerned that future rebels against him might also hide in the Sierra Maestra. He answered:

> *We would handle it differently. We would give guns to guajiros and tell them to go get the rebels. We would tell them to do this if they wanted to avoid bloodshed in their area. Besides, we know all the hiding places in the Sierra.*

Castro was asked whether he had recently said that he intended to hang his hammock at Havana's busiest intersection at Galiano and San Rafael streets. He grinned and answered: "I said it to annoy the Habañeros. I would like to see guerrillas descend on them, cooking their stews in streets and sleeping in Parque Central. Havana is a problem." Castro said he had wanted to place the country's capital in Santiago but this wasn't practicable.

Castro got to talking about the Dominican Republic's Rafael Leonidas Trujillo, Castro's longtime foe. Said Castro: "We must keep up our defenses. Trujillo might pick a fight. I would like that." Castro indicated it might be interesting to have some Cuban "volunteers" go to the Dominican Republic. He said: "Just half a dozen well-trained men could do much. If we had known 2 years ago what we know now, the Army would not have lasted long."

Who did Castro think might be Cuban ambassador to Washington? "I do not know. It is best not to concern oneself with everything."

Would Colonel Ramon Barquin be called back to active service? [Barquin had led an abortive conspiracy against Batista.] Castro answered: "They thought they could seize power. They named their men to key positions. But who appointed them—by what authority?"

At 5 a.m. we left the cantina. Most of the soldiers had gone. Castro's car was sent to be refueled. Even at this late hour his energy could not be controlled: he kept striding back and forth, chatting with the people around him.

Finally, a four-car caravan pulled away. Castro, Celia, and a driver were in the front seat of a blue and white 1955 Ford, followed by two Chryslers containing soldiers (there were 11 escorts), and then the *Time-Life* car. No sirens sounded. The cars sped up the road toward Santa Clara. Castro dozed against a window. We quietly passed through several towns where even at this hour crowds were waiting for Castro to come by. They did not spot him. Well after daylight the driver of a car coming in the opposite direction pulled over to let us pass, saw Castro, and commented: "There goes the hope of a people."

Three hours after leaving Sancti Spiritus we pulled up in front of the home of a resistance leader who lives on the outskirts of Santa Clara. Castro entered the home for breakfast and talks with the local leaders.

[Ever larger throngs awaited Castro as he approached Havana. The three journalists lost contact with him. Castro, flanked by his top commanders, delivered a victory speech at Camp Columbia.]

chapter three

COMMUNIST TAKEOVER

The 1956-58 Cuban Revolution was fundamentally a revolt of the country's middle class against a despot. Castro himself came from the middle class, as did other revolutionary leaders. The middle class provided most of the young men and women who fought in the streets and in the hills. The resistance movement which functioned in virtually every city and town was composed mainly of business and professional men. They shaped the basic goals of the struggle: an economy freed from governmental corruption and a democracy freed from repression. The new leadership of Cuba, once victory was achieved, was a mix of guerrillas and city civilians. But the most visible figures at the top were the guerrilla chiefs: Castro, of course, his brother Raúl, the Argentinean doctor Ernesto "Che" Guevara, and Camilo Cienfuegos, who had once played minor league baseball in the United States and was considered strongly pro-American. Guevara was a leftist, he resented the United States and he led the veer toward Marxism. How this was accomplished is detailed in this portion of a chapter from *Fortress Cuba*, published in 1965.

It was during these first days of victory that Castro began to utilize a technique which was to become a cornerstone of his power. From the beginning he proved that he possessed surpassing ability to capture an audience. Castro, the orator, was an amazing phenomenon. He handled crowds the way a puppeteer works his marionettes. He drew forth hysterical cheers and chants of support whenever he wanted them. And he called forth roars of rage when he assailed his enemies. Castro's command over his listeners was to develop into his single most potent weapon. No one knows how many mass rallies and nationwide television audiences he has addressed in the 5 years he has been in power, but the number runs well into the hundreds. It is not unusual for him to deliver 2 or 3 messages in a single week, each running in length from 2 to 4 hours. And few people ever leave before he is through talking.

Even his enemies watch him, fascinated. It is like the fascination a cobra commands.

Castro had come down from the hills and occupied the proud and historic city of Santiago. He passed through rich Oriente Province, across the great cattle lands of Camagüey, on past the fertile yellow canefields of Las Villas, and then through the smaller provinces until he arrived in the capital, an old city overlaid by a modern metropolis, its ancient narrow streets crossed by broad avenues lined with glistening new homes built by up-to-date businessmen, or by old-line politicians who had enriched themselves at the public trough.

A million shouting, swarming citizens thronged to greet the victors. Addressing them passionately, Castro told them they now had "liberty, peace, and rights." And most of the people of Cuba believed him, as did many in other lands. For who then could have guessed that this voluble young orator from the mountains would create the first communist state in the Western Hemisphere? Who could foresee that within 3 years he would bring the entire world to the brink of nuclear catastrophe? Who could know that Fidel Castro, the legendary patriot proclaiming the cause of democracy, would launch a vast drive aimed at subverting the free countries of the Western Hemisphere to the cause of communist tyranny, and—most incredible of all—would bring not only Russian missile bases but Chinese communists within 90 miles' striking distance of the United States?

During those first weeks of 1959 hope and optimism were high. The dictator had fled, his government had collapsed, and his henchmen were dead, in prison, in hiding, or in flight. A provisional regime was set up, and it was pledged to restore honest and democratic government, something Cuba had rarely known in its 48 years as an independent country. The provisional government included a number of the most competent and respected figures on the national scene: representatives of business, the professional classes, and the rebel movement. On 8 January Castro exclaimed: "What is it the people want? Is it not an honest government? Well, there it is!"

The new President was Manuel Urrutia Lleó, a former judge from Cuba's centuries-old second city, Santiago, site of the major land and sea battles of the Spanish-American War. Santiago—located near the Sierra Maestra Mountains, long the rebels' stronghold—had valiantly supported the rebel movement despite repressive terror by Batista's police and army. A group of Castro's followers had been brought before Urrutia for trial in 1957, and he had defiantly acquitted them, holding that it was lawful for citizens to rise in arms against a totalitarian regime. After this verdict, Urrutia had to flee the country. Now the heroic former judge was back as Batista's titular successor.

The Premier in the new government was Jose Miro Cardona, who had been one of Castro's law professors and head of the Havana Bar Association. An intellectual revolutionary and an important member of the resistance movement, heavy-set Miro had on one occasion escaped the police by dressing in a priest's robes. Minister of State was Roberto Agramonte, the presidential candidate in 1952 of the reformist

Ortodoxo Party. Minister of the Treasury was Rufo Lopez Fresquet, a man with an astute mind for finance who was an adviser to numerous American companies in Cuba and was married to an American. Fresquet had been one of the chief money-raisers for the rebel movement. Minister of Public Works was quiet-spoken Manuel Ray, a top-notch civil engineer and a leading figure in the rebel underground. Castro himself was technically not a member of the Council of Ministers. He held the vague title of "Delegate General of the President to the Armed Organization."

If this government had been permitted to rule Cuba, the future of the island might have fulfilled the revolution's early promises of peace and liberty. It was not to be so, for a number of reasons, not the least of which was Castro himself, exulting in victory and popularity. He talked and talked. He made speeches and held press conferences, and continually orated before the groups of hero-worshipers he drew around him. And what Castro said was not always in keeping with what the President and the Council of Ministers were trying to accomplish. "What can you do with a man who disclaims responsibility and actually has all of it?" a council member grumbled. Cuba was getting its first taste of government by talk.

Urrutia and Miro, both of whom tried to exercise power and had little, soon began to be troubled by Castro, who claimed no power and had it all. The Communists, waiting in the wings of Castro's stage, were delighted. Banned for 6 years, they now began to come out into the open, and, in fact, they were Cuba's only fully organized political party. Anibal Escalante, a member of the Communist National Committee, prophetically declared, "The dynamic forces of the revolution will sweep away conservatives like Miro Cardona." What Escalante did not foresee was that the day would come when Castro would sweep him away, too!

Urrutia and Miro tried their best to run the government; Castro, meanwhile, was not to be quieted. Finally Miro resigned, was persuaded out of it, and then quit for good. Castro then took the post of Premier himself and has held it ever since. Responsibility, however, did little to alter his ways. He continued to talk, talk, talk, while others labored to keep the country going. Cuba—and the world—was witnessing a unique form of government in which the leader laid down policies in speeches but rarely bothered to implement them. It was up to subordinates to carry out Castro's directives. The hero himself was constantly on the move up and down the island, in the cities and in the fields, talking wherever there was anyone to listen—and there was always someone eager to hear his spellbinding words.

Castro also traveled abroad. He flew to Venezuela and he made a trip to the United States, where he had lived as an exile in 1955. In New York, in April 1959, he declared:

> We want to establish a true democracy in Cuba, without any trace of fascism, Peronism, or communism. We are against all kinds of totalitarianism.

Castro hugely enjoyed his 1959 trip, and bemused Americans enjoyed watching the then still amiable antics of Cuba's *barbudo* leader. He addressed a rally of 20,000 people in Central Park. He visited the Bronx Zoo, rode a kiddy train, patted a Bengal tiger, fed elephants, gorillas, and orangutans. Earlier, during a trip to Washington, he was on his best behavior. He addressed the American Society of Newspapers Editors, put on an unaccustomed tie and a neatly pressed uniform to attend a reception, and met with a group of congressmen, whom he assured: "The 26th of July Movement is not a communist movement. Its members are Roman Catholics, mostly."

What a contrast was Castro's next trip to the United States! In September 1960, when he returned to address the United Nations, he and his party stayed at the Hotel Shelburne. There they plucked chickens and cooked dinner in their rooms, created dirt and disorder everywhere, and when there were protests they stormed out and moved to Harlem's Hotel Theresa. The move to Harlem was a carefully prepared propaganda move—Castro's agents had been dickering with the Theresa even before he checked into the Shelburne. [Soviet Premier Nikita] Khrushchev, who was on his own famous American tour at the time, visited Castro at the Theresa. There the two leaders embraced and the seal was put on the betrayal of the Cuban people.

But back in the early months of 1959, Castro was not yet openly with the communists. He still spoke of rights and freedom and what he called his own philosophy, "humanismo." The words then were reassuring, but the facts were already ominous. The trials and executions of Cuban so-called "war criminals" began almost at once. It was known that many of the Batista police and army men had engaged in torture and murder, and it was reasonable that these pay for their crimes. But the trials became a mockery of justice. They were conducted by "Revolutionary Tribunals" whose members rarely knew the most elementary facts about law or court procedure. Some Tribunal members were illiterate and signed court papers with their fingerprints. Perhaps these procedures could be excused during the first weeks of upheaval following the revolutionary victory, but they were continued month after month. Soon it was clear that Castro, who had talked so much about justice, would do nothing to bring it into being.

There was one notable case that demonstrated the contempt which Castro, himself a graduate lawyer, held for due process of law. Forty-five former members of Batista's air force had been brought to trial in Santiago before a Revolutionary Tribunal, charged with having committed "genocide, murder, and homicide" in bombing and strafing villages during the civil war. The defense argued that the airmen had been carrying out orders in a military campaign, and the Tribunal, composed of three rebels, agreed with this and absolved the airmen, stating, "To do otherwise would not be in line with the principles and humanity maintained by the glorious revolutionary army." This verdict would seem to have been in line with Castro's own convictions. Several weeks earlier, asked about Batista's airmen, Castro had replied: "They had a right to bomb. Could we ask them not to fire on us? Let's be fair about this." But by the time the airmen came to trial, their acquittal no longer suited Castro, who wanted all potentially dangerous opponents to his new dictatorship safely out of the way. He said: "It has been a great error of the Revolutionary Tribunal to absolve those criminal pilots." The airmen were then put back on trial. Most were found guilty and given long prison sentences.

Consistency was not part of Castro's personality. Nor was gratitude. Time and again he viciously crushed men who had been his staunchest supporters. This was dramatically demonstrated when he turned upon President Urrutia.

On 17 July 1959, Cubans were thunderstruck to learn that Castro was resigning as Premier. The official government newspaper, *Revolucion,* covered its front page with two huge words: "Fidel resigns." The paper gave no explanation other than that there were "very serious and justifiable reasons that determine this decision."

Mystified, the country waited. Within hours, it was to be vividly shown another ugly aspect of Castro's new type of "democracy"—mob rule. A crowd gathered in front of the Presidential Palace, loudly chanting support of Castro and carrying pre-readied signs with such slogans as "Fidel, Cuba needs you." President Urrutia addressed the mob and declared: "This revolution cannot be directed by anyone other than Fidel Castro. You can be sure that the resignation he has presented will not be accepted by the government."

President Urrutia had not yet realized the truth: Castro was maneuvering to destroy him. In the Sierra Maestra, Castro had declared that Judge Urrutia was "the person competent to preside over the Republic," and "we will support him at all costs." But Urrutia as President had not pleased Castro. The law-conscious ex-judge had believed he was President in fact as well as in name, and he had held up some of Castro's decrees, arguing over their wording and wanting to go slow on a number of measures. Urrutia was anti-communist, and Castro was moving steadily toward alliance with the communists. In a television interview, Urrutia declared, "I have always said that I reject the support of the communists, and I believe that the genuine Cuban revolutionaries should reject it openly." For Castro this statement was the ultimate provocation, and he launched his scheme to oust the President.

Castro went into seclusion to plan his moves. The mobs were mobilized and then Castro went on a nationwide radio and television hookup. The national hero lashed out at the hapless President. Castro accused him of "bordering on treason," as indicated by a number of points, including the charge that Urrutia was in the process of buying an expensive house. Furthermore, Urrutia was "trying to blackmail us with the problem of communism." Watching the merciless performance on television in the Presidential Palace and knowing its effectiveness on the mobs, Urrutia numbly wrote out his resignation and broke into sobs. With his wife and children, he left the Palace through a side door. Had the crowds seen him, he would have been lynched on the spot. Thus Castro disposed of his one-time protector, Manuel Urrutia.

Castro considered replacing the toppled President with Miro or Treasury Minister Lopez Fresquet, but both men were vetoed by the increasingly powerful communist and leftist elements within the army. Instead, the presidency was given to a minor Council Minister, Osvaldo Dorticos Torrado, a former underground figure but a colorless, unaggressive, and little-known individual. Three months later, speaking of his early career as a lawyer, Dorticos frankly told the Council, "I was affiliated with the Communist Party, and I've never denied it."

Within 7 months after the new government had taken over, the 2 top men, respected and dedicated to democracy, had been driven out, and in his ruthless drive to center power around himself, Castro had destroyed the 26th of July Movement, which he himself created. On 28 October 1959, he told the Council:

The 26th of July was the instrument to achieve power. It no longer exists. Power now resides in the Council. Compañeros Ray and Perez can consider themselves out.

Manuel Ray and Faustino Perez had been devoted to the 26th of July freedom movement and were original members of the Council. The 26th of July had respect and standing because it had been the main instrument in overthrowing Batista. There were members of the movement who had won substantial prestige for themselves at national and local levels. But now that Castro was swinging to total authoritarianism, he could no longer tolerate the existence of individuals or organizations that might compete with him in the public eye, or, potentially, in the political arena. The 26th of July had fought for democracy, and there was to be no democracy in Cuba.

The destruction of democracy was closely linked to Castro's personality. Temperamentally, Castro could not stand criticism of any kind. Hardly had he come into power when he began to display his irritation at any unfavorable comment directed at him or his regime. The American press, antagonized by the continuing lawless executions, was the first target of his indignation. Later he turned his verbal guns on Cuban critics who courageously spoke out against the same brutality. I recall a chilling experience in the town of Cojimar, outside Havana, where Castro maintained one of his residences. Castro was asked about some minor criticism, and he angrily replied, striding back and forth across his living room, his arms slashing:

They are with us or they are against us. Those against us are against the revolution, and those against the revolution are counter-revolutionaries.

There was to be no middle ground. You were for the government, or you were a counter-revolutionary—and counter-revolutionaries were condemned by Castro's mobs, shot, or given long prison terms.

By 1964, of the 18 members of the original Council, only 3 still held their posts. One, Agriculture Minister Humberto Sori Marin, had been executed; one had died in a plane crash; and the rest had fled into exile or settled into obscurity. Both Urrutia and Miro eventually went into asylum in foreign embassies and then escaped to the United States. Miro became a leader of anti-Castro forces and was President of the Cuban Revolutionary Council, which would have established a new government for Cuba had the Bay of Pigs invasion succeeded.

Castro was now indisputably in control. He ruled the country by talk and television, only occasionally concerning himself with official conferences and paper work. He obviously regarded himself as expert on all matters. He spoke with equal authority on agriculture, economy, industrial production, and international affairs. And what he said became the law of the land. A single Castro speech was sufficient to precipitate the break in relations with the United States. Another speech was enough to convert his regime openly to communism. And still another later speech almost resulted in a rupture of the ties between Castro and his communist cohorts.

Paralleling Castro's absolute control of the government was the takeover of powerful institutions within the country. The first, and probably most important, was the army.

It is an unfortunate fact of political life in Latin America that the bullet has traditionally been more potent than the ballot. Generals and colonels have ruled through tight military dictatorships, and some of the smaller countries have served as little more than private estates for their overlords. Only in very recent years have democratically elected governments outnumbered army-dominated regimes in Latin America. Even in 1963 there were four military coups.

The armed forces of Cuba were as politically powerful as in most Latin American countries. The army had thrown out Dictator Gerardo Machado in 1933 and put in Dictator Fulgencio Batista. Batista ruled from 1933 to 1944. Then he was ousted, but in 1952 he and the army staged another coup that put him back in power. He remained until the Castro-led rebellion finally forced him to flee on New Years' Day, 1959.

The army, having fought its unsuccessful campaign in support of Batista for 2 years, was decimated, disorganized, and demoralized. Once-proud soldiers stood quietly by while bearded rebels, wearing makeshift uniforms and carrying a motley collection of weapons, took over military establishments across the island. I remember one sentry, natty in khaki uniform and white helmet, who was standing guard at one of the gates of Havana's huge Camp Columbia, watching unkempt barbudos roar back and forth in jeeps. The soldier said, with hopeful bravado, "I won't bother them if they don't bother me."

Within days of Castro's arrival in the capital the old army was no more. The top commanders, with few exceptions, fled abroad or into asylum in foreign embassies. Most of the lesser officers were imprisoned. Several hundred were charged as "war criminals" and brought to trial before the Revolutionary Tribunals. The soldiers of the old army who wanted to continue as soldiers, and who were acceptable to the *barbudos,* doffed their khakis and put on the olive-green uniform of the rebel forces, while the rebels themselves, many of them illiterate young peasants from the mountains, became the new army of Cuba. Vestiges of the old army remained, but even these were eventually erased in later trials and purges.

But this rebel army was not yet a communist army. Many of the *barbudos* openly wore crucifixes on their chests when they rode into Havana. Few probably even knew what communism was. There were communists and far-leftists among the guerrilla officers, notably *Comandantes* Raúl Castro and Ernesto "Che" Guevara, but the head of the new army, *Comandante* Camilo Cienfuegos, had lived and worked in the United States and was considered pro-American. In general popularity, and thus in influence, Cienfuegos then ranked second only to Castro himself. The day would soon come, however, when Cienfuegos would mysteriously be removed from the Cuban picture. Che Guevara and Raúl Castro would then be the dominant figures immediately under Castro.

Che Guevara (the meaning of the nickname "Che" is akin to "pal") was an Argentine doctor who followed an adventurous trail long before his destiny crossed that of Fidel Castro. In 1952 Guevara broke off his studies at the University of Buenos Aires Medical School, and with a friend took a motorcycle and hitchhiking trip over the Andes and through Chile, Peru, and other countries. They wound up flying from Venezuela to Miami, but Guevara was refused admittance to the United States and returned to Argentina to complete his studies. After he graduated in 1953, he again left the country and gradually drifted north. Guevara considered himself a Marxist and threw in his lot with leftist groups. Like Raúl Castro, he was also vehemently anti-American.

Though the Cuban army was not communist when Raúl Castro and Che Guevara seized control, no time was lost in changing its character. In July 1959, Raúl bluntly declared:

> *We are a political army.... It is not possible to be apolitical, since to be apolitical means to have no interest in the march of public affairs. And that is precisely why we fought: to transform the economic and social structure of the nation.*

The communists concentrated heavy efforts on indoctrinating officers and men. The communist daily, *Hoy* (Today), was distributed free of charge at army camps. Movie clubs were formed, and the movies shown almost always adhered to the Party line. The head of the movie club at Santiago's Moncada Barracks was a communist, and among the films he selected were Charles Chaplin's *Modern Times*, the Japanese movie *Hiroshima*, and the French *If All Men of the World*, which had a racial theme. After each showing, soldiers discussed the film. *Hiroshima*, they were told, depicted American ruthlessness and brutality in atom bombing that city, while *Modern Times* proved the mechanical cruelty of industrial capitalism. The movie club at Camp Columbia was named after Chaplin, and among the films exhibited was *El Megano*, made by the Cuban Communist Party about 10 years earlier to show the exploitation of peasants.

Indoctrination schools were set up at military posts. Guevara, who commanded Havana's La Cabana Fortress, was also named head of the *Departamento de Instruccion* of the Armed Forces Ministry, a post which placed him in charge of the indoctrination program. Soldiers studied an "Economic Bulletin" which differentiated between "capitalism" and "socialism" as follows:

> CAPITALIST REGIME—*The capitalist method of production, which followed the feudal method, is based on the exploitation of the class of salaried workers by the class of capitalists.*

Socialist REGIME—*This is the most advanced system of production known up to the moment. It carries out the elimination of social classes, private property, and the exploitation of man by man.*

A booklet entitled *Objectives and Problems of the Cuban Revolution* taught the soldiers that "large landowners," "big sugar magnates," "big importers," and "foreign companies" were villainous "counter-revolutionary forces." This booklet also informed soldiers that:

Our army is an army formed from top to bottom by the most oppressed groups of our country: workers, students, professionals, poor and middle-class farmers, and others.

The large North American companies which were set up on our soil ... continually used [the old army] to smother the protests of Cuban workers in the face of poor laboring conditions and other abuses.... One of the most negative characteristics of the Cuban economy consists of the fact that an overwhelming and decisive portion of Cuban wealth is not in national hands.

In the past ... the government practically turned over the functions of direction of our armed forces to foreign military missions [i.e., American], and ... our country signed military agreements [with the United States] which did not take into account Cuban interests.

The revolution for independence from the Spanish yoke was strong enough to break control of our land by Spain, but not strong enough to prevent North American military intervention or to evade seizure of our economy by influential U.S. interests.

Thus did the communists utilize all available means to inculcate the Party line upon the officers and soldiers of the new army. Parallel with this, Guevara and Raúl Castro opened doors which enabled communist officers to move into key positions. Among the communist indoctrination personnel at Campo Libertad were Rafael Rivero Pupo and his wife Nilsa Espin de Rivero. Rivero was once a communist youth leader in Santiago and his wife was the sister of Raúl Castro's wife, Vilma. Raúl's wife was an attractive and determined woman, one of the most picturesque and intelligent female figures of the revolution. Daughter of a middle-class Santiago family— her father had worked for the Bacardi Rum Company—she studied chemical engineering at Oriente University, followed by a year at Massachusetts Institute of Technology. Using the *nom de guerre* "Deborah," Vilma headed the rebel underground in the pro-Castro city of Santiago and then went into the hills to join Raúl Castro's guerrillas on their "second front" in eastern Oriente. Vilma's quarters were always protected by guards and Raúl's posted order, "Please do not pass through here." After the rebel victory, Vilma and Raúl were married in a civil ceremony in Santiago. The bridegroom wore the traditional uniform of the mountain fighters, complete with his .45 automatic.

In spite of the flood of new communist officers who swarmed into the army, there were many non-communists remaining from the original forces which had put Castro into power. Prominent among these was Luis Diaz Lanz, chief of the air corps. Diaz Lanz had been a commercial pilot, but later he joined the rebel cause and began ferrying weapons from the United States to the guerrillas in Oriente. He flew Urrutia into the Sierra Maestra early in December 1958, and when the rebel cause was victorious, Castro named him Air Force Chief. He also served as Castro's pilot.

But Diaz Lanz was not acceptable to the communists, and as their power spread through the army, he expressed his fears. In June 1959, Lanz became ill, and during his absence a foot soldier, *Comandante* Juan Almeida, was named "Supervisor" of the air force. Lanz feared that he was being replaced, and on a day when Almeida was away from headquarters, Lanz returned and declared:

> *Those who love liberty cannot agree to any dictatorial system, especially the most inhuman one in the world: communism. I am against all types of dictatorship, whether they be called Trujillista or Batistiana or communistic.*

Almeida rushed back to headquarters, and he and Diaz Lanz engaged in heated argument. They then adjourned into Castro's presence, where Castro supported Almeida as more insults were traded. Lanz then departed and went into seclusion to write a letter of resignation addressed to President Urrutia. He declared that "by express order of *Comandante* Fidel Castro" he had been subordinated to Almeida, and he added:

> *I consider that all these actions against me are due only and exclusively to the fact that I have always been against an attitude which permits communists to occupy prominent positions within the rebel army and within dependencies of the government.... We all know well who they are, what they are, and what ends they pursue.*

Urrutia issued a statement noting his own anti-communist position ("I absolutely reject communist ideology") but calling Lanz a "deserter." Shortly afterward this statement was withdrawn, obviously under communist pressure, and a new one was issued which still condemned Lanz but omitted Urrutia's own anti-communist convictions. Meanwhile, Diaz Lanz, fearing for his life, fled into exile in the United States.

When Castro became Premier in February 1959, and his brother Raúl took over as chief of the army, navy, and police, Raúl began attending meetings of the Council of Ministers. On October 20, he achieved formal Council rank by being named Minister of the Armed Forces. Upon being appointed, Raúl declared, "We will not be satisfied until ... our nation is in a position where it is respected militarily by the small and the powerful." Within 4 years, with Soviet assistance, Raúl would build up the second largest military force in the western hemisphere.

With Raúl Castro as their Council minister, the communists' takeover of the military was assured. In April, Raúl had made known his views. He declared:

> *If I were a communist, I would stand here and say clearly, 'Yes, I am a communist,' because we have fought for the free expression of ideas. But even though I am not a communist, as a revolutionary, as one of the leaders of the revolutionary armed forces, I must confront this anti-communist campaign, I must confront this divisionist campaign, because it is the pretext used by enemies of our revolution to turn some of us against the others.*

Thus, even in the earliest days, as far as the Castro regime was concerned, anti-communism was "divisionism," and this was not to be allowed.

Diaz Lanz was not the only important officer who understood the communist advance. Another was *Comandante* Huber Matos, army chief in Camagüey Province. A capable guerrilla leader who had laid siege to the city of Santiago during the civil war, Matos repeatedly complained to Castro about the communist infiltration, but instead of being heeded, he found that officers loyal to him were being transferred to other areas. Finally, when Raúl was appointed to the Cabinet, Matos resigned, bitterly writing to Fidel Castro, "No one can talk to you about the communist issue." Matos declared:

> *I do not want to become an obstacle to the revolution, and believing that I must choose between adapting myself or going into a corner in order not to do damage, the honest and revolutionary thing to do is to go.... I have done for Cuba everything I can, now and always.*

But Castro was unwilling to let Matos leave the scene peacefully. He flew to Camagüey and had him arrested. Then he went on television and made a long speech assailing Matos, charging that he had been attempting "a political maneuver" in order to satisfy "personal ambition." In December, Matos and 34 officers were brought to trial. Matos declared: "I always fought communism.... The communists are trying to steal the revolution." But the Castro brothers testified against him, and he was sentenced to 20 years in prison. Twenty-one other officers also received prison terms, and thus ended the last open effort by anti-communists within the army to stem the communist advance.

One day in October 1959, Army Chief Camilo Cienfuegos set out in a light plane on a flight to Havana from central Cuba. He was never seen again. A wide search in which United States Navy planes and ships participated failed to find his body or even the wreckage of his plane. In view of the communist takeover, a suspicion arose that the communists had had a hand in the disappearance of the one remaining outstanding rebel commander who was a political moderate. This suspicion gained ground later when Cristino Naranjo, a trusted Cienfuegos aide, was shot and killed at the gate of the main army camp. The government claimed the killing was an accident, but to those who had observed the usual pattern of the rise of totalitarian governments the meaning was clear. The fastening upon a people of a rule by terror is made of such "accidents," reinforced by demagoguery and mob fanaticism. With all these tools Castro was becoming an expert. He was beginning to qualify as the practiced head of a totalitarian regime, unscrupulous and insatiable in his grasp for the power to weld his nation into one unit, in which only he would have freedom to choose the direction of public policy.

By now propaganda was a major Castro weapon, and it was drummed into the citizens through every available means: television, radio, cinema, newspapers, magazines, loudspeakers, and billboards. Taped messages were even transmitted on telephone lines, bedeviling every hapless person who picked up a phone to make a call. Sports articles, television shows, nightclub spectacles—nothing was unworthy of the attention of the propagandists. An entire nation was brainwashed. Mob rule was another weapon now used habitually. The organized mobs were called out to intimidate potential opposition; they were called out to shout acquiescence to governmental measures; they were called out to give Castro the adulation upon which he had learned to thrive. "Elections, for what?" roared a crowd, and Castro, looking back over the sea of faces, declared ecstatically, "This is democracy!"

In Cuba three civilian forces had balanced the army as traditional repositories of power, retaining some measure of autonomy under even the most narrow of the island's previous dictatorships. These were the union, the press, and the Church. To them Castro now turned his attention.

Cuba's unions (*sindicatos*) had long been powerful. No employer willingly tangled with them. No government tried to exist without their support. Over the years the benefits secured by the unions for their members had steadily improved working conditions and standards of living. A special mission of the International Bank for Reconstruction and Development reported in 1950 that the per capita income of Cuba was "undoubtedly higher than that of any other tropical country and among the highest in all Latin America."

Batista had maintained a tight rein on the unions through leaders loyal to him, and when he fled, they had to flee also. Members of the 26th of July emerged from the underground and took control. In April, May, and June 1959, elections were held in all of Cuba's 1,800 unions. The communists put up their own nominees, but they won control or near-control in only about 100. Cuba's 1,200,000 organized workers were overwhelmingly anti-communist. The communists tried to capture the powerful, 450,000-member Sugar Workers Federation by placing the name of Conrado Becquer, an old-time, non-communist labor leader, at the head of their slate of candidates, but Becquer denounced the communist maneuver, and he was elected Secretary-General on the 26th of July ticket by a vote of 885 to 13.

The communists were irked by their losses. The 26th of July Movement had spoken for "unity at the base," and the communists had hoped this would enable them to place a foot in the door of labor's traditional power. In May, Communist Party Secretary-General Blas Roca, writing in the official Communist Party paper, *Hoy*, angrily declared: "The alleged unity at the base is a subterfuge to sabotage and combat unity that is necessary"—by which was meant of course that the "necessary unity" was a communist unity dominated by communist leaders. Spokesmen for the 26th of July Movement assailed Roca's article, pointing out quite truly that he had proposed that "there is no other solution than ... the communist one."

The breach between the communists and the 26th of July widened, and the communist effort to seize control of the unions was frustrated—for the moment. Castro, for the time being, was on the side of the unionists. He spoke out against a plan the communists had been advocating to create an armed workers' militia.

But in the months that followed, as the communist takeover proceeded in most phases of the Cuban life, Castro himself began openly to veer further left, and the unions began to stand alone in their anti-communism. On 18 November 1959, the National Congress of the Confederation of Cuban Workers (CTC) was scheduled to convene. Thirty-three union confederations made up the CTC, and all held elections for delegates to the Congress. Three thousand one hundred were elected, and of these, 2,784 were members of the 26th of July, 224 were communists, and 192 belonged to other groups. The communists thus by popular election had less than seven percent of the delegates, and it was obvious they would have little influence. A pro-communist Labor Minister, *Comandante* Augusto Martinez Sanchez, appointed a month earlier, tried to postpone the Congress, but he was forced to back down when the labor leaders threatened to resign en masse.

The Congress convened as scheduled and heard speeches by Fidel Castro, Raúl Castro, Martinez Sanchez, and the CTC Secretary-General, David Salvador, a 26th of July stalwart. The routine business of the Congress proceeded, but backstage a bitter struggle was under way between the communists and the anti-communist faction of the 26th of July. The anti-communists had the upper hand because of their numerical superiority, but the communists were receiving powerful support from Raúl Castro and Martinez Sanchez. The communists were also getting advice from a number of pro-communist "observers" from abroad. Among these was a three-man Russian group, two "observers" and an "interpreter." The "interpreter" used the name Vadim Vadimovich Listov, but I broke a story revealing that his true identity was Vadim Kotchergin, an agent of Soviet Intelligence.

The communists wanted 3 places among the 36 top officers and members of the Executive Committee to be elected to head the union Congress. Despite the fact that Salvador, in accordance with government line, pressed for the slate including the communists, the majority refused to accept it. A number of delegates appeared on the floor bearing melons, to demonstrate that the revolution was "green outside, red inside." Copies of a pamphlet documenting the old communist alliance with Batista were circulated. The situation became increasingly ugly as fights broke out and angry catcalls resounded through the meeting hall.

Finally, Castro himself returned in an effort to restore order. But even as he spoke, yells of *"Unidad!"* were answered by cries of "26!" Castro said angrily, "Shut up, all of you!" He charged that "this looked like a lunatic asylum," and declared that there were "irresponsible voices that cannot be revolutionary and that can only be the echo of counter-revolutionary voices originating, perhaps, from the chorus of war criminals." The threat was clear: there was to be no further dispute; those who argued would be labeled counter-revolutionaries.

A new slate was presented to the Congress, and it was approved. Although it did not contain the names of the communists previously proposed, it did include several fellow travelers, and the communists had put a substantial foot in the door. With Castro backing them now, it would not be long before they were running the house.

Again they resorted to their favorite tactic, striking at individual labor leaders and unions one at a time. Rump sessions were held, guarded by armed *milicianos* who permitted only communists and their friends to attend. Anti-communists were charged with being *Batistianos* or *contra-revolucionarios*, or they were accused of supposed crimes. The rage of the workers rose as they saw union after union thus deprived of its most effective and popular leaders. Finally more than 2,000 unionists staged a demonstration, marching to the Presidential Palace and chanting, *"Cuba, si, Rusia, no!"* They lifted an anti-communist union leader to their shoulders and shouted, *"Elecciones! Elecciones!"* They were calling for labor elections, but onlookers thought they were demanding national elections, and they also took up the chant. Unlike mob assemblies with official backing, this spontaneous demonstration was futile. The head of the powerful Electrical Workers' Federation, Amaury Fraginals, had a confrontation with Castro's hand-picked President, the colorless Dorticos, then left. Soon afterward, following a conference with other federation leaders, he went into hiding. The boss of the CTC, David Salvador, who had been an active member of the July 26th underground, at first went along with the regime's "unity" policy, but finally became disgruntled at the steady communist takeover. His authority was cut back and then he was given a "leave of absence." He set about organizing a clandestine anti-Castro group, but he was captured when he tried to leave Cuba. He was expelled from the CTC, brought to trial, and given a long prison sentence. This ended overt resistance by old-time union leaders.

Parallel with the communist crushing of union officers, the government tightened its direct control over the workers themselves, destroying rights they had won in past years. Since the regime had seized all important industrial and commercial concerns, the workers now found themselves mere employees of the administration. Strikes were prohibited. Wages and hours were set by the government, which also determined who worked where. Further control was established by the creation of the People's Militia, which brought many workers under direct military command. Further anti-communist demonstration by unionists became impossible, because the unions were in actuality ceasing to exist. In February 1963, *Comandante* Guevara announced the future of unions in communist Cuba. "The destiny of the union," said Guevara simply, "is to disappear."

The destruction of the independence of the labor unions was itself a goal of the Castro regime. In addition, however, this provided a key means in the destruction of yet another dangerously free entity, the press. The unions now were communist controlled, and newspaper workers, from reporters to linotypists, were all union men. Freedom of the press in Cuba was to die of slow strangulation.

En route to Havana after Batista's downfall, Castro had declared in January of 1959:

> When a government acts freely, it does not fear any freedom. If it does not rob nor murder, it does not have to fear freedom of the press, because no one can call it thief, murderer, or traitor. When it is called thief, murderer, or traitor, then it does not want the truth to be known.

A mere 17 months later, the last of Castro's outspoken press foes was crushed, and freedom of the press ceased to exist in Cuba.

The process by which the press was destroyed began the day Batista fled. No less than 15 general-circulation daily papers were being published in Havana, a substantial number for even a large city. Five of the dailies were directly owned by *Batistianos,* and these at once ceased publication or were seized by the rebels. *Alerta,* one of Batista's press outlets, became *Revolucion,* official spokesman for the government. *Hoy,* the Communist daily which had been banned under Batista, immediately resumed publication.

One reason there had been so many newspapers was that it had been the official policy of successive Cuban governments to grant most of them subsidies. The Castro regime abolished this system, and the papers began to feel an economic pinch. They now had to rely solely on advertising and circulation for revenue, and the large number of papers reduced the amount of revenue available to any one paper. Then, as the Castro regime proceeded with its confiscatory policy toward private enterprise, revenue for the papers dropped as private companies disappeared. Several papers were anti-government, to a lesser or greater degree, and the remaining companies hesitated to advertise in these. They were also of course deprived of government advertising. As a result, economic problems were a major factor in the demise of a number of dailies.

The newspapers which attempted to maintain their integrity faced additional problems and pressures. The regime's paper, *Revolucion,* was not only supported by the government, but was also favored by news breaks, and this factor was a built-in circulation booster. In their sweep of the labor movement, communists took over the unions connected with publishing, including the printers, and thus could exert powerful pressure on newspaper policies. The government viewed any opposition as treasonable—"counter-revolutionary." In October 1959, Education Minister Armando Hart bluntly told a group of newspapermen: "Impartiality is a myth of civilization.... When Dr. Castro speaks, he speaks for the people, and therefore, makes public opinion known." There has seldom been a balder exposition of the traditional function of the press in a country being welded together under a totalitarian leader. Far from "speaking for the people" in the ordinary democratic meaning of first sounding out majority opinion and then expressing it, Castro in his harangues spoke for himself and his increasingly open leftist ideas and drew half-comprehending mobs along by the force of his ego, the skill of his oratory, and the almost constant hysteria in which he kept his listeners. In the traditional 20th-century pattern of total dictatorship, no separate currents are allowed in this vast tide once it begins to sweep over a country.

Those newspapers which now dared to express independent opinions came under increasingly heavy attack. As early as February 1959, Castro publicly assailed a comic weekly, *Zig-Zag,* because of a cartoon he did not like. In March, at a mass rally, he attacked *Prensa Libre* because it had urged the calling of elections. *Diario de la Marina,* more than a hundred years old, was the conservative dean of the Cuban press and generally considered to be the unofficial spokesman for the Catholic Church. In August 1959, *Marina* struck at the Communist daily, *Hoy,* and *Revolucion,* the paper of Castro's regime, charging that "one defends Moscow from Cuba and the other defends Cuba from Moscow." In September, *Marina* assailed the government's economic policies, warning of the "consequences and repercussions which result from too vigorous ... economic controls." Castro, spluttering and gesticulating, went on television to attack all opposition papers. Crying, "...rascals ... cynics ... shameless ones ... Machiavellian," Castro charged:

> *They play the game for vested interests, the privileged ones, the enemies of Cuba.... What they want is this: that the revolution fail due to the conspiracy of foreign interests.*

Castro's previous oratorical attacks had usually been met with silence on the part of those assailed, but *Marina's* editor, Jose Ignacio Rivero, courageously replied to Castro with a front-page editorial, which stated:

> *We are already very tired of so many threats, so much intolerance, and so many unjust and gratuitous accusations. In an epoch such as this, when our rulers want it to be known that there is true respect for freedom of expression, this attitude [on the part of Castro] is not conceivable.*

The following day, the *Marina* again spoke out, declaring: "The morale of freedom of expression is being crucified in Cuba with a cross of terror."

There was swift public approval of *Marina's* stand. Copies of the paper sold out. Congratulatory phone calls from Havana and across the island jammed its switchboard, and operators were surprised at the number of people who simply blew kisses into the phone. Rivero's home was flooded with flowers from well-wishers. A group of women offered to sit in front of the Marina Building and defend it from attackers. Close to 6,000 new subscriptions were taken out within 3 days. I visited Rivero at this time in his office on the fourth floor of the Marina Building in downtown Havana. Wearing a white suit with an open shirt, he discussed informally the nature of the press situation. He said:

> *In Cuba, freedom of the press exists physically, but not morally. It is a press freedom which does not please me or other newspapermen. Many would prefer outright censorship. If you speak out, you are not subjected to physical attack, but to public discredit.*

Nevertheless, *Marina* continued lashing out at the Castro regime. The government, bothered though it was by *Marina's* popularity, still hesitated to shut down the paper. It knew that *Marina's* stand had attracted worldwide attention. Early in May 1960, Rivero told Hal Hendrix, an American correspondent:

> *I don't think the government will close the paper because it knows the free world is watching Diario de la Marina. To silence it completely would cause very bad world reaction, as well as in Cuba.*

The time was to come very soon, however, when the government would decide that world reaction weighed less than the necessity of doing away with the outspoken daily. In the May 11th issue Rivero planned to run an editorial calling for free elections, plus a statement of support for *Marina* signed by a majority of the paper's 300 workers. The government got wind of this, and a group of union and government officials appeared at the Marina Building, demanding that the editorial and the statement not be published. The editors refused. The men withdrew, but soon returned with reinforcements carrying sub-machine guns. The plant was taken over forcibly, and the plates containing the documents were smashed. *Marina* was now in the hands of the government. Rivero, who was not at the plant at the time, sent telegrams of protest to President Dorticos and other officials and then went into asylum at an embassy.

The following day, the government, through its organized mobs, staged a mock funeral for *Diario de la Marina*. A crowd surged through the streets, carrying a coffin from the Marina Building to the University of Havana, where it was placed face down on a speakers' stand. Sixty thousand people—including workers, students, uniformed militia, and the army band—were present, cheering wildly. On May 16, armed militiamen also entered the plant of *Prensa Libre*, and that paper was seized. The free press of Cuba was henceforth moribund.

The *Diario de la Marina*, whose extinction was followed by the demise of other, lesser opposition dailies, had been generally regarded as the voice of Cuban Catholicism, and the Church was the last of the repositories of public power with which the regime came into direct conflict. It was also the last to be crushed. The Church, while perhaps not as powerful in Cuba as in other Latin American countries, nevertheless was an important influence, particularly among Cuban women. The government did not want to clash with it. Castro had been educated in Catholic schools, and as late as November 1959, he attended a midnight Mass honoring Cuba's patron saint, the Virgin of Charity. The Mass, held on a cool, rainy night, followed an impressive torchlight procession bearing the image of the saint to the Plaza of the Republic. Castro did not participate in the parade, but he came to the plaza for the Mass.

The Church, on its side, did not want a conflict with the government. It realized that the regime was highly popular with a majority of the citizens and that some of its measures represented real social progress. The Church's single most important figure was Santiago's Archbishop Enrique Perez Serantes, and he, speaking of the government's new agrarian reform program, declared in June 1959, "We do felicitate the Maximum Revolutionary Leader for the inspiration he has had."

Though there were minor differences between the Church and the government during 1959, both sides were obviously striving to avoid a head-on clash. It was, however, inevitable. The Church and the communist state represented opposing ideologies, and the supremacy of one had to result in the submergence of the other. Even while praising Castro for his Agrarian Reform Law, Archbishop Perez Serantes warned of communist influences, declaring, "Dr. Castro, certainly free from Muscovite orientations, should know perfectly well that this orientation in no way favors the success of the revolution."

As communist control increased, the Church showed greater concern. In November 1959, a National Catholic Congress was convened in Havana, and one of its events was the immense torchlight parade followed by the Mass to which Castro came. Although a Catholic youth leader declared that the Congress had "no secondary intentions of a political nature," the meeting was obviously intended to be a rededication to the faith as well as a Catholic show of strength to impress the government. Two hundred thousand people attended the Congress, and on one occasion they set up another vast chant of *"Cuba, si, Rusia, no!"*

From this time on the conflict between Church and State grew more bitter. In February 1960, a small group of pro-Castro priests and laymen set up an organization called *Con la Cruz y con la Patria* (With the Cross and With the Fatherland). This was intended to be the forerunner of a national church, but the move expired for lack of recruits. Of Cuba's 6 million Catholics, only a few thousand joined. In April, addressing a Communist Youth Congress, Party President Juan Marinello declared, "The Catholics have nothing to fear from the Popular Socialist Communist Party, nor from the Socialist Youth, as long as they remain within their temples adoring their images." But, added Marinello ominously, "He who raises the anti-communist banner does not deserve from an honest Cuban any other name than that of a traitor." Then, in May, the government seized and shut down the paper which was regarded as the voice of the Church, the *Marina*.

The Church struck back. In Santiago, Archbishop Perez Serantes issued a pastoral letter: "It can no longer be said that communism is at the door, because in truth it is within, speaking powerfully, as one who is on his own property." The Archbishop warned his diocesans, "Have nothing to do with communism, absolutely nothing." Perez Serantes was the most respected figure in Cuban Catholicism, but Cubans knew that he was now speaking for more than the Church. In a real sense, he spoke for all the moderate elements of Cuban life, and particularly the many non-communists who had participated in the revolution. Archbishop of the city in which the rebellion against Batista first flared and which in later years sustained the rebel cause, Serantes was identified with the revolution: He had encouraged it and he symbolized it. When Castro's original 26 July 1953 attack on Santiago's Moncada Barracks failed, Serantes obtained guarantees for the lives of some of the rebels who agreed to surrender. Among these was the young rebel, Fidel Castro Ruz.

In the months that followed Serantes' May Pastoral, he struck hard at the communists in successive letters to his diocesans. As he read one of these, "Rome or Moscow," in Santiago's Cathedral, militia entered and suddenly began to sing Cuba's national anthem in an effort to drown out the Archbishop's words. Serantes ordered them to leave. There were scuffles between the militia and the congregation, and police who arrived promptly arrested five of the latter for creating a disturbance.

By the end of 1959 it had become clear to all but the most naïve that a vital issue had been drawn: the communists had moved in on all phases of Cuban life, and the question for each citizen was whether to accept this or to fight it as best he could. The ruthless police state was well on its way. Prisons were crowded with tens of thousands of opponents to the regime. A year after they had been started, the brutal executions were still continuing. And as of December 1959, those being killed were no longer "war criminals," but merely opponents of Castro, those he termed "counter-revolutionaries." His rabble howled, *"Paredon! Paredon!"* (the execution wall), the Revolutionary Tribunals churned out their death sentences, and the firing squads continued their grisly work, while the revulsion of decent citizens steadily grew.

In July 1960, a Mass for the victims of communism was held at the Cathedral of Havana. While worshippers prayed within, a mob gathered outside and sang the *"Internationale."* When the congregation emerged after the service, rioting broke out. Ugly incidents occurred at other churches. Mobs yelled, *"Viva Rusia!"* and Catholics replied with their now habitual *"Cuba, si, Rusia, no!"* Outside one church a crowd gathered at night and shouted insults until the priests turned out the lights, including the one that shown on the steeple cross.

Cuba's nine bishops until now had hesitated for fear of provoking all-out conflict with Castro, but in August a joint pastoral letter was issued, signed by all the bishops. Noting that Cuba had established "close commercial, cultural and diplomatic relations with the principal communist nations" and that government officials "have repeatedly and warmly praised the systems of life existing in those nations," the bishops stated:

> *Catholicism and communism respond to two totally different concepts of man and the world which it will never be possible to conciliate. We condemn ... communism ... because it is a doctrine which is essentially materialistic and atheistic ... [and] because it is a system which brutally denies the most fundamental rights of the human being.... The absolute majority of the Cuban people, who are Catholic, are against materialistic and atheistic communism, and only by deceit or coercion could be led to a communist regime.*

The day after the Pastoral was read, the regime's daily, *Revolucion*, charged that the letter was "a plan contrived by those privileged ones whose interests have been affected by the revolution" and who were leading "some ecclesiastical authorities" into a position "of opposing the people." Castro delivered a four-hour harangue in which he said:

> *You know that the revolution is being repeatedly and systematically provoked by a group of counter-revolutionaries who have wanted to seek refuge in temples in order to fight the revolution.*

The crowd broke into cries of *"Paredon, paredon!"* and Castro continued, "The public know perfectly well how respectful the government has been in matters of religion." He declared that there were "two types of priests," those who served "poverty" and those who served "great wealth." Said Castro, "To serve wealth is to betray Christ." Lashing out at Spanish-born priests, for it was a weakness of the Church in Cuba that it had never been able to train the majority of its priests on Cuban soil, Castro declared: "There is no doubt that [Spanish dictator Francisco] Franco has a sizeable group of fascist priests in Cuba." "Fascist priests" thenceforth was to become a familiar epithet.

The abortive Bay of Pigs invasion in April 1961 led to a reign of terror. Executions multiplied, with hundreds of thousands arrested and herded into stadiums, theatres, and the buildings. The government moved against the Church with a vengeance. Archbishop Perez Serantes was placed under house arrest, and other bishops and priests were imprisoned. Militiamen occupied churches, convents, and other religious edifices. Altars were profaned and wrecked, valuables were stolen, and statues destroyed. In the weeks that followed, an exodus began, as virtually all of the country's 500 foreign-born priests and 2,000 nuns left the island. Only the minority of native Cuban clergy remained behind to try to maintain a semblance of religious life.

In September 1961, Havana's Auxiliary Bishop Eduardo Boza Masvidal, a native Cuban and a leader in the Church's struggle against communism, sought official permission to hold an annual procession honoring Cuba's patron, the Virgin of Charity. The permission was refused. Nevertheless, services could be held and were scheduled at the Bishop's own Church of Charity in downtown Havana. Scores of worshippers arrived, then hundreds, then thousands. A police captain made his way into the church, found the bishop, and then, to the surprise of everyone, ripped off his own insignia and declared, "I'm with you." The jubilant crowd lifted the officer onto their shoulders. There were cries of *"Libertad, libertad," "Cuba, si, comunismo, no,"* and *"Viva Cristo Rey!"* An impromptu procession got under way, despite urgings by the bishop that the demonstrators go home quietly.

Militiamen fired into the air and sniped at the crowd. It scattered, then reformed. A communist goon squad was overwhelmed, and the crowd continued forward, heading for the Presidential Palace, some 18 blocks away. Night fell and a number of the marchers lit candles and torches, singing hymns and waving white handkerchiefs, symbols of Church militancy. Onlookers burst into applause, bus drivers honked their horns. Police cars followed, but did not interfere. Nevertheless as the sniping continued and as emotional fervor subsided, more and more of the marchers dropped away. By the time the procession reached the Palace, it numbered only a few hundred people, and guards talked these into dispersing peacefully.

This type of spontaneous demonstration was intolerable to Castro. His paper, *Revolucion,* assailed "the vile activity of Falangist clerical counter-revolutionary groups which carry out the instructions of imperialism." The Interior Ministry charged that a priest had fired shots, and that a 17-year-old boy who had been killed had been shot by "counter-revolutionaries." Another roundup of priests was launched. Native-born Cuban Bishop Masvidal was arrested, released, and then re-arrested. He and more than a hundred other priests were taken to the Spanish liner Covadonga and placed aboard it, bound for exile in Spain. When the bishop arrived at the dockside, hundreds of onlookers who had gathered kneeled for his episcopal blessing. Then they broke into anti-communist cries. Watching militia did not interfere.

Today, in spite of popular feeling and sporadic resistance, there are only about a hundred priests left in Cuba for the country's nearly 6 million Catholics. Yet Castro at no time directly attacked the Catholic religion, or even the Church as a whole. The offensive was always cleverly directed against "priests," or "churches," or the "Church hierarchy." The destruction of the Church was a classic example of what Communists call "salami" tactics. The Church was not destroyed overnight: Castro whittled it away. Perhaps if the Church had acted with unified and determined opposition from the start, it might have been able to resist better. But it hesitated, and in its hesitation lay its destruction, because when it did act, it was already too late.

It was the same story in all phases of Cuban life. Sheltered by Castro's harangues, his mobs, and the hysteria he knew how to induce, the communists inched in, spread out, and took over. The breach with the United States was also the result of a step by step process in which relations were steadily frayed, until finally the diplomatic break came in January 1961. A vicious and all-pervading anti-American campaign, which was maintained for over a year, prepared the Cuban people for enmity toward a nation that until 1959 they had always considered their friend and ally.

At no time did the communists make a full-scale attack against a powerful foe, whether it was the labor unions, the Catholic Church, or the United States. Rather, a relentless policy of infiltration and attrition was utilized. The anti-communists were often slow to realize their peril, or they simply closed their eyes, and when they finally awakened it was too late. One may well wonder as to what course history would have taken if, in the early months of 1959, the anti-communists had spoken clearly, stood firm, and remained united. If the press, the Church, the unions, and the anti-communist elements within the army had formed a brave alliance for the defense of democracy, surely the communists would have had considerably more difficulty in their drive for conquest. Perhaps the communists would have won in the end anyway, but at least democracy would have died, not with a whimper, but with a battle cry.

The warning and the lesson are there for the other Latin American countries, and for all free nations. Cuba is one of the few countries conquered by communism from within, instead of because the Red Army was there to prepare the way. In historical perspective, the communist takeover of Cuba, less than 100 miles from the United States, was little short of astounding. No Latin American can now safely say, "It can't happen here." It can.

The communists cannily turned to their own advantage the victory of the 1956-1958 revolution and the rise to power of Fidel Castro. Castro, for his part, seeking to further his own glory and win a place on the world stage, was easily swayed by the attractions of communism, which provided a ready-made ideology and a tried expertise in the seizure of personal power. If the path to a personal niche in history must be reached through the destruction of democracy, elimination of the existing social systems, and eradication of friendly ties with the hemisphere nations, then, decreed Castro, democracy must be destroyed, the social system demolished, and friendly relations torn asunder and replaced by ties with the Iron Curtain countries.

The argument that the United States drove Castro into the hands of the communists is nonsense. The American government and its ambassador, Philip Bonsal, did everything that was reasonable in its vain effort to maintain good relations. But the United States could not give Castro what he wanted, and the communists could offer: an alliance so designed that he could obtain absolute power within his country and support and encouragement in his Caesarean dream to become *El Líder de las Américas.*

The communists proffered Castro unconditional support, and as his drastic policies turned more and more of his former allies against him, he was happy to accept communist assistance. The revolution against Batista had been fought to restore free and honest government, but the communists leaped on the wave of popular victory and soon were able to mutilate and transform the revolution, turning it to their own uses. Under the cover of la revolucion, the communists accomplished their gains, and the democrats, fearful of opposing la revolucion, said little and did less, until they were engulfed and destroyed.

Democracy was thus lost in Cuba, and the loss was Cuba's tragedy. It was also a loss for the whole free world, a point which was dramatically underscored in October 1962, when the world was thrust close to the brink of nuclear war. Today the communists seek to convert Cuba into a springboard for conquest—not nuclear conquest now, but subversive conquest of the entire hemisphere—and they hope to use many of the techniques that succeeded in Cuba.

"Never send to ask for whom the bell tolls. It tolls for thee."

chapter four

Raúl Castro Ruz has always been overshadowed by his charismatic, grand-standing, loquacious older brother, Fidel. He has also been generally under-estimated; in actuality he has played and continues to play an important role in events in Cuba. The following biographical sketch was published in *Strategy for Conquest* in 1970.

On 22 June 1958, Major Raúl Castro Ruz, commander of the rebel "Second Front" in the eastern portion of Cuba's Oriente Province, issued "Military Order No. 30." This instructed his troops to carry out "the detention of all U.S. citizens" in the area. As the reason for the roundup, the order claimed that almost 100 air raids had been carried out against "the defenseless peasant population" by government planes. The order assailed "inhuman North American rulers" and charged that the United States had supplied the bombs used by the Cuban government. This, according to Raúl Castro, was a "shameful crime ... against the defenseless Cuban people." (Together with Military Order No. 30, Raúl Castro issued a manifesto titled *"Call to the Youth of the World."* This, like the order, was a bitter attack against the United States and alleged U.S. "domination of Latin America.") Raúl Castro's action was a harbinger of the course Cuba would follow once the Castro brothers were in power.

Rebel troops proceeded to seize 48 Americans and 2 Canadians. Two American consuls traveled into the hills to confer with Raúl Castro and to seek the release of the prisoners. After drawn-out negotiations, Castro began releasing the prisoners in small groups until all were free.

Ostensibly the kidnappings had been aimed at forcing the United States to cease shipping weapons to the government of dictator Fulgencio Batista. But, in fact, the United States had already embargoed weapons shipments to Cuba 3 months earlier.

More important were two other goals that the rebels achieved. In forcing the United States to negotiate with them, they won *de facto* recognition of sorts. And in seizing 50 foreigners and holding them with impunity, they demonstrated to the world the weakness of the Batista regime and the extent to which the rebel movement had developed.

Like his older brother Fidel, Raúl was born (3 June 1931) on the family sugar plantation at Birán, near Mayarí in Oriente. Raúl was the fourth child (of seven) of planter Angel Castro and his second wife, Lina Ruz. Raúl was baptized a Catholic, and he studied at Catholic schools in Oriente and Havana. Then he entered the University of Havana, where Fidel was an important student activist. Raúl listened to his brother's ideas and met Fidel's politically-minded friends. It was a left-leaning student crowd, bent on reforming the world. There were almost certainly communists among the students.

Raúl moved to the left, and possibly during this period joined the youth branch of the *Partido Socialista Popular*, Cuba's Communist Party. In 1953 he traveled to Europe to attend the communist-sponsored "International Conference for the Defense of the Rights of Youth" held in Vienna March 22 through 27. After this, Raúl went to Bucharest to attend another communist meeting, the "World Festival of Youths and Students."

Raúl returned to Havana aboard a steamship, and upon his arrival on June 6 he was detained by customs officials. His baggage was found to contain communist literature. The literature was confiscated, but Raúl was released.

Batista had staged a successful coup the year before, and Fidel Castro, a member of the opposition *Ortodoxo* Party, was organizing an uprising to take place in the island's second city, Santiago de Cuba. Raúl plunged into the conspiracy.

On 26 July 1953 the rebels attacked Moncada Barracks in Santiago and other strategic points. Raúl led a small group that captured the Provincial Courthouse. The uprising failed and the Castro brothers were captured. They were brought to trial, convicted, given 15-year sentences, and sent to prison on the Isle of Pines.

Cuba entered a period of relative tranquility, and, in May of 1955, Batista granted amnesty to a number of political prisoners. Fidel walked out of prison, followed by Raúl.

The brothers remained in Havana, and then, on 17 June, Raúl went into asylum in the Mexican embassy. He flew to Mexico a week later and was joined by Fidel. There followed months of planning a new struggle against Batista, organizing a group of followers, raising of needed funds, and guerrilla training by Alberto Bayo [a veteran of Spain's civil war].

In November of 1956 the yacht *Granma* sailed for Cuba with 82 expeditionaries who landed early in December on the western shore of Oriente. Batista's troops and air force went into action, dispersing and pursuing the rebels, killing or capturing many of them.

During a skirmish at a place called Alegría del Pío, Fidel and Raúl were separated. Later—so the story has been told—sitting in a farmer's shack, Raúl heard a radio report that Fidel had surrendered, whereupon he angrily swore that he would seek out his brother and kill him. But Fidel had not surrendered, and the brothers were later reunited.

During the months that followed, the rebels slowly built their guerrilla strength in the Sierra Maestra mountains. Semi-independent commands—"columns"—were set up under the leadership of *Granma* survivors. One of the columns was led by Raúl. He was a harsh commander, but he held the loyalty of his men. He was efficient, he had a talent for organization, he was indefatigable. Despite jungle sores, he marched with his men for days and nights, with only brief pauses. He fought side by side with his troops, and they fought well, in contrast with the slapdash troops commanded by Fidel.

By the first months of 1958 the rebels were in firm control of the Sierra Maestra and looking for new areas to conquer. In March of that year Raúl set out with about 100 men. They crossed the Central Highway, hid in cane fields, finally made their way to the Sierra del Cristal in the northern portion of Oriente Province.

The rebel group remained in the Sierra del Cristal a while, then headed eastward to the extensive mountainous area of Oriente's far corner. Encountering only token resistance from government troops, most of whom were concentrated in the Sierra Maestra region, Raúl rapidly established control over an area much larger than that held by Fidel. This was the rebels' "Second Front," where Raúl staged the kidnapping of the Americans and Canadians.

Raúl put his organizational abilities to work, established administrative offices, set bulldozers to leveling new roads. A rural intelligence service and the first rebel indoctrination schools were established.

Raúl executed suspected government informers. At the Soledad sugar mill a list of 39 executed men was openly posted on a wall. During 2 years of guerrilla operations, Raúl was probably responsible for over 100 executions, more than were carried out by all the other rebel commanders combined. On one occasion a young lieutenant balked at commanding a firing squad, saying that he couldn't deliver the *coup de grace*. "It's easy," said Raúl, "you just do this," and he pointed his own gun at the ground to demonstrate. On another occasion three prisoners were blindfolded and lined up, ready for execution. The firing squad, however, fired over their heads. Someone shouted: "You missed one! He's still alive." Each of the prisoners thought he was the one that was still alive and presumably would be killed by a new volley. The terrifying mock execution was only meant as a warning, however, and on this occasion, at least, no one died.

As an independent area commander, Raúl Castro was able to indulge his delight in irritating the United States. He kidnapped Americans. He turned the water supply for the United States base at Guantánamo on and off (the water was pumped from a river within Raúl's territory). He attacked the American-owned Nicaro nickel works, forcing the evacuation by the U.S. Navy of American civilian personnel. He kidnapped a Cuban lawyer employed by the Guantánamo base. In effect, Raúl was leading the rebel movement into an increasingly anti-American position.

On 1 January 1959 Batista fled Cuba, and the revolution was victorious. While Fidel and other guerrilla leaders traveled to Havana, Raúl remained in Santiago as commander of all "land, sea, and air" forces in Oriente. He promptly carried out the execution of some 70 Batista followers, who had been given little or no trial. They were buried in a mass grave, not far from famed San Juan Hill.

On 21 January, addressing a mass rally, Fidel declared Raúl to be his heir apparent (a status which still prevails). On 26 January Raúl married Vilma Espín, a fanatical young woman who had played a leading role in Santiago's clandestine movement and later joined Raúl in the mountains. Immediately after the wedding, the couple flew to Havana, where Raúl took up a new post as assistant chief of the armed forces under Fidel. Later, when Fidel became prime minister, Raúl took command of all the country's military and police forces.

While Fidel made speeches and traveled around the country and up and down the hemisphere, Raúl built a new military establishment. Raúl saw to it that the troops received political indoctrination. He declared:

> We are a political army.... It is not possible to be apolitical since to be apolitical means to have no interest in the march of public affairs. And that is precisely why we fought, to transform the economic and social structure of the nations.... The armed forces play an important role in the public life of a nation.

Raúl attended cabinet meetings, and on 20 October he was officially given cabinet rank when he was named minister of the revolutionary armed forces, a position which he continues to hold. Cuba began making mass purchases of weapons in Europe. At the same time, under Raúl's benevolent eye, communists steadily gained in power and influence within the Cuban military establishment.

Raúl's activities were not limited to military affairs. He had an important voice in all policy making, he received foreign dignitaries, he was involved in labor affairs, and he even flew to Chile to a meeting of the Organization of American States (but arrived a few hours too late to attend it).

Raúl's greatest power—and the same was true of Ernesto "Che" Guevara—lay in knowing how to handle egocentric and unstable Fidel Castro. Fidel is susceptible to suggestions, and nobody was more adept at guiding him than Raúl and Guevara. After years together with him, they knew how to play on his vanity, how to lead his thoughts, how to convince him to do things without telling him outright to do them. They utilized the fact that Castro seizes and makes his own the thoughts of other people. A true anecdote illustrates how Raúl could influence his brother. Their younger sister Emma was due to be married in April of 1959, and she had asked Fidel to attend the wedding. He agreed to do so and even told friends that he was going to dress up and give the bride away. But Raúl talked to Fidel and asked him, "Do you want your enemies to take pictures of you kneeling in church?" Fidel showed up at the wedding slovenly and 20 minutes late.

Raúl, who had once volunteered to fight with the Allied forces in Korea, became more strongly anti-American as Cuba veered increasingly leftward. On one occasion, he told friends, "It is my dream to drop three atomic bombs on New York." In

July of 1960 he flew to Moscow, and there arrangements were made for Cuba to receive over $100 million worth of Communist weapons, ranging from mortars and anti-aircraft guns to heavy tanks and supersonic MiGs. Cuba was to become the most powerful military nation in Latin America. But even this was not enough for the communists. In 1962 Raúl again flew to Moscow, and now preparations were made for Russia to send troops and missiles to Cuba—a move which precipitated the nuclear crisis of October 1962.

Raúl Castro today commands a military organization that numbers approximately half a million troops and militia. In addition to heading the armed forces, he is also deputy prime minister and a member of the Cuban Communist Party's Politburo, Secretariat, and Central Committee. He is also president of the party's Armed Forces and State Security Commission.

Fidel and Raúl neatly compliment each other. Fidel is the dreamer, the speechmaker, the demagogue. Raúl, however, is the better fighter, organizer, and administrator. Fidel prefers to move around the countryside, to visit farms, to make speeches, to talk with people, to play baseball. Raúl, meanwhile, maintains tight personal control over the military forces that help maintain the Castros in power. Fidel provides the charisma. Raúl provides the muscle.

chapter five
FAILED TRUMPET

In 1954, the Eisenhower Administration had succeeded in overthrowing a leftist regime in Guatemala by launching an invasion of Guatemalan exiles from neighboring Honduras. With the Castro government in Cuba veering toward communism, plans were drawn up to launch an invasion of Cuba from Central America. When it came into office, the Kennedy Administration continued the planning and preparation. Finally launched in April 1961, the invasion failed totally. There were mistakes of planning and of execution. An additional reason for the debacle was brought to light in the following article, published in March 1974 in the *Tropic* magazine supplement of the *Miami Herald*.

> *Even while troops were fighting in the Bay of Pigs, the vast Cuban underground was still awaiting orders to join the fight. So says a longtime observer of Cuba, who here reveals for the first time why the CIA deliberately kept the underground out of the battle.*

In the days of the Cold War, the United States was committed to preventing the establishment of a communist-run government anywhere in the western hemisphere. This was a commitment rooted in historical tradition (the Monroe Doctrine), strategic necessities, and treaty agreements with other nations of the hemisphere. This commitment led the United States to help organize and support an exile invasion of Guatemala in 1954. And it was this same commitment that caused the United States to attempt to overthrow the regime of Fidel Castro in Cuba in 1961.

The disastrous results of that attempt are well known. The real reason the effort failed, however, is not known. In fact, it has never been revealed that the landing at the Bay of Pigs was doomed before the first expeditionary splashed ashore.

Public, press, and political attention to the events that occurred in Cuba the third week of April 1961 have long centered on the landing itself. Largely overlooked in the wake of the military debacle was the vital role that the internal resistance movement was preparing to play—but was prevented from playing. And therein lies the real reason the Bay of Pigs failed.

The Bay of Pigs was the Pearl Harbor of Cuban resistance. But whereas the United States recovered from Pearl Harbor and went on to eventual victory, the Bay of Pigs was so devastating that it enabled the Castro regime, in danger of being overthrown at the time, to pull itself together and tighten its control over the population. Never since then has Fidel Castro faced a serious challenge from rebellious citizenry.

Castro came to power in 1959 amidst an atmosphere of national euphoria following the overthrow of dictator Fulgencio Batista. By the end of the year, however, disillusionment was setting in among many Cubans. A year later the new revolution was under way, this time directed against Castro.

In the United States, the Eisenhower Administration decided to overthrow Castro, who was moving toward establishment of a communist regime in Cuba. The CIA was selected as the instrument to be used in this effort, just as it had been the organization utilized to overthrow Jacobo Arbenz in Guatemala in 1954. The CIA's subsequent planning, in fact, was heavily influenced by the successful Guatemalan affair. Arbenz was brought down by means of an invasion launched from neighboring Honduras; Castro would be attacked similarly: by trained fighters dispatched from bases in Central America.

The CIA began recruiting Cuban exiles and sending them for training to a base in—appropriately—Guatemala. To head this force the CIA picked Manuel Artime, onetime officer in Castro's army who broke with Castro over the communist issue. Artime now headed a clandestine organization called the Movement for Revolutionary Recuperation (MRR).

Inside Cuba the opposition to Castro had developed into open resistance. Cubans had overthrown two dictators previously through resistance and revolution (Gerardo Machado in 1933, and Batista), and now the people were using the same tactics in an effort to rid themselves of Castro.

Guerrillas operated in the Escambray mountains of central Cuba and the Sierra Maestra of eastern Oriente Province. Underground organizations proliferated; no one knows precisely how many there were but they numbered over 50. Because of the large number of groups, their actions were generally uncoordinated. Nevertheless this worked to their benefit: Castro's G-2 (secret police) was hard put trying to keep track of all of them. Bombs exploded in theaters, stores, and other public places. Clandestine literature was circulated. Two major Havana department stores, La Epoca and El Encanto, went up in flames, demolished by incendiary materials expertly placed by saboteurs. Castro was seen on one occasion livid with rage at the mounting acts of resistance.

Just 2 years earlier Batista had toppled as the result of a combined urban resistance and rural guerrilla campaign, and as the new campaign against Castro grew, increasing numbers of Cubans were becoming confident that this campaign would also succeed.

The resistance in Cuba was rooted in the populace as a whole. Its leaders were men on the scene, hiding from Castro's police, moving from house to house every few days, but very much in control of their respective organizations. The CIA had only tenuous connections with these groups, and no control. Only the MRR could be considered linked with the CIA, because its chief was Artime. But even here the MRR's clandestine organization was autonomous to some extent and had its own "military chief," Rogelio Gonzalez Corso, who used the *nom de guerre* "Francisco."

Sometime in October or November 1960, an engineer named Rafael Diaz Hanscom slipped out of Cuba and arrived in the States. He had been the intelligence officer of the MRR, which meant that his duties were to gather information as well as to uncover government infiltrators. In the United States, Hanscom received training from the CIA and was entrusted with a highly important mission. After about 2 months Hanscom returned to Cuba.

He contacted other rebel leaders and told them he was setting up a new group, to be called *Unidad Revolucionaria.* Its function was to draw together the many clandestine organizations in Cuba and to coordinate their activities. Although he did not reveal this, Hanscom was now acting entirely for the CIA. The CIA had two basic reasons for setting up UR: (1) If the various groups could be coordinated, they would make a more effective weapon against Castro; (2) The CIA, through Hanscom, would be taking control of the Cuban underground. The CIA would then be in command not only of the men in the Guatemalan camp but also of the freedom fighters inside Cuba. Once Castro was overthrown and victory achieved, the CIA could pick Cuba's new leaders and determine the political path they were to take.

To induce the clandestine groups to come in under the UR umbrella, the CIA offered to provide the weapons and other supplies they needed.

By December 1960, 27 organizations had agreed to join *Unidad Revolucionaria.* They formally signed an "act of consolidation" in which they declared:

> That as of this historic moment all the revolutionary groups which we represent, as well as the men and women participating in them, agree to and do hereby consolidate the revolutionary unity that with the slogan "Fatherland and Liberty" shall fight until we gain triumph or death.

The united groups issued a "Declaration of Principles," as well as a general program to be followed once Castro was overthrown. Stated the UR:

> We declare that we shall raise as our flag respect for man himself, as a human being, without discrimination due to race or social condition; to acknowledge men's rights to social advantages ... to exercise his right to work, to education, and to security for himself and for his family ... to have the right to free thinking and free opinion; to exercise the right to elect his own rulers through free elections...

An organization was set up under Hanscom to coordinate clandestine activities of the various groups and to arrange for them to receive weapons from the States. UR even printed its own "currency": small paper bills ranging in value from $1 to

$100. These bills would be given to sympathizers contributing funds to the UR, and they were to be redeemed once the revolution was won.

The CIA carried through on its promise to ship arms to Cuba. The yacht *Tejana* made two or more trips to secluded spots on the coast of Matanzas province, and there the shipments were brought ashore. According to an officer of the UR: "Each shipment was large enough to fill two trucks. The ship brought in .30 and .50 caliber submachine guns, M-1 Garand rifles, C-3 and C-4 plastic explosives, and incendiary materials. Some of the weapons were distributed to the groups. The remainder was hidden for future use."

Early in 1961, the United States and Cuba broke diplomatic relations. The two countries were increasingly hostile toward each other, and this added fuel to the flames of resistance inside Cuba. Not many Cubans believed Castro could last long in the face of open American opposition.

The UR was engaged in a widening plan of activity. There would be a continual step-up of terrorism and sabotage in the cities. In the hinterlands the guerrillas would also increase their operations as they received more weapons and recruits. It was expected that the men in the Guatemalan camp would be sent to Cuba to bolster the guerrilla movements. The UR leadership—with the possible exception of Hanscom himself—did not expect a full-fledged invasion.

The general plan was to intensify armed resistance against Castro to the point a general uprising could take place. In line with this, the underground was already secretly in touch with officials of the Castro government itself and with military officers. At the proper moment, these conspirators would join the uprising, the military bringing their units with them. Virtually nothing has ever been said about this aspect of the anti-Castro revolution; even today details must be kept hazy because a number of individuals involved are still in Cuba. But this much can now be revealed:

- An air base was to be seized by rebel air force officers;
- The University of Havana was to be taken over by rebellious students;
- Navy ships were to raise the flag of rebellion and sail from their ports;
- Key positions in Havana, including radio stations, were to be seized by rebel units;
- Rebel police officers were to take command of several police stations.

Contacts had been made and plans were being developed. As of March 1961, however, there was still a great deal to be done. The rebels knew that they must not act prematurely, for to move before success was assured would result in destruction of the clandestine apparatus.

In his efforts to unify the underground, Hanscom was faced with a troublesome obstacle. "Francisco," the MRR military chief, did not want to accept Hanscom's leadership, claiming rather that the united organizations should be placed under his own command. Finally the disagreement was settled by the CIA: it sent word to "Francisco" that Hanscom was to be the leader. The order came nominally from

Artime, but it clearly emanated from the CIA's operations officers abroad.

"Francisco" bowed to the decision and requested to be placed in command of operations in Pinar del Rio province. A meeting to decide this and other questions of coordination was called. On the afternoon of March 18, nine persons gathered at the home of Pedro Echegaray in the Alturas de Biltmore suburb of Havana. Echegaray, who owned a machine shop, was a minor figure in the rebel movement and was not at the meeting. Among those who were present were Hanscom, "Francisco" and Humberto Sori Marin, former agriculture minister under Castro and now military chief of the UR.

One other person arrived at the meeting, saw that nine persons had gathered and refused to stay: it was too dangerous, he felt, for so many clandestine figures to be together in one spot.

The person was right, and it was now in Echegaray's house that the fate of Cuba was sealed. Police arrived and surrounded the house. Either they had been tipped off by an informant or someone had spotted an unusual number of people arriving at the house and had become suspicious. Whatever the reason, all nine persons were captured. Sori Marin attempted to flee and was wounded by a gunshot.

With the capture of Hanscom the CIA lost its top man in Cuba, and control of the underground movement. Another rebel, Andres Zayas ("Justo"), took over the leadership, but there is no indication he was as close to the CIA as Hanscom was.

Having lost Hanscom, the CIA apparently decided to stake everything on a landing of the trainees who were in Guatemala. The CIA might have waited and tried to reassert control over the underground, but it was under the pressure of time. MiG fighter planes were reportedly to be brought to Cuba from Russia, thus bolstering Castro's military strength. Furthermore, the men in the Guatemalan camp were restless, even near rebellion, and to forestall trouble it was necessary that they be thrown into action as soon as possible.

The original invasion plan called for a landing near the town of Trinidad in Las Villas province. Trinidad was near the guerrilla-filled Escambray mountains, and the invading force would have been able to seek the shelter of the mountains and reinforce the guerrillas if it was unable to hold its beachhead.

When the U.S. Joints Chiefs of Staff reviewed the plan, they concluded that the landing itself had about a 50 percent chance of success, and that the long-range success of the plan depended on support from the people of Cuba in the organized clandestine movements. Otherwise, additional troops would be required; that is, the United States would have to intervene with its own forces.

President Kennedy, however, did not care for the Trinidad plan and asked for alternatives. In mid-March the CIA presented the Joints Chiefs with three alternative plans, and the Joint Chiefs, after studying these, reported that none was as good as the Trinidad plan. In the words of Admiral Arleigh Burke (Ret.), who was then chairman of the Joint Chiefs, "the best of the poor lot was the Bay of Pigs plan." The CIA briefed Kennedy on the new plan, and after some modifications were made at his suggestion, the plan was prepared for action.

Kennedy approved of the modified plan March 16. Hanscom and the other underground leaders were captured March 18.

The Trinidad plan had envisioned support from the underground. The Bay of Pigs plan needed this support even more acutely because the new landing spot was considerably removed from the mountainous area.

Many people inside Cuba believed the men being trained in Guatemala were to be gradually infiltrated into Cuba to reinforce the guerrillas already operating inside the country. Hanscom, however, probably knew that a direct invasion was planned. Nevertheless, for security reasons he kept this to himself, giving no indications to men close to him in the UR. He did not even inform Arturo Villar, his intelligence chief, in whose home he hid for 3 weeks. The men who took over after Hanscom was captured did not know and were never informed that an invasion was coming and therefore did not make appropriate preparations.

Despite the plans which supposedly called for a general uprising, it is apparent that the CIA, after Hanscom was captured, did not want an uprising to take place. The CIA did not want the underground, and the mass of the Cuban people, to partici-pate in the liberation of the country. Instead, the CIA wanted the invaders to dis-embark and hold out for 72 hours, after which time a CIA-sponsored exile "govern-ment" would call for outside help and the United States would land Marines to sup-port the exile force at the Bay of Pigs. Castro would be overthrown by direct military intervention on the part of the United States, and the U.S. government—specifi-cally the CIA—would control the new Cuban government.

Hopelessly outnumbered and outgunned, their air support shot down, and receiv-ing no assistance from inside Cuba, the invaders were unable to hold out even for 72 hours.

Dramatic evidence that the CIA was bypassing the underground came at the time of the invasion. On Saturday, 15 April 1961, planes from Nicaraguan bases bombed several military airfields in Cuba. The underground was as much caught by surprise as were the Castro forces. Villar, the UR intelligence chief, met "Guillot," intelli-gence chief for the MRR, and, according to Villar:

> I asked him what was happening. He didn't know. He didn't know what we should do. In those days the groups were in touch with the CIA through telegraphy. The telegraph operator for Alberto Muller's group contacted the CIA and asked what was going on. The only reply he got was a stream of names of Cuban vegetables—bananas, yucca, malanga.

When the invaders disembarked in the early hours of Monday morning, the underground received no forewarning. That afternoon, puzzled and concerned, sev-eral leaders met at the Hong Kong restaurant in the Vedado section of Havana and discussed possible action. Not even certain that a landing had really taken place, fear-ing this might be a ruse by Castro to draw them out into the open, the leaders decided to do nothing except try to get information or guidance from the CIA. The telegraph operators made contact but the only instructions they received were: "Don't do anything. Wait for news. Maintain your positions."

Three days later the CIA went off the air. The invasion had failed.

By now the underground had been smashed. Castro's police and militia had rounded up a quarter of a million people suspected of being disloyal to the regime. Many underground fighters were caught in the net. Others fled to Latin American embassies seeking asylum.

Hanscom, "Francisco," and Sori Marin were put in front of a firing squad and executed.

Never again was there to be a significant resistance movement inside Cuba. The Bay of Pigs had saved Fidel Castro.

chapter six
SUBVERSIVE CAMPAIGN

From Argentina to Canada, from the Dominican Republic to Zanzibar, subversive activities were undertaken by Cuban agents or local nationals trained in Cuba. Castro and company were determined to extend the Cuban Revolution—or at least its communist aftermath—to far corners of the globe. The following article, published in the November/December, 1973, issue of the *Air University Review*, provided details about the big campaign launched by a small country, a small country governed by a man with a gigantic ego.

Few countries in the world in recent history have carried out programs of subversion with the consistency and determination of communist Cuba under Fidel Castro. Subversion, directed especially against other Latin American countries but also reaching as far away as Africa and even into the United States itself, has been a primary policy of the present Cuban government almost from the day it came into power.

Less than a month after the revolutionary movement took control in Cuba early in 1959, Ernesto "Che" Guevara declared, "The revolution is not limited to the Cuban nation." And in March 1959 Fidel Castro stated, "The Caribbean is ours." In July 1960 Castro bluntly declared, "We promise to continue making [Cuba] the example that can convert the Cordillera of the Andes into the Sierra Maestra of the American continent." This was not mere rhetoric; the Castro regime matched actions to words. Exiles of diverse nationalities and political stripes flocked into Cuba following the rebel victory, and those deemed to be ideologically acceptable—especially by Guevara, the government's in-house international expert—received moral support and military assistance in the form of training and equipment.

The first Cuban aggressive effort was directed against Panama. In an amateurish and near-comical venture 84 expeditionaries, 82 of whom were Cuban, landed at Nombre de Dios, an almost inaccessible village on the Caribbean coast of Panama. The invaders had to be "rescued" by the Panamanian National Guard, which utilized a landing barge borrowed from U.S. authorities in the Canal Zone. After a brief stay in a Panamanian jail, the invaders were sent back to Cuba with a stern warning. One Cuban stayed behind; he decided to marry a Panamanian girl he had met at Nombre de Dios.

Cuba was not deterred by this fiasco. In June 1959, coordinated air and sea landings of expeditionaries, armed in and launched from Cuba, took place in the Dominican Republic. All but a few of the invaders were killed by Dominican forces. In August 1959 another invasion group infiltrated Haiti from Cuba, and it, too, was wiped out. In Nicaragua also an insurgency, which had received an arms shipment by plane from Cuba, was quelled.

These four attempts to establish guerrilla operations in Caribbean-area countries having failed, the Cuban government developed more sophisticated subversive techniques. No more filibustering expeditions would be launched from Cuba. Instead other tactics were employed: Cuban diplomats provided financial aid to pro-Castro groups in the Latin American countries. Cuban fishing boats slipped weapons ashore to be used by insurgent movements. Propaganda was beamed from powerful Cuban shortwave radio stations, circulated through Cuban diplomatic missions, and distributed by the *Prensa Latina* news service. (*Prensa Latina* was organized by Jorge Ricardo Masetti, an Argentine friend of Guevara's who would die a few years later leading a Castroite guerrilla movement in Argentina.)

The greatest emphasis, however, was on the instruction of Latin Americans in guerrilla warfare. To this end, hundreds, and then thousands, of men were brought to Cuba, trained in special schools and camps, and returned to their homelands to start insurgencies or join campaigns already under way. Venezuela, Colombia, and Guatemala were among the nations most seriously affected by Cuba-assisted guerrillas; however, few countries in Central and South America escaped at least minor outbreaks.

The first Cuban efforts at subversion in 1959 appeared to have resulted from a combination of factors: the exuberance of the revolutionaries after their victory against a regime considered to be militarily superior; a belief on their part that it was up to them to set right what was wrong in other countries; a desire by Castro to become, as signs in Havana proclaimed, *El Líder de las Américas;* and the eagerness of Guevara to export Marxist revolution. As Cuba moved toward communism and became alienated from the rest of Latin America, the support of insurgency developed into an integral part of Cuban foreign policy. It was a policy which aimed at the communization of other countries, but it had practical as well as ideological motivations. Cuba needed allies that could provide it with support and break its hemispheric isolation. Venezuela was a particular target of Cuban subversion because of its vast oil reserves. Obtaining access to these would have made Cuba less reliant on the Soviet Union, Cuba's sole provider of vitally needed petroleum. Blas Roca, a leading Cuban communist, stated in 1963:

> If their [Venezuelan] struggle is a help to us today, their victory will give us an even more tremendous help. Then we shall no longer be a solitary island in the Caribbean con-

fronting the Yankee imperialists, but rather we shall have a land of support on the mainland.

Because of its geographical proximity, the Dominican Republic was another priority target for Cuba's insurgency program. First came the abortive June 1959 expeditions. Then, in November 1963, another guerrilla operation was launched with full Cuban support. Cuba had trained a number of the guerrillas who participated and attempted to send them a shipload of weapons; these were intercepted by Dominican forces. This guerrilla movement also was defeated. In 1965 an unexpected opportunity for Cuban subversion occurred. Late in April of that year the government of Dominican President Donald Reid Cabral was overthrown as the result of a military uprising. No clear-cut change of authority took place, however, and the situation in the capital city deteriorated rapidly. Mobs swirled through the streets, stores were looted, policemen were killed. The United States, supported by the Organization of American States, intervened militarily in the conflict, probably preventing what might have become a communist takeover of the entire country.

The Dominican uprising was an aberration—a move by military men which degenerated into near-chaos and a resulting opportunity for the communist movement. Other countries suffered Cuba-directed or -assisted insurgencies, but in these countries, too, the subversive efforts failed to achieve their objectives, the establishment of pro-Castro communist regimes. The Latin America of the sixties was not Cuba of the fifties, where the army of strongman Fulgencio Batista was unable to cope with the guerrilla movement. Farsighted Latin American governments were undertaking significant social programs. Armies, acutely aware of the danger inherent in guerrilla movements, moved with determination to wipe these out whenever they appeared. The United States, on its part, developed counter-insurgency concepts, including civic action, and instituted effective means of teaching these to the Latin American military.

Castro, however, was not discouraged. His regime was, in fact, prepared to make an attempt to institutionalize subversion. What could only be termed an international conference to foment subversion was held in Havana from 3 to 15 January 1966. Officially, it was called the "First Conference of Solidarity of the Peoples of Africa, Asia, and Latin America," but for brevity's sake it came to be known as the "Tricontinental Conference." From 82 countries came over 600 representatives, chosen by local Communist parties and "liberation movements." The tone and purpose of the conference were indicated by the agenda, which included such phrases as:

Struggle against imperialism ... Struggle for complete national liberation ... Intensification of all forms of struggle ... Ways and means of aiding the liberation movements in Africa, Asia, and Latin America ... Burning issues of the struggle.

The Tricontinental adopted 73 resolutions aimed at "the system of imperialist, colonialist, and neo-colonialist exploitation against which it has declared a struggle to the death." Castro told the delegates that the conference had been "a great victory of the revolutionary movement."

Two permanent organizations grew out of the conference. The first, created by resolution of the conference as a whole, was the Organization of Solidarity of the Peoples of Africa, Asia, and Latin America, whose task was "to unite, coordinate, and further the struggle" on those three continents. The second organization was created by the 27 Latin American delegations; on 16 January they announced [the] setting up of the Latin American Organization of Solidarity (*Organización Latinoaméricana de Solidaridad*—OLAS).

The OLAS was of special interest to Castro. Through its establishment a façade of international respectability, at least in communist eyes, was given to the subversive efforts Cuba directed against other Latin American countries. The headquarters of OLAS was set up in Havana, and the First Conference of Solidarity of the Latin American Peoples was held in that city 28 July-5 August 1967. A "general declaration" issued after the conference proclaimed "that it is a right and a duty of the peoples of Latin America to make revolution."

The holding of the Tricontinental conference graphically demonstrated that Castro's subversive interests extended beyond Latin America. In the Guevara-Castro view, undeveloped nations were particularly susceptible to communist take-overs via guerrilla movements. Acting in accordance with this concept, Cuba has given a full measure of attention to Africa. As early as 1961 a Zanzibar National Party office, headed by a former Mau Mau, John Okello, was opened in Havana. By mid-1962 men from at least nine African countries, including Zanzibar, were receiving subversive training in Cuba. In January 1964 a rebel movement in Zanzibar led by Okello overthrew the pro-Western government and set up the "People's Republic of Zanzibar." Cuba has also been involved in the Congo (Brazzaville), where Cuban troops help maintain the leftist government in power, and in Portuguese Guinea, where Cubans serve with the guerrilla forces (eight Cubans were reported killed early in 1973 when they were intercepted trying to infiltrate the colony).

The United States hardly qualifies as an undeveloped country, but even here Castro's agents have been active. In November 1962 the FBI arrested three Cubans in New York, including an *attaché* of Cuba's United Nations mission, and charged them with planning to place bombs in stores, oil refineries, and the New York subway system. A cache of explosives and incendiary devices was seized. In 1968 two other Cuban representatives at the UN were barred from the United States because they had been providing guidance and financial assistance to American black extremist groups.

Through the first half of the sixties Guevara masterminded Cuba's operations abroad. Then, apparently tiring of the successive failures in Latin America, he decided to go into the field himself once more. He chose Africa as his new battleground, feeling that this continent was comparatively far from the United States' sphere of power and influence and close to communist and other sympathetic countries. Leading a group of Cubans, Guevara involved himself in the struggles in the Congo.

The African adventure also failed—Guevara was evidently there 6 months—so Guevara returned secretly to Cuba, where he began preparations for yet another guerrilla movement. This one would be in Bolivia, where he believed the government of President René Barrientos could be overthrown much as that of Cuba's Fulgencio Batista had been brought down in 1959. Furthermore, Bolivia was centrally and strategically located so that, in Guevara's view, it could serve as a base for spin-off operations in adjoining countries, especially Argentina.

The full extent of the Cuban operation was revealed later when Orlando Castro Hidalgo, a defector from the Cuban intelligence service, disclosed that at approximately the time Guevara was preparing to go to Bolivia, two *comandantes* of the Cuban army, both of them members of the Cuban Communist Party's Central committee, were infiltrated into Venezuela to assist guerrillas in that country. Guevara's movement in Bolivia had been part of a two-pronged attack on South America. The Venezuelan effort, like the one in Bolivia, ended in failure (although, unlike Guevara, the two *comandantes* in Venezuela eventually got back to Cuba).

Castro, aided by Guevara, Raúl Castro, and other able lieutenants, had led a guerrilla movement which was part of the revolution against Batista. The movement was a major factor in Batista's eventual overthrow, but it was not the only factor: effective operations by urban clandestine organizations, a substantial decline in the Cuban economy, and the United States' cutoff of arms and support for Batista also contributed to his fall. Upon coming to power, however, Castro and Guevara overlooked these other factors, preferring to emphasize the guerrilla role in the revolution. Out of this grew a mystique of guerrilla invincibility, a mystique in which Castro and Guevara really believed (so much so that Guevara staked his life on it, and lost). It was this mystique that was the conceptual foundation for much of Cuba's subversive effort during the sixties. Start a guerrilla movement, support it, and it will eventually succeed—thus thought the planners in Havana. But not one such guerrilla operation in Latin America succeeded, and with the death of Guevara and the failure of the grand plan (Bolivia-Venezuela), Havana was forced to accept the fact that other methods were needed.

Cuban subversion entered a new phase. There would be more sophistication and selectivity in the program. Substantial numbers of men would no longer be sent abroad to start guerrilla operations.[1] Funds, weapons, and trained agents would still be sent to existing movements, but not on the scale of previous efforts.

A doctrinal shift also occurred. In a speech on 13 March 1967 Castro faulted

[1]*In special cases Castro seems still willing to try to set up new guerrilla operations. After the termination of the 1965 Dominican uprising, rebel chief Francisco Caamaño Deño went to London as Dominican military attaché. In October 1967 he took a trip to The Hague, where he disappeared from public sight. He went to Paris in disguise and from there was spirited by the Cuban intelligence service to Cuba via Prague. Evidently Castro wanted to use him in the Dominican Republic again one day. Early in February 1973 Caamaño did land on the Dominican coast with a small group of armed men. Pursued by Dominican forces, he was killed in a battle a fortnight later.*

Venezuelan revolutionaries because in their strategy there had been "an over-estimation of the importance of the capital and of the struggle in the capital and an under-estimation of the importance of the guerrilla movement." The death of Guevara was a severe blow to the guerrilla mystique, and now Cuba reluctantly turned its attention to the cities of Latin America as a potentially fruitful battleground. A case in point was Montevideo, Uruguay, where the Tupamaro clandestine organization was growing in strength, boldness, and operational capability. A number of Tupamaros were trained in Cuba; an interrogation manual used by the Tupamaros was written in Cuba or by a Cuban. The Uruguayan army's intelligence department learned that Castro, during a trip through Africa, met with a Tupamaro representative and gave him $265,000 in cash to support the insurgent movement.

The Tupamaro movement was crushed by the Uruguayan army in 1972. Castro, however, seems intent on continuing to use urban terrorism as a major method of subversion. In February 1973 a U.S. State Department official reported that "several hundred" persons in Cuba were being trained in urban terror tactics.

Castro's persistence in pursuing a policy of subversion has a direct bearing on relations between Cuba and the United States. These relations were broken in January 1961 and American officials have repeatedly stated that they will not be resumed until Castro, among other things, ceases trying to subvert Latin American countries. Castro, however, has indicated no interest in doing this. He stated bluntly in 1971, "Cuba maintains its policy of support to the revolutionary governments and also support of the revolutionary movements of Latin America." Subversion continues to be an operational policy of the Cuban government.

chapter seven
DOMINICAN TARGET

The Cuban revolutionaries had succeeded in overthrowing President and General Fulgencio Batista. Ergo, it would be possible to overthrow Generalissimo Rafael Leonidas Trujillo on the nearby Dominican Republic, too. Or so thought Castro and cohorts. In June 1959 they launched an air and sea invasion of the country. It was quickly defeated by Trujillo's forces. This did not deter Castro, nor did the assassination of Trujillo. Cuba's subversive efforts continued, and eventually led to American military intervention in April 1965. Mallin covered the U.S. action, and on one occasion was caught in a rebel ambush with troopers from the U.S. 82nd Airborne Division. The following is a chapter from *Caribbean Crisis*, published in 1965.

Cuban dictator Fidel Castro Ruz had been in power only 3 months when he declared, "The Caribbean is ours," and ever since then he has been working hard to make that statement come true.

Castro's primary target in the Caribbean has been the Dominican Republic, which, because of its unstable condition, has become particularly susceptible to subversion. The 1965 rebellion marked the third major effort by Castro to subvert that country.

The first attempt was described in my book *Fortress Cuba*:

> *Late in the afternoon of 14 June 1959, soon after Castro solidified his power in Cuba, 80 men wearing olive-green uniforms boarded a gray C-46 at an airfield near Antilla, in the northern part of Cuba's Oriente Province. The plane bore Dominican markings. The men wore armbands which displayed a red and blue shield and the letters "UPD," representing the Union Patriotica Dominicana, a Dominican exile group. Loaded aboard the plane were food and ammunition sufficient for 15 days, and the men carried FN Belgian rifles, M-1 Garands, bazookas, and machine guns.... In command of the group of men was Enrique Jimenes Moya, a Red-tinged Dominican exile who had served as a captain with Castro's guerrillas.*

The plane took off and headed eastward, holding close to the route and timetable of a regular Delta Airlines' flight in order to avoid radar detection. Two hours later, the C-46 landed at an airfield outside Constanza, a town of 3,000 people set in the Dominican Republic's Central Mountain Range. The expeditionaries piled out of the plane and quickly overcame the small handful of surprised soldiers on guard at the field. They captured several vehicles and used these to race into town, where they attacked a garrison of about 15 men, killing or wounding most of them. Other troops, stationed outside of town, headed toward Constanza, but were ambushed by the rebels. Following this fight, the rebels retired into the surrounding hills.

Two hundred additional rebels who had sailed from Cuba on 13 June in two converted yachts carried out landings at two points on the northwest Dominican coast. The regular Dominican military were, however, the best in the Caribbean at that time, and Dictator Trujillo soon had them in determined pursuit of the rebels. Within weeks all of the rebels were killed or captured, and Castro's first effort to subvert the Dominican Republic had failed.

The second major attempt was made in 1963. A pro-Castro political party had been formed, the *Agrupación Política Catorce de Junio* (June 14th Political Group, named after the 1959 expedition). The June 14th sent a group of approximately 25 men to receive 6 months of guerrilla training at the Minas del Frio camp in Cuba's Sierra Maestra Mountains.

Using false identity papers, most of these men returned to the Dominican Republic, where they served as the hard core of a guerrilla operation which was launched on 29 November 1963. Over 120 guerrillas began operating in 6 areas: Altamira, Bonao, Enriquillo, San José de las Matas, San Francisco de Macorís, and Miches. The government—the Triumvirate [a three-man *junta* which ruled after Trujillo had been assassinated on May 30, 1961]—charged that the goal of the rebels was "to establish a communist dictatorship."

Once again the Dominican armed forces moved effectively, and within a month the guerrilla bands had been wiped out. On the night of 21 December Army patrols located the last substantial group in the mountains west of San José de las Matas, and in the resulting action 5 guerrillas were captured and 15 were killed. Among the dead was Manuel Tavárez Justo, head of the June 14th and "supreme commander" of the rebels. Altogether, the government reported, 31 guerrillas had been killed and 92 captured (most of whom were subsequently deported the following year).

Not only had Castro trained the guerrillas and sent them to launch the uprising, he also attempted to send them weapons. On 6 December a shipment of arms and ammunition was captured which had been sent from Cuba aboard a Cuban Navy vessel and transferred at sea to a Dominican fishing ship, the *Scarlet Woman*. Four men who had landed with the weapons were also captured.

When did the planning for the April 1965 uprising begin? Since communists are always in a state of conspiracy, the moment when the plot was spawned cannot be pinpointed. In all likelihood, however, the conspiracy was given a considerable impetus at a secret meeting held in Havana of representatives of all Latin American Communist parties. At this conference, in November 1964, a decision was made to step up subversive efforts throughout the hemisphere, and this included the Dominican Republic.

The communists probably did not plan to launch their own rebellion openly. Undoubtedly aware of the pro-Bosch conspiracy [Juan Bosch had been elected President in December 1962 and ousted by a military coup in September 1965], they would wait until this got started, and then move in—much as they had moved into the Cuban government once Castro had already come to power. Highly significant is a "manifesto" issued on 14 March 1965—over a month before the civil war began—by the *Partido Socialista Popular*, another of the Dominican Republic's Communist parties. Ominously and prophetically, the statement declared:

> *A growing popular clamor is rising throughout the country in favor of the return of Professor Juan Bosch.... This victory can only be achieved through the mobilization and the active struggle of all the patriotic sectors of our country.... Concrete actions by the masses ... [are] imperative.... All the people, fight in the streets, in the plazas, in the factories, in the fields, for the return of President Bosch at the front of the constitutional government!*

The return of Bosch, the communists admitted, however, "does not signify the solution of the national problems." The return of Bosch through "popular action" would be "a step of extraordinary advance in the integration of the forces which will lead to the general emancipation of the Dominican people." Bosch's return, the communists were saying, would be a step, but only a step, toward their eventual goal: "socialist democracy," i.e., communism.

Within hours after the pro-Bosch military made its move [overthrowing the government of President Donald Reid Cabral] in April, the communist presence in the rebellion became apparent. The executions, the arming of civilians, the attacks on foreigners, the setting up of strongpoints, the leading of mobs to the offices of anti-Castro newspapers and political parties—all of these were traditional communist tactics in a revolutionary situation. The rebels took over Radio Santo Domingo and it became an echo of Radio Habana Cuba: denouncing of the "oligarchies," calls to the "masses," violent attacks on the United States, abolishing the rank of general (*á la* Castro), declaration of "the dictatorship of the proletariat" and the "Free Territory of the Dominican Republic" (*á la* Cuba's claim to be the "Free Territory of the Americas").

There are three Communist parties in the Dominican Republic. The largest is the June 14th (APCJ), with a membership estimated at somewhere around 4,000 militants. Its strength lies among students and workers, and Castro's influence is considerable. The *Partido Socialista Popular Dominicano* (PSPD), with approximately 1,000 members, is Moscow-oriented. The *Movimiento Popular Dominicano* (MPD) has only about 500 members, but it closely follows the aggressive communist Chinese line. (A fourth party that is occasionally mentioned, the *Partido Nacionalista Revolucionario*, is inactive and largely a paper organization.)

Despite any ideological differences they might have, the three Communist parties worked in unison when the rebellion broke out. The rapid and effective manner in which they began operating demonstrated the careful planning with which they had prepared themselves for revolution.

As soon as the military launched their uprising on 24 April the communist leaders went into action. They armed themselves and their key followers, who were assigned to tasks in various parts of the city. Communists were ordered to incite civilian crowds that were gathering on the streets, and to organize rallies and demonstrations in favor of Bosch.

The following morning, armed PSPD members harangued crowds gathered in the downtown Parque Independencia. Among the speakers were Diomedes Mercedes Batista (who had traveled to Cuba in 1963), Narciso Isa Conde (a member of the PSPD Central Committee), and Asdrúbal Ulises Domíngues Guerrero (who had received training in Russia in 1962). Later, communist mobile loudspeaker units drove through the city urging the citizenry to join the rebellion.

It was on this second day of the uprising that the communists engineered an event that almost completely placed the revolt in their hands, at least for a while. Several thousand weapons, ranging from hand grenades to machine guns, were loaded on trucks at the 27th of February Army camp and driven to downtown Santo Domingo. There they were handed out to civilians. Top communists helped Army rebels to distribute the weapons, and in some cases they actually controlled the distribution, thus seeing that their fellows received arms. Among the communists who took part in the handing out of weapons were: Fidelio Despradel Roque (a founder of the APCJ who had received guerrilla training in Cuba and was a leader of the abortive 1963 guerrilla operation); Félix Servio Ducoudray Mansfield, Jr. (a PSPD leader who had received indoctrination in Russia, worked for Cuba in 1960 for the New China News Agency, then visited communist China, traveling on a Cuban passport); Juan Ducoudray Mansfield (Félix's brother, also a PSPD leader who had traveled to Russia, communist China, and Poland, and to Cuba, where he prepared scripts for broadcasts beamed toward the Dominican Republic); Hugo Tolentino Dipp (PSPD leader, guerrilla training in Cuba); Daniel Ozuna Hernandez (APCJ leader, survivor of the 1963 guerrilla operation); and Buenaventura Johnson Pimentel (member of the PSPD's Central Committee, possibly also a member of the APCJ).

To further prepare for street fighting, bottles (many removed from a Pepsi-Cola plant) were distributed to civilian rebels. These were filled with gasoline taken from tank trucks and filling stations, and they thus made "Molotov cocktails," particularly useful when fighting tanks.

The rebel radio station issued a call for a march on the National Palace, and several thousand civilians, armed with everything from clubs to rifles, responded and seized the building. Among the civilians was an armed communist group, including PSPD members who had received guerrilla training in Cuba.

Leaders of Bosch's *Partido Revolucionario Dominicano* (PRD) arrived at the Palace and advocated setting up a temporary government under Rafael Molina Ureña until Bosch could be brought back. Other factions urged different steps, including the establishment of a military *junta*, but the PRD view prevailed, and Ureña took over as Provisional President. Communists actively participated in the heated discussions, siding with the Bosch people. Among the communists present were Facundo Gomez (PSPD member who was part owner of the *Scarlet Woman*, the vessel which landed the Cuban weapons in December 1963); Luis Gomez Perez (PSPD Central Committee, trained in Czechoslovakia); Antonio Emilio José Isa Conde (PSPD student agitator who received guerrilla training in Cuba and money in Prague) and his brother Narciso (PSPD Central Committee); Ema Tavarez Justo (APCJ student agitator and sister of APCJ Leader Manuel Tavares Justo, killed in the 1963 guerrilla operation); and a number of other leading figures from the Communist parties, including Mercedes Batista, Ozuna Hernandez, and Lora Vicente. "President" Ureña appointed Alejandro Lajara Gonzalez (an APCJ member who earlier in the day had been busy distributing weapons to civilians) to the post of Deputy Director of Investigation.

Communist agitators incited the armed mobs to burn and destroy property. Civilians looted stores and homes, and communists and hoodlums made a special point of killing policemen. The plant of the anti-communist newspaper, Prensa Libre, was seized, and communists immediately made preparations to print propaganda leaflets. The offices of three anti-communist political parties, *Union Cívica Nacional, Partido Liberal Revolucionista,* and *Vanguardia Revolucionaria Dominicana,* were sacked by mobs.

The communists prepared themselves militarily. Additional weapons were obtained and distributed, para-military units were organized, strongpoints were established at strategic locations. Directing the communist military activities was Manuel Gonzalez Gonzalez, a veteran of the Spanish Civil War who came to the Dominican Republic in 1940. A communist, he joined the PSPD and rose to membership in the Central Committee. He was reported to be an agent of G-2, Castro's intelligence service. Assisting Gonzalez was Manuel Escobar Alfonseca, a prominent PSPD member who had received training behind the Iron Curtain in 1963.

Strongholds were established in a building in Arzobispo Portes Avenue (PSPD), on José Gabriel Garcia Street in the Ciudad Nueva low-cost housing area (APCJ), in a building at the corner of Arzobispo Merino and Luperon Streets (machine guns were set up on the roof), and at Arzobispo Portes and Sanchez Streets. Juan Miguel Roman Diaz (a member of the APCJ Central Committee and survivor of the 1963 guerrilla operation) commanded a combination prison, arsenal, and strongpoint at the corner of Estrelleta and Arzobispo Nouel Streets. Gonzalez Gonzalez set up a comando in a building on the corner of El Conde and Hostos Streets. Another communist group, calling itself the Luperon Comando, was established at the corner of Hostos and Luperon Streets. Strongholds were established on Caracas Street, on Juan de Morpha Street, and on Bolivar Avenue, as well as at other locations.

On 26 April General Wessin [Elías Wessin y Wessin] made his first move, sending his planes to bomb and strafe rebel positions. Public resentment was aroused, and the air attacks provided the communists with a propaganda weapon. The rebel radio gave the names and addresses of Wessin's fliers and urged the public to sack these houses.

The distribution of weapons and the making of Molotov cocktails continued. Ema Tavarez Justo, Antonio Isa Conde, and other agitators continued haranguing crowds, and distributing mimeographed flysheets. These called for the formation of "common units of soldiers and civilians" and of "people's combat units" (militia á la Castro).

The effectiveness with which the communist apparatus operated, combined with the arming of communist-led rebels, caused a major shift within the top leadership of the rebel movement. Faced with mob violence which it could not control, frightened by the attack's of Wessin's warplanes, the PRD leadership dissolved. Molina Ureña gave up the "presidency," and several other PRD leaders, including José Pena Gomez, Maximo Lovaton Pittaluga, and Antonio Martínez Francisco, abandoned the rebel side. Martínez Francisco, secretary-general of the PRD, went to the loyalist Air Force base at San Isidro and appealed to the rebels to lay down their arms.

Approximately a thousand troops of the Regular Army had participated in the original revolt. As the communists poured out weapons to civilians, these latter soon greatly outnumbered the soldiers. The rebel Army officers could not control the mobs; the communists could. The fomenting and directing of mob violence is a tool with which the communists have had considerable experience over the years in many lands.

Still in exile in Puerto Rico, Juan Bosch, symbolic leader of the rebellion, seemed little aware of what was happening in his country. Visited on 2 May by a special emissary of President Johnson's, John Bartlow Martin, Bosch spoke meaninglessly of "a meeting of the congress," "general amnesty for everybody," and the return of "Molina to the palace." Concluded Martin: Bosch "was still dreaming of the old days."

The Communists, by 28 April, dominated the rebel movement, but they were unable to—and it probably was not yet their purpose to—restore order. Shooting was widespread, and armed mobs roamed the city, terrorizing it, sacking stores, firing on foreign embassies. The junta, based at San Isidro, notified the American ambassador that it could no longer provide protection for American citizens, and the wheels were quickly set in motion for the landing of U.S. Marines.

On 29 April an armed mob launched an attack on the last loyalist stronghold in downtown Santo Domingo, the police-held Ozama Fortress on the Ozama River. The attack was directed by MPD leaders who had been in Cuba but APCJ and PSPD members also participated. After heavy fighting, the fortress fell on 30 April and with it the communists captured a large amount of weapons and ammunition.

On 29 April a mob looted a large church and, roaming through the Ciudad Nueva area, echoed slogans so familiar in Cuba: "Fatherland or death!" and *"Viva Castro!"*

But a new element was now entering the scene of the Dominican tragedy. To protect its citizens and those of other countries, and to block the communist takeover, the United States began to pour troops into Santo Domingo. Some 3,000 Marines and paratroopers were flown into the city and San Isidro on 29 and 30 April and more would arrive in the following days.

In order to discuss this new turn of events, leaders of the APCJ, PSPD, and MPD met with Benjamin Ramos Alvarez on 29 April. Ramos was a high-level APCJ member and head of that party's District Committee for Santo Domingo. Leading communists, including Gonzalez Gonzalez and the Ducoudray brothers, also conferred with rebel Army officers.

Although the rebel radio station instructed rebels not to fire on the American forces, attacks and sniping continued. The U.S. troops did not fire unless fired upon first, but once they had been shot at, they replied, and it was estimated that rebel casualties in these incidents were running at two to one for every American casualty. Two APCJ units were especially active, one of which was led by Central Committeeman Roman Diaz (who was killed in a firefight on 19 May).

In Havana, Fidel Castro, addressing a May Day rally, admitted the communist link with the Dominican rebellion. He said:

> We do not know how many communists there are in Santo Domingo. It is possible there are few communists. But without a doubt of any kind, any communist in a struggle like that one does not side with the imperialists, does not side with the gorillas [military]. He fights because it is his revolutionary duty—alongside the Constitution, alongside the party that defends the Constitution, although that party declares itself non-communist, although that party swears that it has nothing to do with the communists.

The rebel radio asked that U.S. troops not be fired on, but a shortwave transmitter gave contrary instructions, urging rebels to shoot at "Yankees" on sight. In the Parque Independencia, a violent anti-American speech was delivered before a crowd by Edmundo Garcia Castillo, a member of the PSPD.

During the first days of May rebel leaders held a series of conferences regarding their future moves. Considerable thought was given to improving the structure of their "government" so that it could make a greater claim to legitimacy. There was also discussion around this time as to the advisability of the top communist leaders withdrawing from open participation in the rebel movement. Two reasons seemed to counsel this move: to prepare for the possibility that the communist leaders might have to go underground and to lend credence to rebel disavowals of the communist role in the rebellion.

Although the lesser communists were to continue fighting, a number of top communists went into hiding, and others attempted to go into the interior of the country. They were under instruction to organize local party members for eventual guerrilla action. False identity cards were prepared for these top leaders.

MPD leaders, as well as those of the APCJ and the PSPD, began to go underground. In addition, MPD members were urged to obtain as many weapons as they could, to be hidden for possible use in future guerrilla warfare.

Having been prevented from seizing control of the Dominican Republic, the communists were now laying the groundwork for new subversive efforts.

On 11 May, in a radio address, Colonel Caamaño [rebel military commander Francisco Alberto Caamaño Deno], declared:

> Despite the tremendous propaganda by U.S. publicity organs based on the erratic or ill-intentioned reports by Ambassador [W. Tapley] Bennett [Jr.], our revolutionary government is eminently democratic. I do not have to tell the people this, because they know why they are fighting and what flag they are under. It is superfluous to insist further on this, but in this respect I can only say that there is no deafer person than the one who does not want to hear. That version [regarding the communist role] is a specious fabrication ...

By Caamaño's side when he delivered the speech was Héctor Aristy, who held the post of minister of the presidency. Ordinarily, this would be an administrative position—sort of a general manager of the presidential office—but Aristy appeared to play a considerably more important role. Invariably when Caamaño talked with foreign diplomats or correspondents, Aristy would be with him, ostensibly as a translator (although Caamaño speaks English well), but actually to counsel him and sometimes even to speak for him.

Before the rebellion, Aristy had been a playboy, a minor politician, and a sometime conspirator. Once the rebellion started, the smoothness with which Aristy handled matters around Caamaño was noted, and there was some suspicion that he was a trained communist agent, but most qualified observers labeled him simply as an "opportunist."

John Bartlow Martin, the U.S. presidential emissary, conferred with Caamaño and noticed the ubiquitous presence of Aristy. On one occasion Martin and the nuncio were trying to convince Caamaño to confer with General Imbert, but Caamaño insisted that before he would do this, Imbert had to get rid of General Wessin and two other officers. [Antonio Imbert Barreras had participated in the assassination of Trujillo and became a powerful political figure.] Writing in *Life* magazine, Martin recalled:

> The nuncio said, "... We must talk about peace. Will you talk at the nunciatura?"
>
> Caamaño said, "No, I cannot go there."
>
> I said, "Well, where can you go? Let's find a place," and touched his sleeve and said, "Let's look at the map."
>
> I wanted to get him alone—for the first time. I took him to the far end of the table and asked him in a low voice, "Are you a free agent?"
>
> He said, "I am a free agent."
>
> "Can you leave here?"
>
> He hesitated, said, "My people say that talking won't do any good as long as those three are there. If I did, I'd be out."

"That's what I'm asking you—are you a free agent? Who would put you 'out'? Who are 'your people'?"

"My militantes. The cabinet. Some senators."

Militantes, *in this cloudy context, could mean either soldiers, like himself, who had defected, or Castro-communists. I asked, "Who are the militantes?"*

Caamaño hesitated again, then said, "The officers."

I said, "Not the communists?"

He said, "There are no communists."

I said, "We know there are. What I am asking is whether you are free of them."

He said, looking away, speaking hesitantly, "There may be individual communists in my area. But they are not in the leadership. After we get over this, we get rid of them."

I was far from sure. And I think he was, too.

This was not the only time that Caamaño admitted to the communist presence in the revolution. The Organization of American States sent a special committee to Santo Domingo, and when it later returned to Washington, Mexico's OAS ambassador raised the question of communist infiltration in the rebel movement.

To this, the chairman of the committee, Argentina's OAS ambassador, Ricardo M. Colombo, replied:

... We spoke with the different men who were in this rebel grouping and, a notable thing, from the head of the revolution, Colonel Caamaño, to someone known as minister of the presidency, they recognized that they [the communists] were their great problem. They explained to a certain extent briefly the process of the history of the Dominican Republic, then confessed to us how gradually a number of elements were being incorporated with them whom they called communists, and that their problem was to avoid infiltration for the purpose of springing a surprise and seizing control. They said this clearly, and even at one point ... I spoke with Colonel Caamaño and asked him in a friendly way whether he honestly believed that such infiltration existed. He confirmed this to me, but he gave me the impression that he had the courage to face it.

The communists had again failed in their effort to conquer the Dominican Republic. But Ernesto Guevara, the master planner and wily executor of Cuban subversion, once wrote:

The result of the struggles of today does not matter. That one or another movement be put down transitorily is not important for the final result. Decisive is the resolution for struggle which ripens day by day ...

In the Dominican Republic, the communists were already preparing for a new effort, a new struggle, a new battle.

[Caamaño died in 1973 leading another Cuban-sponsored expedition against the Dominican Republic.]

chapter eight

Apart from Castro, no figure that emerged from the Cuban Revolution was more fascinating and influential than Ernesto "Che" Guevara. Guevara joined Castro's group as a doctor. Within a year or so he was one of the top guerrilla captains. With victory, Guevara helped handle Cuba's official finances and at the same time masterminded and directed a hemisphere-wide subversive program. He was a guerrilla theoretician, as well as practitioner, as related in the following excerpts from *"Che" Guevara on Revolution*, which was published in 1969.

WARRIOR TURNED THEORIST

Guerrilla warfare, basically, is conflict between irregular forces and regular armies. Germans waged guerrilla war against the Romans; the French waged guerrilla war against the British toward the end of the Hundred Years' War; the Indians waged guerrilla war against the American settlers; the American settlers used it against the British; the Spaniards and Russians against Napoleon; the Cubans against the Spaniards, the Filipinos against the Americans, the Yugoslavs against the Nazis, and on and on, innumerable instances throughout recorded history.

The communist contribution has been to adopt and adapt guerrilla warfare to communism's political purposes, utilizing it as a concept for conquest, endowing it with ideological overtones, broadening it to fit into the theory of revolutionary warfare. For undeveloped regions, guerrilla warfare has come to be for communists the prime mover of revolutionary warfare, although revolutionary warfare also encompasses a wide variety of tactics ranging from the ancient arts of diplomacy and espionage to modern techniques of sabotage and propaganda, and ultimately must include, according to most tacticians, the build-up and use of regular armies capable of crushing in open battle the forces of the enemy.

Soviet Premier Nikita Khrushchev publicly, albeit reluctantly, committed communists to the use and support of this type of warfare—he used the euphemistic term "national liberation wars"—in a speech delivered on 6 January 1961. He stated:

> There will be wars of liberation as long as imperialism exists, as long as colonialism exists. There are revolutionary wars. Such wars are not only possible but inevitable, since the colonialists will not voluntarily grant the peoples independence. Therefore, the peoples can win their freedom and independence only through struggle, including armed struggle.... Can such wars occur in the future? They can. Can there be such uprisings? There can. These are precisely wars of popular rebellion. Can conditions in other countries come to where the people exhaust their patience and rise up with arms in hand? They can. What attitude do Marxists have toward such uprisings? The most favorable. These uprisings must be identified with wars among states, with local wars, because in these uprisings the people are fighting to exercise their right to self-determination and for the social and independent national development; these are uprisings against rotten reactionary regimes and against colonialists. Communists fully and unreservedly support just wars and march in the van of the peoples fighting wars of liberation.

There is a belief that guerrilla warfare is primitive. This is erroneous. The basic techniques of guerrilla warfare are ancient—hit, run, hide, hit, run, hide, until you wear down your enemy—but these techniques are as applicable in the nuclear age as they were in ancient Rome. Since World War II there have been over a score of major guerrilla campaigns around the world, and in several of these, ill-trained, lightly-equipped guerrillas eventually achieved successes against modern armies employing planes, tanks, and other modern equipment.

Guerrilla warfare is a flexible, sophisticated type of struggle, adapting itself to the contemporary age, utilizing automatic weapons or old firearms. It is a directly human type of combat: the guerrilla sees in his gunsight the soldier he is shooting at, or is in close proximity to the target of his mortar shells. He does not direct military barrages against distant points nor aim bombs to be dropped through 30,000 feet of clouds. The effective guerrilla needs to be the most dedicated of soldiers. He is ever in peril and usually in discomfort, he may be long separated from his family, he has little to go on except faith and hope. The guerrilla pits his shrewdness and his endurance and his cause against the regular soldier. Brigadier General Samuel G. Griffith has remarked:

> Guerrilla warfare is ... suffused with, and reflects, man's admirable qualities as well as his less pleasant ones. While it is not always humane, it is human, which is more than can be said for the strategy of extinction.

The leading communist theoreticians of guerrilla warfare have been China's Mao Tse-Tung, Viet Nam's Vo Nguyen Giap, and Cuba's Ernesto Guevara. All three have written extensively about guerrilla warfare; all three have experienced successful campaigns.[1]

General Griffith holds that Mao produced "the first systematic study of the subject" of guerrilla warfare. It must not be understood by this that Mao was the first person to originate or set down thoughts on the processes of guerrilla warfare. Mao was himself influenced by the ancient Chinese military philosopher Sun Tzu. Whereas

Sun counseled, "Uproar [in the] East, Strike [in the] West," Mao wrote, "In guerrilla warfare, select the tactic of seeming to come from the east and attacking from the west ..." Other works had their influence on Mao and his associates—even one on George Washington. Robert S. Elegant stated that the "first textbook on large-scale partisan warfare" used by Chu Teh, Mao's top lieutenant, was "a short work on the tactics employed by General George Washington in the Revolutionary War." Mao himself is not well read. He uses no foreign language and thus has had advantage of only such foreign works as have been available in Chinese translation. For his formative years he concentrated principally on Lenin and Stalin, particularly Stalin. He had, however, some knowledge of Clausewitz. Mao's main contribution has lain, as Katzenbach and Hanrahan have said:

> ... in pulling together a group of previously unrelated and unstudied techniques—shaping these into a single operational pattern. He is the man who has written it down for others; the man who has presented the communist revolutionary with the workable blueprint.

Mao set it down—the limited things he learned from others and what he had learned from personal experience in China's drawn-out struggles—and others proceeded from where he left off. One of these was Vo Nguyen Giap, the North Vietnamese military leader in the wars against the French and the American and South Vietnamese forces.

Giap, as a refugee from French Indochina, may have spent some time in Yenan, Mao's stronghold in China, and had the opportunity to observe at firsthand Chinese guerrilla operations. But whether or not this was so, Mao's thinking strongly influenced Giap's writings and the tactics he would one day himself employ. Mao, for example, was the first military theorist to define the three stages of revolutionary warfare. Writing within the context of the Sino-Japanese War, he set these forth:

> The first stage covers the period of the enemy's strategic offensive and our strategic defensive. The second stage will be the period of the enemy's strategic consolidation and our preparation for the counter-offensive. The third stage will be the period of our strategic counter-offensive and the enemy's strategic retreat.

Giap, in his own writings, echoed Mao thus:

> The long-term revolutionary war must include several different stages: stage of contention, stage of equilibrium, and stage of counter-offensive.

---

[1]*Fidel Castro is not usually included in this group. Although he came to power through a guerrilla campaign, and although he subsequently used guerrilla warfare as a major means of subversion in other countries, his own military leadership in the Cuban revolution consisted primarily in surviving as a symbol of resistance. More aggressive maneuvers and decisive campaigns were conducted by his brother Raúl, Guevara, and other rebel officers. Castro has been a vociferous exponent of guerrilla warfare, but he has written virtually nothing on the subject and done little to add to or define this concept of combat. The concepts of European communist theoreticians, beginning with Marx and Engels and continuing on through the twentieth century leaders, including Lenin, Stalin, and the modern-day Russians, were rooted in the experiences of the French Revolution of 1789, the revolution of 1848, and the French Commune of 1871, with their urban upheavals, street barricades, defections of regular armed forces, etc. Lenin and Stalin placed some emphasis on guerrilla operations, but only in terms of assistance to a main revolutionary effort on the part of urban masses.*

Both Mao and Giap viewed guerrilla warfare as of only limited potential. Under conditions of enemy superiority, guerrilla methods were basic from the standpoint of both weakening the enemy and building up one's own capabilities. But guerrilla operations would have to give way at some stage to more sophisticated operations if victory were to be attained. Thus Mao said of the "people's struggle" against the Japanese:

> Among the forms of warfare in the anti-Japanese war mobile warfare comes first and guerrilla warfare second. When we say that in the entire war mobile warfare is primary and guerrilla warfare supplementary, we mean that the outcome of the war depends mainly on regular warfare, especially in its mobile form, and that guerrilla warfare cannot shoulder the main responsibility in deciding the outcome.

Giap spoke in similar terms of the strategy that led to Communist success against the French in Indochina, although he laid greater stress on a straight-line evolution from a guerrilla strategy to a regular strategy than did Mao.

> From the strategic point of view, guerrilla warfare, causing many difficulties and losses to the enemy, wears him out. To annihilate big enemy manpower and liberate land, guerrilla warfare has to move gradually to mobile warfare. As our Resistance War was a long revolutionary war, therefore guerrilla warfare not only could but had to move to mobile warfare. Through guerrilla activities, our troops were gradually formed, fighting first with small units then with bigger ones, moving from scattered fighting to more concentrated fighting. Guerrilla warfare gradually developed to mobile warfare—a form of fighting in which principles of regular warfare gradually appear and increasingly develop but still bear a guerrilla character. Mobile warfare is the fighting way of concentrated troops of the regular army in which relatively big forces are regrouped and operate on a relatively vast battlefield, attacking the enemy where he is relatively exposed with a view of annihilating enemy manpower, advancing very deeply then withdrawing very swiftly, possessing to the extreme dynamism, initiative, mobility, and rapidity of decision in face of new situations. As the Resistance War went on, the strategic role of mobile warfare became more important with every passing day. Its task was to annihilate a bigger and bigger number of the enemy forces in order to develop our own, while the task of guerrilla warfare was to wear out and destroy the enemy's reserves.

Both Mao and Giap emphasized the totality of modern warfare, the need for meshing political, economic, and ideological efforts. Mao referred to "revolutionary war waged by the whole nation," and Giap wrote of "combining military operations with political and economic action." The writings of both men dwell on the use of propaganda, the ideological content of revolution, and the role of the peasantry.

The strategic thinking of both rested upon the concept of using the countryside to engulf the cities. Mao saw as one means to this end enlisting the sympathy and support of the peasants through exemplary conduct on the part of revolutionary forces, including direct assistance to local populations in a variety of ways. Giap stressed the usefulness of terror and violence to bring civilian masses into line: " ... We firmly upheld local people's power, overthrew men of straw, eliminated traitors..."

He bluntly explained what this involved:

> ... *The most correct path to be followed by the peoples to liberate themselves is revolution-ary violence and revolutionary war. This path conforms strictly to the ethics and the fun-damentals of Marxism-Leninism on class struggle, on the state, and on revolution. Only by revolutionary violence can the masses defeat aggressive imperialism and its lackeys and overthrow the reactionary administration to take power.*

The Viet Cong have utilized terror so extensively in South Viet Nam that violence has become a major instrument of policy and power in that country. Probably never before have terror tactics been so widely used by a political faction bent on achiev-ing control of a country.

The third man in the communist guerrilla triumvirate was Ernesto "Che" Guevara. It is not clear how much, if at all, Mao and Giap influenced the Cuban guerrilla cam-paign itself. Guevara has asserted that the Cuban leaders did not then know the the-ories of those two men. In the prologue he wrote for a Cuban edition of Giap's *People's War, People's Army*, Guevara stated:

> *Cuba, without knowing these writings [by Giap] nor others on the same subject that had been written on the experiences of the Chinese revolution, set out on the path toward its liberation through similar methods ...*

A contrary statement reportedly made by Guevara was contained in an interview published in a communist Chinese journal. According to this journal, Guevara con-fessed:

> *We have always looked up to Comrade Mao Tse-Tung. When we were engaged in guer-rilla warfare we studied Comrade Mao Tse-Tung's theory on guerrilla warfare. Mimeographed copies published at the front lines circulated widely among our cadres; they were called "food from China." We studied this little book carefully and learned many things. We discovered that there were many problems that Comrade Mao Tse-Tung had already systematically and scientifically studied and answered. This was a very great help to us....*

Whether this statement was more accurate than the former or was invented by the zealous Chinese cannot be ascertained.

Whether or not Guevara knew of Mao's and Giap's writings at the time of Castro's guerrilla campaign, it is clear that they had a considerable impact on his subsequent thinking and writing. Note the echoing of Mao's three-stages concept:

Guerrilla warfare or war of liberation will, in general, have three stages: the first, a strategic defense, in which a small hunted force bites the enemy; it is not protected for a passive defense in a small circle, but its defense consists in limited attacks which it can carry out. After this, a state of equilibrium is reached in which the possibili-ties of action of the enemy and the guerrilla unit are stabilized; and later the final moment of overrunning the repressive army that will lead to the taking of the great cities, to the great decisive encounters, to the total annihilation of the enemy.

Guevara's first book, *Guerrilla Warfare*, was less a theoretical work than a basic guidebook for guerrilla warfare. It contains detailed comments and instructions on tactics, techniques, weapons, training, propaganda, indoctrination, morale, and even "the role of the woman." The book was specifically written for use by future guerrillas in actual operations. As such, the Cuban government printed at least one small-sized edition which would fit handily into any guerrilla's pockets. A note at the end stated:

> *Compañero: This book seeks to be a synthesis of the experiences of a people; if you believe anything should be added or changed, communicate it to the Department of Instruction of the MINFAR [Ministry of the Revolutionary Armed Forces].*

Guerrilla Warfare was nevertheless a foretaste of the views Guevara would later project. There was a warning of things to come in his statement that the guerrilla goes to battle "with the intention of destroying an unjust order, and, therefore, more or less surreptitiously with the intention of putting something in place of the old," i.e., establishing a communist regime.

Two years later Guevara brought his ideas to full fruition. He published an article entitled "Guerrilla Warfare: A Method" in *Cuba Socialista*, at that time the leading doctrinal publication of the Castro regime. In compact form, Guevara described how a guerrilla campaign can be started and carried out:

> *Relatively small nuclei of people choose favorable places for guerrilla warfare, either to begin a counterattack, or to weather the storm, and thus they begin to act. The following must be clearly established: at first, the relative weakness of the guerrilla movement is such that it must work only to settle in the terrain, establishing connections with the populace and reinforcing the places that will possibly become its base of support.*

Guevara agreed with Mao and Giap on basic tactics. But whereas they referred to the "three stages" as qualitatively different phases of a revolutionary war—the evolvement of guerrilla forces into regular armies and a changeover from guerrilla methods to more sophisticated methods of conventional warfare—Guevara thought in terms of a continuing guerrilla effort with the "stages" differing only in the sense of size and strength of guerrilla forces. Guevara used "guerrilla war" and "liberation war" and "revolutionary war" interchangeably. Mao and Giap viewed a "guerrilla war" as but one of the three stages of a "revolutionary war," or "war of liberation," although they allowed for the use of guerrilla methods and tactics in support of the conventional type of operations of the later stages.

Guevara echoed Mao in his listing of the conditions necessary for guerrilla survival: "Constant mobility, constant vigilance, constant distrust." He advocated the utilization of terror on the model of Giap. He saw terror not only as a means of intimidating civilians to support and help the guerrilla forces but also as a means of forcing increasingly harsh and indiscriminate countermeasures on the part of government forces. He explained this tactic on grounds that in Latin America there exists "a state of unstable balance between the oligarchic dictatorship and the popular pressure," and this balance "must be upset." Guevara said:

The dictatorship constantly tries to operate without the showy use of force; forcing the dictatorship to appear undisguised—that is, in its true aspect of violent dictatorship of the reactionary classes, will contribute to its unmasking, which will intensify the struggle to such extremes that then there is no turning back. The manner in which the people's forces, dedicated to the task of making the dictatorship define itself—to hold back or to unleash the battle—carry out their function depends on the staunch beginning of a long-range armed action.

Guevara believed that a small nucleus of well-trained men could be formed in, or introduced into, any country, and that this nucleus, with the use of proper tactics, would with surety grow into a revolutionary movement and would step by step weaken and ultimately destroy opposing government forces. Guevara argued that it was "not always necessary to await the existence of all the conditions for revolution; the insurrectional focus can create them." An insurrection in the form of a guerrilla movement can lead to a general revolution—so thought Guevara. In this, he differed importantly with both Mao and Giap and indeed with communist thinking generally. He here reflected a naïve faith in a sort of magic or mystique about guerrilla warfare that Fidel Castro and he had built up over the years, and which indeed became the foundation for much of Cuba's foreign policies. The mystique may be expressed as faith that any guerrilla operation, no matter how small or weak at its inception, can generate the means to its own success, that is, to a Castro-like takeover of power.

Castro and his followers, in speeches and writings, carefully nurtured the legend of the guerrilla "victory" in Cuba. Quite evidently the Castroites came to believe this legend, as evidenced by the fact that since 1959 efforts have been made to launch similar guerrilla campaigns in more than a dozen Latin American countries. Every one of these attempts has failed. In concentrating on rural guerrilla activities (with the partial exception of Venezuela, where "urban guerrillas" were also highly active for a period), the Castroites chose to overlook the fact that in Cuba the guerrilla campaign was but a phase of a general popular movement against Batista. Popular resentment against the Batista regime found expression in steadily widening clandestine activities: terrorism, sabotage, strikes, propaganda, passive resistance. It also found expression in the supply of the guerrillas with men, funds, and weapons. If it was true that the guerrillas were a major element in the wearing-away of the Batista army, it was also true that Castro rode—but did not generate or direct—a groundswell of national unrest.

Guevara's ideas became the practical, as well as theoretical, guide for the Castro-communist drive for power in Latin America. His article was a blueprint for revolution. Tactics might vary somewhat from country to country, but basic emphasis was on fostering guerrilla warfare: "guerrilla warfare is ... the central axis of the study," he declared.

... The war [said Guevara] would be continental. This means also that it will be prolonged; there will be many fronts, it will cost much blood, innumerable lives for a long time.... In fact, the birth of the American struggle has begun. Will its vortex be in

Venezuela, Guatemala, Colombia, Peru, or Ecuador...? Will these present skirmishes be only manifestations of an unrest that does not bear fruit? It does not matter, for the final result, that one movement or another may be momentarily defeated. What counts is the decision to struggle that ripens day by day; the awareness of the need for revolutionary change, the certainty of its possibility.

ADVENTURER, AGAIN

Ernesto Guevara, a wanderer as a youth, continued traveling after the Castro regime came to power. Now he was a high official of that government, and as such he conferred with foreign leaders and attended international conferences. On 9 December 1964 he flew from Havana to New York to address the United Nations. In two speeches he covered a wide spectrum of topics dealing with Cuba's foreign relations—he was Guevara, the international revolutionist, now giving his views before the entire world. He denied charges of Cuban "interference in the internal affairs of other countries," but significantly added:

... We sympathize with those people who strive for their freedom, and we must fill the obligation of our government and people to state clearly and categorically to the world that we morally support and feel as one with people everywhere who struggle to make a reality of the rights of full sovereignty proclaimed in the United Nations Charter.

Perhaps at this moment Guevara was already thinking of the international role he would attempt to play, first in Africa and then, finally, in Bolivia.

From New York Guevara flew to Algiers, and thus began a trek that would take him to countries in Africa, Europe, and Asia. For 3 months Guevara traveled, talking to leaders of nations, preaching revolution and communism wherever he went.

On 14 March 1965 he flew back to Havana, where he was met by Castro, President Osvaldo Dorticós, and other high officials. This was the last time Guevara was seen in public in Cuba.

Weeks and then months went by, and there was no further word about him. He did not appear to be in disgrace. He was mentioned favorably by Castro in speeches, his pictures were prominently displayed during the annual 26 July celebration, and Cuban publications ran photographs of the Castro brothers with his wife and daughter at a May Day rally. (After divorcing Hilda Gadea, Guevara had married a Cuban girl named Aleida March.)

In a speech on 16 June Castro touched on the speculation regarding Guevara's absence. Castro said, "If the *compañero* does not appear at a public gathering it is because *Compañero* Guevara has some reasons for not appearing at a public gathering." And Castro jibed the United States: "Why don't they take a picture of him with the U-2? Let them look for him and photograph him."

Then on 3 October there was a new development in the mystery. Castro read a letter allegedly written by Guevara and received by Castro on 1 April 1965. Declaring that he felt he had "carried out the part of my duty which tied me to the Cuban revolution," Guevara announced that he was giving up his Cuban citizenship and resigning his military rank and governmental posts. He declared:

Other lands of the world claim the assistance of my modest efforts. I can do what is denied to you [Castro] because of your responsibility at the head of Cuba.... I have always been in accord with the foreign policy of our Revolution, and I continue to be thus.... Wherever I am I will feel the responsibility of being a Cuban revolutionary, and as such I will act.

As time passed and there was not the slightest indication of Guevara's whereabouts, the feeling grew among many Cuban experts that Ernesto Guevara was dead. How could a well-known international figure remain hidden for so long? Even if he had gone behind the Iron Curtain, surely after 2 years some inkling of his presence there would have filtered out. It appeared increasingly logical that Guevara had died at a time and under circumstances unknown.

Suddenly, in April 1967, the baffling affair took a new turn. The official Cuban daily *Granma* published a set of photographs—not too clear—allegedly showing a beardless Guevara in the jungles of an unidentified country. Gloated *Granma*, "Like the Phoenix, he arose from his ashes, battle-hardened, a guerrilla fighter." The newspaper also published a lengthy statement from Guevara written for the magazine *Tricontinental*, an offshoot of the Tricontinental Conference which had been held in Havana in January 1966.

The main point of Guevara's article was reiteration of the coming battle for the Western Hemisphere:

... The struggle in Our America will achieve ... continental proportions. It will be the scene of many great battles fought for the liberation of humanity.

Guevara foresaw growing U.S. involvement in this struggle:

Little by little ... the U.S. military 'advisers' will be substituted by U.S. soldiers until ... they will be forced to send increasingly greater numbers of regular troops to ensure ... relative stability....

Guevara declared:

Our aspirations to victory may be summed up thus: total destruction of imperialism by eliminating its firmest bulwark: imperialist domination by the United States of America.... What a luminous near-future would be visible to us if two, three or many Viet Nams[2] flourished throughout the world with their share of death and their immense tragedies, their everyday heroism and their repeated blows against imperialism obliging it to disperse its forces under the attack and the increasing hatred of all the peoples of the earth!

Why had Guevara left Cuba? There has been speculation that he might have broken with Castro—a clash of strong personalities

—but no evidence of this has ever appeared. Indeed, for nine 9 Guevara accepted Castro's leadership, and Guevara's power in Cuba was due to a major degree to his

---

[2]*Although this phrase—"two, three, or many Viet Nams"—is generally credited to Guevara, Castro, in a speech delivered on: 18 December 1966, had declared, "[imperialism] will be defeated when instead of one Viet Nam there will be in the world two Viet Nams, three Viet Nams, four Viet Nams, five Viet Nams ..." It is possible that at this time Castro already had the Guevara message which was to be released later.*

ability to influence Castro quietly without displacing him from the public spotlight that Castro loves. Some speculation has centered on the dispute within the Cuban government over the relative merits of moral versus material incentives for workers—Guevara advocated moral incentives as being appropriate in a "socialist" society. But the Cuban government finally did adopt the theory of moral incentives, after toying with material rewards, so Guevara was the victor in the dispute. This issue, at any rate, would hardly have seemed to merit his abandoning the island. The theory has also been expressed that criticism by Guevara of Russia and other communist nations for not adequately assisting underdeveloped countries might have caused Moscow to pressure Castro into exiling Guevara. Attempts to pressure Castro, however, usually have a reverse effect, and in this case probably would only have served to tighten the bonds between the two men.

More likely Guevara's departure was the result of a personal decision. He had reached his peak in Cuba, with no place further to go: he could not aspire to a higher position. He may have felt that his capabilities were wasted playing a secondary role; perhaps he concluded that he had been relegated to a hopeless task in attempting to straighten out the Cuban economy. This all may have weighed in Guevara's decision. Surely another factor was the same restlessness that he had displayed throughout his life. Perhaps 9 years in one country was all that he could take. Another consideration may have even more strongly influenced him. Guevara probably did believe, as communists often proclaim, that the age of "imperialism" was ending, that new communist societies would be created, that there were new worlds to conquer. He may well have felt that his official position in the Cuban government placed severe limitations on the personal role he could play and that it would be the better for him if he gave up that position and even disassociated himself from Cuba itself.

Only portions of Guevara's travels during 1965 and 1966 are as yet known. He was in Africa and he was in Europe, and finally he went to South America and to Bolivia. It has been through photographs and documents captured in Bolivia, as well as the statements of men who were with Guevara, that it has become possible to piece together a partial picture of his journeys during the period that he was missing.

Ciro Roberto Bustos, an Argentinean who joined the guerrillas in Bolivia and was subsequently captured, wrote a lengthy, detailed report for Bolivian intelligence officials. In it he recalled a conversation with Guevara in which Guevara explained that his theories of guerrilla warfare were best applicable in Africa and Latin America, but that Africa was preferable because of its greater distance from the United States and its nearness to communist and sympathetic countries. And so, according to Bustos:

> During his extensive voyage through Africa and Asia before disappearing from Cuba, Guevara arranged for his voluntary incorporation in the struggle in the Congo; that is, he chose Africa. But the experience turned out to be negative, because, he said, the human element failed. There is no will to fight, there is nothing to do. After 6 months Guevara left Africa.

On 2 December 1965 a balding, slightly chubby man using the name Ramón Benítez Fernández obtained a Uruguayan passport (No. 130220) in Montevideo. On 22 December 1965 the same man obtained a second passport (No. 130748), also in Montevideo. This one was in the name of Adolfo Mena González. Although the names were different, the same handwriting signed both passports, and both had identical pictures of a bespectacled man. That man was "Che" Guevara.

For several months afterward, the story of Guevara is a blank. Possibly he was behind the Iron Curtain. Perhaps he was somewhere in Asia. At any rate, at some point he secretly returned to Cuba. According to the Bustos statement, when Guevara failed in his efforts in Africa, he sent one of his aides, "Ricardo" (Roberto Aspuru—first name not certain), to prepare the ground for the launching of a guerrilla operation in Bolivia. Bustos recalled:

> It seems that during a trip that Ricardo made to Cuba he said that Ramón would have to enter Bolivia then or never. Thus, in order to assure his entry into Bolivia ... he [Ramón] decided to come. This happened in October of last year, I think.

By the time "Ricardo" made his report to Guevara, a special guerrilla team had been put together and given training at a camp somewhere in Cuba. The diary of one of Guevara's lieutenants, Eliseo Reyes Rodriguez (nom de guerre: "Rolando"), was later captured by the Bolivian army, and it contained this entry:

> September
>
> We met with Ramón [Guevara] at the S. Farm. We were extra-ordinarily moved when we recognized him. We continued our training until 22 October 1966, at which time we went on leave after having been visited by C. [Castro], who spent 3 days with us.

Still in disguise, still traveling secretly, Guevara again left Cuba. Dates stamped in his passports indicate that he entered Spain through Madrid's Barajas Airport on 9 October 1966. On 19 October he left through the same airport. Curiously, both of his passports—now in the hands of the Bolivian military—bear identical entrance and exit imprints.

Guevara next appeared in Brazil, entering Sáo Paulo on 1 November 1966. He left there on 3 November and was on his way to Bolivia.

Guevara apparently crossed the border and made his way to La Paz, where he stayed at the downtown Copacabana Hotel, right on the capital's main street. Like any other tourist, Guevara, a camera bug, took pictures of local scenes and buildings. He then headed south to begin his operations. He was still in disguise and he wore a jaunty hat, and he had a driver to handle his jeep.

A farm had been purchased in an isolated area near the town of Camiri by Roberto Pedro Leigue, a leader in the Moscow-oriented wing of the Bolivian Communist movement. This would be Guevara's base camp, and it was here that he began to train the recruits that were brought in, some evidently by "Tania" (Laura Gutiérrez), an Argentine girl who may have become Guevara's mistress. Guevara adopted the nom de guerre "Ramón."

Why had Guevara chosen Bolivia to be his target? The conditions in that country must have seemed ideal to him. The country is one of the poorest and least developed in Latin America. There were the vast jungle areas in which guerrilla units could incubate, grow, and spread out, eventually moving into adjoining countries. The Bolivian army consists mainly of one-year recruits—and the army has never won a war, but has lost three. Turmoil is chronic: in 142 years of independence Bolivia has had 55 different administrations and more than 150 congresses.

So there was Bolivia, strategically located in the heartland of South America, and if Guevara could establish a secure base of operations, the guerrilla movement could be extended into Brazil, Argentina, Peru, Chile, and Paraguay. Guevara had asserted: "The war will be continental ... "

On 23 March the guerrillas staged their first ambush. It was a success, and so were others that followed. As a result of the rebel attacks, the army casualty toll steadily mounted, with more than 40 soldiers dying in action in the next few months. (The Bolivian army consists of 18,000 to 20,000 men, but of these only some 1,200 can be considered regulars, and, until the guerrilla outbreak occurred, virtually none of the troops had had any counterinsurgency training.)

Guevara's guerrillas, at their peak, probably numbered no more than some 50 men. But included were at least 16 Cubans, among them 3 *comandantes*[3] and 6 captains of the Cuban army. Three of the officers had been members of the Central Committee of the Cuban Communist Party. Guevara had established what was, according to his concepts, a high-powered guerrilla "nucleus."

Despite initial success in the way of ambushes of military units, the rebel movement failed to gain any real momentum. Then the tide began to turn strongly against Guevara and his men. They were running short of food; the army had encircled their area with large numbers of troops: clandestine support being provided in the cities was uncovered and broken up. On 28 September Guevara wrote in his diary:

A day of anguish which, at times, seemed to be our last. Water was brought in at dawn and almost immediately Inti and Willy left to explore another possible way to go down to the canyon, but they came back right away because there is a trail all along the hill in front of us and a farmer on horseback was traveling on it. At 10, 46 soldiers carrying their knapsacks crossed in front of us, taking centuries to go on. Another group appeared at 12, this time 77 men, and to top it off, a shot was heard at that moment and the soldiers took positions. The officer ordered a descent, no matter what, to the ravine, which appeared to be ours, but at last they communicated by radio and he seemed to be satisfied and resumed the march. Our refuge has no defense against an attack from above and had we been discovered our possibilities of escape would have been remote.

A number of basic factors were working inexorably against the rebels. The peasants displayed virtually no interest in aiding them. Guevara repeatedly remarked

---

[3]Comandante, *technically the equivalent to the rank of Major in other armies, is the highest rank in Castro's army.*

upon this in his Bolivian diary, noting at the end of September 1967 that "the mass of peasants does not help us at all and they become informers." Over a dozen years previously Bolivia had gone through an agrarian reform, and most of the peasants now owned their own land. Guevara had nothing to offer them. The lack of peasant support was a major element in the eventual defeat of the guerrillas: Guevara himself, in his writings on guerrilla warfare, had emphasized the necessity of basing this type of conflict on peasant assistance.

Another difficulty was that Guevara and others of his hard-core nucleus were Cubans—in a word, foreigners. Even the local Bolivian Communist parties failed to provide support. The diary of a doctor with the guerrillas noted on 31 December:

> Today there arrived Mario Monje, secretary-general of the Communist Party of Bolivia. He conversed with "Ramón." He made known three conditions for remaining with the guerrillas. First, he would resign his position because his party did not support the guerrilla movement. Second, to be recognized as political and military chief of the guerrillas, as long as they operated in Bolivian territory; and third, freedom to talk with all parties in order to obtain their support. To the second condition "Ramón" told Monje, "I am the chief." Later Monje left the camp.

How good a guerrilla, in fact, was Guevara? In Cuba he was brave, he persevered, he was evidently a good leader of men, and he fought well. But it must not be overlooked that Batista's military commanders all but stood aside to permit Guevara to make his famous march across the island without interference. In Bolivia Guevara violated a number of the basic precepts he had enumerated in his own guerrilla textbook. He had said that "the guerrilla soldier should preferably be an inhabitant of the zone." Yet he and the other Cubans were complete outsiders. He chose to be the operational leader of the guerrillas despite the fact that his age (39) and ill health (severe asthma) were hardly in accord with the requirements of campaigning, and he himself had said that a warrior should have "health of iron" and "the best age of the guerrilla fluctuates between 25 and 35." He had written, "Fundamental characteristic of a guerrilla group is mobility," but he persisted, during the early days of the campaign, in remaining at the *finca*, "read[ing] all day in his hammock," as Bustos later recalled.

Guevara believed in the guerrilla mystique. Despite the discouragement reflected in his diary in the last months, there is no evidence that he ever doubted that final victory would be his. Well might he have heeded the admonition Karl Marx had written long ago:

> Hegel remarks somewhere that all facts and personages of great importance in world history occur, as it were, twice. He forgot to add: the first time as tragedy, the second as farce.

Guevara undoubtedly imagined that the Bolivian army was a carbon copy of the inept, corrupt army that crumbled in Cuba in 1958. The Bolivian army, with the specter of what had happened to the Cuban army at the hands of the Castroites before it, poured troops into the troubled area. Although Bolivia had no forces specifically prepared for counterinsurgency operations, the Second Ranger Battalion (about 640 men) entered, with the assistance of American advisors, into a 4-month period of training for jungle fighting.

Sent into action upon completion of their training, the Rangers patrolled aggressively. The guerrillas already were on the run. The climax came with a relentless 5-day pursuit by 120 Rangers seeking to catch Guevara and the 16 men who were with him. The guerrilla movement had splintered, and most were dead or had deserted, and this group with Guevara were all that were left.

On 7 October Guevara noted in his diary:

> We completed 11 months of our guerrilla operation without complications ... until 12:30 o'clock, at which time an old woman leading goats came into the canyon where we were camped, and we had to pressure her. The woman has not given any trustworthy word about the soldiers, answering to everything that she does not know, that it has been a long time since she has been there, but she gave information about the roads. As a result of the report by the old woman, we figure that we are approximately one league from Higueras and another from Jagüey and about two from Pucará.... The 17 of us left under a very small moon and the march was very tiresome and we left many traces in the canyon where we were, which has no houses nearby but there are some potato fields irrigated by canals of the same creek. At 2:00 we stopped to rest as it was now useless to continue advancing.

The next day, 8 October, in mid-morning, government troops caught up with Guevara and his men. In the attacking group were two Ranger companies, with a third in reserve. The Rangers, commanded by Captain Gary Prado Salmon, had Guevara trapped in the Yuro Canyon a few miles from La Higuera. In the first exchange of fire two soldiers were killed. The guerrillas, however, were forced into making an attempt to break through the Rangers' lines.

The first to brave the Rangers' fire were Guevara and a former union leader from the mining town of Huanuni named Simón Cuba (*nom de guerre:* Willy). Guevara fell almost instantly with a bullet in the leg, his shattered carbine shot out of his grasp. Simón Cuba tried to pull Guevara back to safety but succeeded only in dragging his leader to a spot where four Rangers were concealed. Guevara is reported to have gasped: "Stop! I'm Che! I'm worth more to you alive than dead."

The forward troops radioed their colonel, "Hello, Saturn, we have 'Papa.'"

Incredulous, the colonel radioed back, "Ask 'Skinny' [Captain Prado] to confirm that news."

The news was confirmed. "Che" Guevara had been captured.

Placed on a blanket, he was carried by four soldiers to the town schoolhouse at La Higuera. Simón Cuba had also been captured, as was a third guerrilla, Aniceto Reynaga Gordillo (nom de guerre: Aniceto), a member of the National Executive Committee of the Bolivian Communist Youth. Cuba and Reynaga were also taken to La Higuera.

In the town, the three guerrillas were quickly separated. Cuba and Reynaga were put in a shed adjoining the schoolhouse where Guevara was imprisoned. Having identified himself to his captors, Guevara became the object of considerable interest. He parried an inevitable *barrage* of questions with noncommittal replies, giving little satisfaction to his captors. When the opportunity presented itself, he directed the cleaning and dressing of the bullet wound, a relatively superficial injury, in the calf of his left leg. Guevara was interrogated almost continuously by Bolivian officials. He took out his pipe and asked the officers to fill it with tobacco from Astoria cigarettes which he carried in his pockets. He pipe-smoked one cigarette after another.

An officer asked him what he was thinking. Guevara did not reply, barely moving his head.

A second officer came up and asked what was the matter. The former replied, referring to a Spanish story, that Guevara "must be thinking of the immortality of the burro."

Slowly, in a low voice, Guevara said, "No, no, I'm thinking of the immortality of the revolution."

Guevara, however, was not immortal.

Sometime in the late morning, a short burst of gunfire from Sergeant Bernardo Huanca's carbine terminated the guerrilla career of Simón Cuba and grimly announced the beginnings of executions. Guevara blanched; he finally understood that he was not to be spared, that it was the end of the road. This realization was emphatically punctuated a few minutes later by the sound of a single shot coming from the shed; Aniceto Reynaga had been dispatched. Guevara's ordeal continued for another hour until, at last, Sergeant Mario Teran, who had fortified himself by downing several bottles of beer, entered the schoolhouse with carbine raised. Recognizing Teran's intention, Guevara stood up to face his executioner, his hands still bound. There was a brief exchange of angry words. Guevara declared: "You are killing an *hombre.*" Teran fired a burst of bullets that ended the life of Ernesto "Che" Guevara. Teran left the schoolhouse and went and got another beer.

Time may well show that the death of "Che" Guevara marked a historic turning point. Not only was this the first occasion that a major communist leader had been captured in battle—it was also the first time that a leading theoretician and advocate of guerrilla warfare had been captured. Since Castro came to power in 1959, he and Guevara had launched or encouraged more than a dozen guerrilla operations throughout Latin America. Not one of these has succeeded in overthrowing a democratic government; several have been wiped out completely (notably in Peru, Argentina, and the Dominican Republic); and a number still sputter along (Venezuela, Colombia, and Guatemala). When Guevara personally entered the lists of battle, this was the master himself engaging in combat. Now he had failed. Would this not be a deterrent to others who might think of taking to the field of combat?

Far off in Cuba, where Guevara might have lived out a life of power and prestige, his friend and former comrade in arms, Fidel Castro, stated: "Who could deny the significance to the revolutionary movement of the blow of Che's death? ... It is a fierce blow, a very hard one ..."

There is, however, another side to the matter, the full import of which cannot yet be judged: the buildup of a "Che" Guevara myth.

The reality of "Che" Guevara is one thing; the growing fiction quite another. The real Guevara came out of an unproductive obscurity, shared, through an accident of history, in a successful uprising against a corrupt and inept dictatorship that was in the process of collapsing of its own weight, and played a large—perhaps decisive— role in the imposition of a communist system on Cuba and the voluntary submission of Cuba to a colonial-like status as against the U.S.S.R. He then failed in a succession of assignments and personal undertakings, including management of the Cuban economy, the use of Cuba as a base and lever to get a viable revolutionary movement underway throughout Latin America, a direct effort to influence the rise of a revolutionary tide in black Africa, and finally as leader of a guerrilla war in Bolivia. In real world terms, the near comic opera circumstances of Guevara's last days and the decidedly unheroic appearance presented by his lifeless body sprawled on a bare table would have seemed the best antidotes to any romanticizing about him. The world of fantasy, however, can make a mockery of the real world. Viewed subjectively, photographs of the frail warrior lying in death could be made to take on a saintly hue. And the ill-conceived and poorly executed brigand-like foray in the wilds of Bolivia could be reshaped in the imagination so as to provide a bold new dimension to the Guevara figure.

Within weeks after the news of Guevara's death, placards proclaiming "Che is alive" and *"Viva Che,"* together with appropriate portraits, became standard features of protest demonstrations everywhere. In Rimini, Italy, two priests presided over a mass for Guevara; a Brazilian bishop asked for prayers "for our brother Che Guevara," and a Brazilian archbishop declared, "I find that Che Guevara was sincere." In Lima, Peru, grammar school children held hands, danced in a circle, and chanted, *"Con cuchillo y con cuchara, que viva el Che Guevara"* (With knife and with spoon, long live Che Guevara). In Santiago, Chile, a bookstore sold photographs of Guevara mounted on a wooden base at the rate of 500 per month, and in Italy close to 15,000 copies of Guevara's *Guerrilla Warfare* were sold in a fortnight. In the United States, adherents of the New Left adopted Guevara as their new symbol. In Rome and Milan Guevara clubs were organized by a Socialist party, in Naples activist students splintered from the regular Communist Party and formed a "Che Guevara Club," and in Paris a student group named itself the "Cercle Che Guevara," while Parisian advocates of black power incorporated *"Guevarisme"* in their credo. A poll published in Spain showed Guevara to be the "most popular international figure of the year," and the student bulletin of the medical school of the University of Salamanca declared:

> *There is a man of this century who looked above and beyond his political party. From the point of view of dedication to the sick, to the weak, to his fellow men, this Ernesto Guevara ... doctor by profession and guerrillero by necessity, can be a lesson for us all.*

In Bolivia the commander of the army that had destroyed Guevara, General Alfredo Ovando Candia, declared, "He was a brave man but God was not with him."

The irony of the Guevara myth is that its strength appears to spring from yearnings the exact opposite of those that moved Guevara himself. He has become the symbol of those who profess hatred of war and violence, while his own life was dedicated to the principle and practice of both. Anti-militarists disregard his obsession with things military and see him as one of their own. He worshipped at the shrine of big technology and wanted to make Cuba a big mill town with its masses rushing in and out of bleak factories. Yet he is taken to heart by those who would escape the age of modernization with its automation, nuclear energy, space travel, laser beams, computerization, and ZIP codes, and who would end the inequities of the world by turning all mankind back to an underdeveloped state. Guevara as a communist was above all else a collectivist, but he is cherished as a staunch individualist. He is pictured as a dreamer, a romanticist who abdicated great power to follow his lonely destiny to a far corner of the world, while in fact power was his god and in leaving Cuba he was reaching for the far greater power that he believed was for the taking in the vast continent that lay beyond the tiny island in whose affairs he had become enmeshed, with little personal success or glory. He is even hailed as a good family man—a loving father who noted the birthdays of his children in his Bolivian diary—although he left those same children and his wife without means of support and in faith that his friend, Castro, would take care of them. He is treated as a lover of humanity, but he did not disguise his arrogant contempt for the blacks who spurned his leadership in Africa, and he flaunted in his diary his disgust with the peasants he sought to "liberate" in Bolivia. His lament to his executioner, "you are killing a man," is taken as epitomizing his life philosophy; ignored is the evident glee with which he recorded the deaths inflicted on Bolivian recruits in ambushes arranged by his professionally trained "guerrillas."

Given the recasting of Guevara the man in the mold of Guevara the myth, the influence of his writings regarding revolution will doubtless be far greater than their intellectual content would justify. Guevara wrote well, sometimes brilliantly.... But he was neither an original nor a profound thinker. Most students would argue that he had a poor understanding—in fact a large measure of naïveté—with regard to the world in which he lived and the great forces that shape its destiny. He knew nothing of economics, and his notion of history bordered on the grotesque. Most striking of all, he was ill-versed in the tenets of communism. He leaned heavily on what he thought to be the concepts of the leading theoreticians of the movement, but what came through in his own writings and speeches was heavily marred by oversimplifications, near-distortions, and ill-digested parrotings. He either did little homework or else lacked the capacity to understand much of what he read.

But how important are deficiencies as these in a case like Guevara's? Historical happenstance and his own strange behavior are surrounding him with a charismatic mystique that for many, and particularly among the young of all lands, sets him above ordinary standards of judgment. For these, not the logic or truth or plausibility of what he says determines its worth: the decisive thing is that he has said it. It may well be, of course, that this Guevara phenomenon is a peculiar product of this peculiar moment in history and will soon pass. On the other hand, the phenomenon may turn out to be more deeply based. In a sense, in romanticizing Guevara, the present generation of radicals—those who pride themselves on membership in the category "Under Thirty"—has recreated him in its own image. Guevara and his writings may thus prove more acceptable and enduring as a hero figure for those-who-would-change-the-world in the last decades of the 20th century than the somewhat shop-worn hand-me-downs from previous generations such as Lenin, Stalin, Tito, Mao, and even Ho Chi Minh.

chapter nine

REACHING SOUTH

Castro's long arm reached to Grenada in the southern Caribbean and Suriname on the northeast coast of South America. The Cuban ambassadors to these countries—both America Department agents—helped steer them into the Cuban orbit. Mallin visited both countries and wrote the following article for a national magazine. It was not published, however, because on 25 October 1983 American forces invaded Grenada and began its liberation. Mallin flew on the first U.S. Air Force plane that took in journalists. In Suriname, Desi Bouterse, heeding events in Grenada and under pressure from neighboring Brazil, rapidly moved away from his Cuban connection. The Castro empire had begun to crumble. Later would follow the reduction in number and final withdrawal of Cuban troops from Ethiopia and Angola, and then, eventually, the defeat of the Sandinistas at the polls in Nicaragua.

The strip of dry, brown earth extends for more than 9,000 feet. To add to its length an American dredging company filled in part of a bay. The bright blue waters of the Caribbean Sea sparkle offshore. Gray sandstone hills were bulldozed and the leveling of the land is now completed. Five layers of asphalt, compacted volcanic ash, and other coverings are now being put down. Nearby, a tower and fuel storage facilities are almost built. Scores of workers are hammering, pouring cement, and running wires to complete the five or so adjoining, hangar-like structures that will be a large terminal building.

The airport is on Point Salines, the southwestern tip of the island of Grenada. Grenada is only a speck in the Caribbean: 133 square miles populated by 110,000 people. But the island has assumed major strategic importance, partially because of the airport. There are about 350 Grenadians at work on the field. It is, however, primarily a Cuban project. Cuban engineers oversee the work, Cuban laborers man the equipment and do the technical tasks. Cuba is bearing approximately half the cost

($71 million) of the project, providing not only knowhow and manpower but also 100 pieces of heavy equipment made in Russia and elsewhere. The airfield will substantially enhance the flying range of Cuban military aircraft. It will provide a logistical stepping stone for supplying Cuba's forces in Africa, especially Angola. And the field will be an important link to the latest country to fall to Cuban Dictator Fidel Castro's expansionist drive: Suriname.

Some 400 miles to the southeast of Grenada, on the South American mainland, lies a former Dutch colony, now called Suriname. Suriname, which covers 63,251 square miles, has a population of 350,000 persons that are a variegated ethnic mix, a true melting pot—Indians (known locally as Hindustanis even if they are Moslems), Creoles, Suriname-born persons of European, African, or other descent, Indonesians, Bush Blacks, Chinese, Amerindians, and Europeans. The Dutch culture remains strong: the official language is Dutch (although a Creole dialect is popularly used), driving is on the left side of the street, the guilder is the basic unit of currency. This colorful country, once a tranquil land, is now ruled by a dictator who models himself after Fidel Castro and is rapidly swinging his country within the orbit of communist Cuba.

Castro is reaching out for new countries. In Central America he already has Nicaragua and is trying for El Salvador. Not content with this, he is making an enormously important move down through the Caribbean and onto the mainland—a goal he has cherished virtually since the day he came to power almost 25 years ago. Suriname will provide Castro with a military base, if he needs it, and even more important, for a base from which subversion can be conducted throughout South America. Only a few hundred miles from Suriname lie the vast Venezuelan oil fields, a most tempting target for Castro.

For Castro the road to Suriname—and beyond—has been through Grenada. Grenada is a "typical" West Indian island. Green foliage covers most of the island, beaches are white and bright, the sky and the seas are blends of blue. Wooden shacks are the housing of the interior; there are open-air markets and cows on the beaches and women washing clothes in streams; roads are narrow, winding, and pocked.

The visitor arriving by air passes through a dilapidated airport. The questioning by immigration officials is more thorough than in any other West Indian country, and there are revolutionary slogans at the airport, as there are on the walls of the capital city: "The revolution must be respected," "Defend the gains of the revolution," and so on. Pearls Airport is about 26 miles from the capital, Saint George's, and the road between twists over a mountain range and through thick jungles. The scene at Saint George's is almost Mediterranean: modern ships in the harbor and old buildings right up to the edge of a waterfront road. Behind but nearby stand the mountains.

Grenada was discovered by Columbus in 1498; it evidently derives its name from the Spanish city of Grenada. The island alternately flew the French and British flags and then by the Treaty of Versailles of 1783 firmly became British. It achieved full independence on 7 February 1974. Known as the "Isle of Spice," Grenada exports about one-third of the world's nutmeg. Although tourism provides some income, the basis of the economy is agriculture, with cacao, cinnamon, bananas, and other products growing in the rich volcanic soil.

Grenada was ruled by parliamentary government until 13 March 1979. That day members of the New Jewel (Joint Endeavor for Welfare, Education, and Liberation) Movement ousted the government of Prime Minister Sir Eric Gairy, a regime known for its corruption and its leader's deep interest in flying saucers. A military barracks was attacked and captured, the country's one radio station was seized, and the police were called upon to surrender, which they did. The New Jewel Movement was headed by Maurice Bishop, a politician having a friendship with Fidel Castro dating back a decade or more.

The constitution was suspended and Grenada became a totalitarian state. The sole opposition newspaper was banned; efforts to start others have been squelched. In one case the editor and lawyers of a newspaper were jailed (in July 1981) and they are still in prison, with no charges filed against them. The country's only television station was purchased by the regime, and the only radio station was already government-owned, so no public voice can now be raised against Bishop's rule.

Alister Hughes, a newspaperman associated with one of the papers that was closed, the *Grenadian Voice*, has reported the harassment to which he has been subjected:

> *All copies of the newspapers were seized together with duplicating machines, paper, typewriters and ... four cars, one of which was mine....*
>
> *... For 10 days after the closure of the* Grenadian Voice *any package carried by any person entering or leaving my house was searched. For 6 weeks my home was under 24-hour-a-day surveillance and my wife and I were "trailed" wherever we went. The details of my income tax return ... [were] broadcast over national radio ... I was banned from foreign travel for 2 months.*

Three buildings up in the hills overlooking Saint George's harbor are of particular interest. One is Butler House, formerly a motel, where the prime minister now has his offices. Another is Fort Rupert, military barracks which insure control of the city. The third building is Richmond Hill, a prison. Here is where political prisoners are held. No one outside the government knows precisely how many there are; the best estimate is some 85. Ten or so have been there since the 1979 revolution and are kept in mind-bending isolation.

About a month after Bishop seized power a Cuban ship made port carrying weapons for the members of the New Jewel Movement. Since then the Cuban presence in Cuba has grown rapidly and today is so extensive that Grenada has become a Cuban satellite. Cuba has provided 10 fishing boats and 40 tractors. It has given Radio Free Grenada a 50-kilowatt transmitter to add to its 10-kilowatt transmitter, and Cubans trained the radio personnel. Grenada now has a voice that can be heard throughout the southeastern Caribbean. Grenadian youths by the hundreds have gone to Cuba on scholarships. There are some 20 Cuban doctors and dentists on the island providing health care. Cubans sit in every government ministry, exercising influence and even control: one in the Ministry of Trade, two in the Ministry of Planning, several in the Education Ministry, and so on. In 1982 there were approximately 350 Cuban civilians on the tiny island. Today there are about 600, including workers on the new airport. The Cubans set up a plant which manufactures building blocks for the airport; a second plant is in the works which will provide blocks for military housing and other construction.

The Cuban embassy—the new viceroyalty—is located in a white, modern, ranch-style house high in the hills of Morne Jaloux, a suburb of the capital. From here Cuban operations are controlled by Julian Enrique Torres Rizo, the sociable, tennis-playing ambassador. Torres Rizo, who once served with the Cuban mission at the United Nations and whose wife Gail is American, is a longtime intelligence agent and is now an operative of the America Department. The No. 2 Cuban, Gastón Díaz González, is also an agent of the America Department, the principal Cuban intelligence organization whose primary responsibility is to conduct subversive operations in the western hemisphere. Formerly he served in the Caribbean section of the department. Grenada and Suriname are most important to Castro; the ambassadorships are too vital to be left to mere diplomats.

In 1982 there were 10 Cuban military advisors in Grenada. This year the figure has more than tripled, thanks to the rapidly growing strategic role of the island. On the southern coast, the Cubans built the Calivigny military camp which includes barracks, administration buildings, an anti-aircraft emplacement, vehicle sheds, firing ranges, and a Soviet-style obstacle course. Here Grenadian soldiers receive training; it is expected that the Cubans will also instruct Castroite militants from nearby islands. The camp is but four miles from the new airport.

Some Grenadian military have gone to Cuba for training. Cuba has provided the Grenadian army with Soviet trucks (still bearing the C.C.C.P. label), armored personnel carriers, and anti-aircraft weapons. Occasionally, when blackouts occur at the waterfront, it is believed additional arms are being unloaded.

In January of this year the army, police, coast guard, and People's Militia were united in a single organization, the People's Revolutionary Armed Forces. This was in line with the military organization in effect in Cuba. The army has 500 to 700 men; the other services about 500 in all. The militia, set up by Bishop, numbers about 2,000, with units in every industrial sector and geographical area.

Construction of the new airport began in January 1980. It is hoped that the installation will be ready for use on the fifth anniversary of the revolution, 13 March 1984. The Grenadian government claims that the airport is essential if the country is to build its tourist trade. Certainly the field will be able to take larger aircraft and will be much closer to the capital, with better roads between, than the airfield used at present. But if the government hopes for increased tourism, foreign observers ask, why isn't it doing anything to upgrade and expand its hotel industry, which has minimal capacity? Why not improve the country's inadequate electric power system?

Fidel Castro, faced with major economic problems at home, is hardly likely to be altruistically concerned with Grenada's tourist trade. The fact is that the airport will be of major strategic importance to Cuba. On 19 December 1981, Grenada's minister of national mobilization, Selwyn Strachan, stated that Cuba would eventually use the new airport to support its troops in Angola. He added that the airport might also be utilized by the Soviet Union. President Reagan in a television speech pointed out that if the airport had been operational at the time, the four Libyan aircraft ferrying weapons to Nicaragua that were seized in April 1983 by Brazil could have flown via Grenada. They would then have been able to complete their mission.

Not only will the Point Salines field assist the Cubans in their African adventures, in Angola as well as elsewhere, it will also be an important link between Cuba and Suriname. In addition, the field will provide Cuban fighter aircraft with a potential base from which they can strike anywhere in the southeastern Caribbean and the northern part of the South American continent. Cuba would be in a position to provide rapid air support for the Surinamese regime. With the availability of airfields in Nicaragua and the new field in Grenada, Castro will have the capability to send airborne troops and fighter aircraft just about anywhere in Central America, the Caribbean, and the northern portion of South America. Of greatest immediate importance, however, is the link to Suriname.

Dictator of Suriname is Lieutenant Colonel Desi Bouterse. Bouterse visited Grenada in 1981 to attend a conference, and then again in 1982 to vacation. He came to know Grenada's Prime Minister Bishop, friend and ally of Castro's. In February 1983 he again flew to Grenada and then he and Bishop went to Cuba to join Castro. The trio—plus Nobel Prize winner Gabriel García Márquez—flew to New Delhi to attend the meeting of the so-called "non-aligned" nations. The journey lasted a little over 38 hours and the 3 leaders used the time to do much talking and planning. Quite likely Castro and Bouterse reached agreements on Cuban assistance to Suriname which would later be refined into some six formal accords. In New Delhi Bouterse was elected one of the four vice-chairmen for Latin America of the non-aligned organization. Returning home, he stopped in Libya and probably conferred with Dictator Mu'ammar Qadhafi. Bouterse would have been seeking Libyan aid for Suriname's troubled economy, hurt by a cut-off of Dutch aid and low world prices for the country's chief product, bauxite.

The role of Grenada in drawing Suriname into the Cuban net was further demonstrated late in April 1983. About 15 Surinamese military men flew to Grenada to witness a demonstration of Soviet military equipment, including anti-aircraft guns and personnel carriers. These had been provided to Grenada by Cuba and it is likely that the Surinamese will be given similar equipment.

Suriname, formerly Dutch Guiana, is the middle country of three Guianas. To the west is independent Guyana, formerly British Guiana, and to the east is French Guiana, an overseas department of France. Centuries ago, in their search for gold, the Spanish and Portuguese *conquistadores* conquered almost all of South America.

There was, however, no gold or other visible wealth in the territory that is now the Guianas, and so the conquistadores did not bother with it. On the other hand, the English, Dutch, and French, eager for a foothold in South America, traded with the area, settled in it, squabbled over it. Finally, by the Treaty of Paris of 1814, the present boundaries were more or less set. (Border disputes continue among the three countries, as well as one between Guyana and neighboring Venezuela.)

Cut off from the rest of the continent by swamps, jungles, and mountains, the Guianas have remained European and Asian (the Asians are descendants of contract laborers). Latino traces do not exist.

Dutch Guiana was a colony until 1954. Its agriculture, worked by slaves until slavery was abolished in the 19th century, provided a flow of wealth to The Netherlands. Then, from the end of the 1920s through World War II, Dutch Guiana prospered as the world's major supplier of bauxite, from which aluminum is made. In 1954 Dutch Guiana became Suriname, a state autonomous and equal to The Netherlands within the Kingdom of The Netherlands. On 25 November 1975 Suriname gained complete independence; it had a constitution and a parliamentary form of government. There was a ceremonial president and a Council of Ministers with executive powers, headed by a prime minister. The Netherlands provided an independence gift: a $1.5 billion development assistance package, to be disbursed at the rate of about $100 million yearly. This, together with exports of bauxite, alumina, and aluminum, were the primary sources of income for the newly independent country. (Suriname not only produces bauxite but also refines it to alumina and reduces the alumina to aluminum. All three products are exported.)

Suriname, wedged into the northeastern part of South America, has rich farmlands along a coastal belt, but most of the remainder of the country—some 80 percent to 90 percent—is undeveloped. This consists of hills and mountains covered with dense forests and intersected by streams of varying sizes. The interior areas are sparsely inhabited by Carib and Arawak Indians and Bush Blacks living in near-primitive conditions. The Bush Blacks are descendents of slaves who escaped from coastal Dutch plantations.

About half of the population of the country lives in the capital city, Paramaribo. The result is an ethnic kaleidoscope. There is the Dutch presence: Dutch businessmen in safari shirts, streets with names like *Zwartenhovenbrugstraat*, and old wooden buildings that make up most of the city. Then there are the Indonesians, eating their *rijsttafel*; the East Indian men in turbans and women in saris; and the Chinese shopkeepers selling American pottery and wood carvings made by Bush Blacks. And now, too, there are the Cubans in their *guayaberas.*

In 1980, after 5 years of independence, the government of Suriname was in trouble. Official corruption was increasingly a public issue, and there was a legislative stalemate. The military demanded the right to have a union, but the government opposed this.

During the early morning hours of 25 February 1980 Sergeant Major Desi Bouterse, a physical education instructor, and 15 other sergeants boarded a patrol boat at a naval base on the Suriname River. They proceeded to nearby Paramaribo with the aim of overthrowing the government. Meanwhile, other military men seized a weapons stockpile and handed out guns to followers. A garrison was attacked and overcome. The prime minister and government officials holed up at police headquarters but by dawn surrendered. "We wanted a union but we got a country," one of the sergeants was quoted as saying.

The sergeants formed a military council and asked a civilian, Chin A Sen, to head the government. A small group of Castroites, however, organized the Revolutionary Peoples' Party and won Bouterse's ear. Bouterse had by now promoted himself to the rank of lieutenant colonel. Chin A Sen publicly warned, "Evil forces will take over." On 4 February 1982 he resigned and Bouterse became the head of the government.

The population had been hopeful that the military-dominated government would correct Suriname's ills, but the ousting of Chin A Sen was a major disappointment. Church leaders assailed the rise of extremist groups "to privilege and influence without any opportunity for public accountability." Over 2,000 people attended the funeral of the leader of the old political party, and other political figures used the occasion to call for a restoration of democracy. In March 1982 the military regime faced its most serious danger when an army officer staged an uprising. After prolonged fighting the rebels were defeated and their leader was captured.

A period of uneasy calm followed the abortive coup but then again voices began to speak out in favor of the restoration of democratic rule. Declarations were made by the Bar Association, the Association of Businessmen, labor federations, academic leaders, and the Council of Christian Churches. When in July 1982 the government began setting up a "people's militia" drawn mainly from the ranks of the Revolutionary People's Party, Cyriel Daal, the leader of the nation's largest labor federation, the *Moederbond*, denounced this development as dangerous, particularly since the Revolutionary Party was "noted for its intolerance."

The spiraling opposition reached a climax on October when Grenada's Bishop made a state visit. Daal publicly denounced Bishop and Bouterse, and he was arrested. Workers promptly went on strike, crippling the docks, public utilities, several factories, and even an airfield where Bishop was due to land. The government bowed to the unions and released Daal. Then, when Bouterse held a rally to honor his guest, Daal held another that drew more people. The situation had become volatile and dangerous.

The opposition to military rule hardened in the weeks that followed. The leader of the bauxite workers called upon the population "to prepare to struggle until real socio-political renewal can be won." On 25 November a *"Bond voor Democratie"* was set up by religious leaders and the associations of businessmen, manufacturers, lawyers, doctors, editors and publishers, farmers, and women. Students staged demonstrations and on 7 December they marched to Revolutionary Square in downtown Paramaribo, the capital city, and there clashed with police and soldiers.

Within hours of the student disturbance armored cars pulled in front of two radio stations, the headquarters of the *Moederbond*, and the offices of *De Vrije Stem*, one of the country's most aggressive newspapers. Using grenades and bazookas, the troops completely destroyed the four buildings.

At the same time the military fanned out across the city to the homes of dissenters and sprayed several of the houses with machine gun fire. There were dozens, possibly hundreds, of arrests. As a Surinamese journalist later reconstructed the events:

> *Whoever resisted was roughly forced into submission. That was the fate of ex-minister [André] Kamperveen, for example ... His arms and legs were broken. Some victims collapsed in terror.*

Many of the arrested were beaten and tortured. The next day there were 15 bodies in the morgue of the hospital; some had knife and burn marks. Among the dead were Cyriel Daal, the head of the Bar Association, the chairman of the University of Suriname, two former cabinet ministers, lawyers, and journalists. In addition to the victims in the morgue, possibly as many as 20 other Surinamese disappeared that night. Bouterse's explanation of what had happened: "A number of the suspects were killed in an escape attempt."

Later Bouterse told a French journalist that "the time has come for speeding up the revolutionary process in Suriname." He said: "We let our opponents have too much freedom. They took advantage of it to regain lost ground."

The massacre caused a national and international uproar. Several officials resigned, some diplomats left Paramaribo, and outcries came from a number of countries. Aristides Calvani, the Venezuelan head of the Federation of Christian Democratic Parties of Latin America, condemned the "Stalinist action" which he said was under "Soviet and Cuban influence." The United States suspended a $1.5 million aid program it had promised. And, most devastating of all, The Netherlands suspended its $100 million annual assistance. On 13 December thousands of courageous mourners had shown up at the cemeteries where the massacre victims were being buried. Afterwards a crowd marched past the Dutch embassy chanting, "Help us, help us."

Today Suriname continues to be ruled by the "Group of 16," although the number has in fact diminished due to deaths and arrests. The only two parties are: the Revolutionary People's Party (RVP) and the Progressive Workers and Farmers Union (PALU), a socialist-type group considered to be a bit more moderate. No visible opposition exists. The country's one television station is now state-owned. There is one daily newspaper and it is state-censored (in addition to the paper that was burned down, one daily and all weeklies were banned), as is one radio station (two stations were burned, three closed).

Following the sergeants' coup a National Military Council was set up. This is headed by Bouterse, whose official position is commander-in-chief of the military (army, a tiny navy, no air force). Bouterse appointed the current civilian cabinet, picking its members from the two accepted political parties.

The official biography of Desire Delano Bouterse is sparse. He was born 13 October

1945 in Suriname. He attended secondary school and a school of commerce, is married, and has two children. He went to The Netherlands in 1968, joined the Dutch army, and attended the Royal Military School. He then served with the Dutch army in West Germany. He returned to Suriname and enlisted in the Surinamese army, serving in the physical education department. He became a union leader, and then came the sergeants' coup.

Bouterse invariably wears olive green uniforms, sometimes with a beret, occasionally with a fatigue cap. The beard and mustache he sports, the uniforms and paratrooper boots he wears, are almost a mirror image of Fidel Castro. But Bouterse is no Castro. He lacks charisma and when he delivers a speech, he reads it. A Surinamese who knows Bouterse describes him thus:

> *Inscrutable, quiet, reserved, careful in talking, hard to fathom. He is not a Communist or a Castroite. His primary concern is, "How do I stay alive?" He has only one interest: survival.*

Bouterse clearly feels that his best chance of survival is in alliance with Castro, and the Cuban dictator has rapidly taken advantage of this opportunity. Suriname has been displaying ever-closer solidarity with Cuba. Official statements and speeches are supportive of Cuba and its allies, such as Nicaragua, and Suriname votes with Cuba in the United Nations. Sports, cultural, and other exchanges between Suriname and Cuba have been increasing. Bouterse has been quoted in the Cuban newspaper *Granma* as stating:

> *The imperialists know perfectly well that a revolution is taking place in this country and that revolutionaries stick together in the struggle.*

Continued and extensive attention given to Suriname by *Granma* attests to the importance with which Cuba views developments in that country.

In September 1982 a Cuban embassy was opened, occupying a modern two-story building at Anton Dragtenweg 25 in the outskirts of Paramaribo. The ambassador is Osvaldo Cárdenas Junquera. An intelligence heavyweight, he was formerly head of the Caribbean section of the America Department.

The staff of the Cuban embassy is relatively large for a mission from one small country to another: 8 to 10 persons (the U.S. embassy in Paramaribo has 13 persons). In addition to the embassy personnel, at any given time there are usually an equal number of Cubans in Paramaribo on temporary duty. Often staying at the downtown Ambassador Hotel, the Cubans work as advisors to various branches of the Surinamese government, as well as to the military. It is believed that they are helping the Surinamese to set up a security/intelligence organization. The rudiments of a peoples' militia have been organized. There is a pervasive fear among residents of Paramaribo about discussing politics; they think that a Cuban-style neighborhood snoop organization is already functioning.

On 15 December 1982 two top America Department officials secretly entered Suriname aboard a small boat from neighboring Guyana. They were Carlos Andres Díaz Larranga, Cuban chargé in Kingston, Jamaica, at the time that country was just about allied with Cuba, and José Antonio Arbesu Fraga, chief of the North American section of the America Department. They were accompanied by a third individual believed to be an aide or code clerk. The apparent purpose of the visit was on-site planning with Ambassador Cárdenas on future Cuban moves. The America Department functions not only in the intelligence field but also engages in other clandestine and in political activities.

On 29 April a *Compañia Cubana de Aviación* plane flew out of Paramaribo with 30 Surinamese soldiers. They were commanded by Captain Paul Bagwandas, a close associate of Bouterse. The Surinamese were to be given indoctrination and training in Cuba and then to return to Suriname to begin the Cubanization of the Surinamese army.

A further tightening of Suriname-Cuba ties took place in mid-May when a 21-man Cuban delegation arrived in Paramaribo to work on agreements between the 2 countries. These accords concerned sports and cultural exchanges; medical, pharmaceutical, and scientific assistance to Suriname; air transport between Havana and Paramaribo; training for the Surinamese army; and advisory help for various departments of the Surinamese government. Cuban purchases of Surinamese rice are also included in the agreements.

The stakes are great in Suriname, and four countries are closely watching or directly involved in what is happening there:

CUBA—The Cubans are moving rapidly to entrench themselves. It is believed that last year they counseled Bouterse to rid himself of enemies but were shocked by last December's massacre of opposing groups. In all probability Castro has urged Bouterse to go easy, not to do anything that would stiffen opposition or again arouse world opinion. Castro particularly does not want a situation that would induce the Brazilian giant to the south to move against Bouterse. Castro needs time to tighten his hold on Suriname. One of Cuba's strongest cards appears to be the personal influence Ambassador Cárdenas exercises upon Bouterse. But Bouterse is a political opportunist, and Cuba must know this. It is possible that Captain Bagwandas is being prepared as a replacement should the Cubans feel it necessary to be rid of Bouterse.

THE UNITED STATES—The strategic implications of Castro's move southward and onto the mainland are a growing worry. Following the December killings the U.S. suspended its promised aid package and in January 1983 two American diplomats were expelled, supposedly for interfering with Suriname's internal affairs. The U.S. and Suriname today still maintain diplomatic relations, which an embassy staffer describes as "correct." Involved with stopping Castro in Central America, the U.S. does not appear to be trying to do much about Suriname, leaving this problem in other hands.

THE NETHERLANDS—The Netherlands continues to have a major interest in Suriname. There still are Dutch holdings, including a bauxite firm, and more important, some 180,000 Surinamese have settled in The Netherlands. The number of visa applications at the Dutch embassy in Paramaribo is mounting as more Surinamese seek to flee. Anti-Bouterse elements are busy among the exiles and the Bouterse regime fears that an expedition might be mounted with Dutch support. The geographical problems of any such effort, however, make it most unlikely. The Dutch no longer appear to have the capability to do much about what happens in Suriname. A Dutch diplomat says:

> *The concern of the Dutch government is human rights. We have asked that there be guarantees that 8 December will not happen again. They have not given such guarantees and there has been no improvement in the situation.*

Any resumption of Dutch assistance would be tied directly to the human rights situation in Suriname.

BRAZIL—"Every nations tries to maintain peaceful situations on its borders. We try to prevent conflicts before they occur." So says a Brazilian diplomat. Brazil lies across Suriname's southern border. A growing military giant with a military establishment that is staunchly anti-communist, Brazil has viewed with displeasure the 8 December killings and Castro's move south, and Brazilian officials have clearly indicated their feelings. Brazil, however, is not just standing by and complaining. Brazilian officials, including the head of the National Security Council, have visited Suriname, and Surinamese officials, including the prime minister, have visited Brazil. The two governments are working on agreements that cover wide areas: economic assistance including Brazilian purchases of rice and aluminum, cooperation in the military field, Brazilian participation in Surinamese hydroelectric development, Brazilian scholarships, improvement of air and sea links, sales of Brazilian goods and services, Brazilian participation in mineral research, and even Brazilian instruction on how to promote sports (this would include the televising of Brazilian soccer games to Suriname). In addition to these moves the Brazilians are evidently trying to work through political elements in Suriname. What is not clear—and the Brazilians are probably deliberately fuzzing this key point—is whether Brazilian aid is conditional on the halting of the Cuban entrenchment. Says the Brazilian diplomat: "We are enticing them. They must make the decision." The decision may have been indicated in an interview with Bouterse which appeared earlier in Cuban publications. Of Brazil, Bouterse said, "... We don't do what Brazil tells us to do nor do we consult anybody before making decisions."

Short of a Brazilian invasion or a Brazil-instigated military coup, it does not appear likely that the Cuban move into Suriname can be stopped. Time is with Castro; each passing day permits him to move more deeply and extensively into the Surinamese government and military establishment.

Cuban expansion relentlessly continues. While the attention of the United States and much of Latin America centers on Central America, Castro is making an end run. Grenada was the springboard to Suriname. Now Suriname will be the springboard to other countries. It provides Castro with a base for possible future use by his air, land, and sea forces. It also gives him a base from which he can extend his subversive activities throughout the continent. And where Fidel Castro is, the Russians are not far behind.

chapter ten

Ernesto "Che" Guevara led the way in 1960, taking a group of Cuban soldiers into the Congo. That particular expedition failed, and Guevara and his men had to flee. This, however, did not discourage Castro. He built up an extensive military presence in Africa, with troops and/or advisors in some 15 countries. In Ethiopia and Angola there were Cuban armies, the largest contingent being in Angola. Because of the sizeable Cuban force in Angola, the war in that country was of particular interest to Radio Martí, a Voice of America program that broadcasts to Cuba. As news director of Radio Martí, Mallin made two trips to Angola to cover the conflict there. On one occasion he flew in a small, darkened plane over Cuban-controlled territory. This paper was published by the University of Miami.

The small aircraft swept down and landed on the dirt strip. It was night and the only lighting was provided by fires burning along the sides of the strip to mark it for the pilot.

The few passengers disembarked, and the plane immediately took off again. The African dawn was beginning to break. A sitting plane would be a sitting duck for enemy aircraft.

The passengers were taken in hand by soldiers wearing overcoats—a necessity in the cold nights. Customs forms were filled out; baggage was inspected.

This was the international entry point into the Free Territory of Angola.

Soon the arrivals boarded a truck for a 2-hour ride over dirt paths to the village of Jamba, capital of the territory.

Contrary to most foreign perceptions, Angola is not a country with a guerrilla problem. Rather, it is a divided country, much as Korea is. The larger portion is controlled by a leftist government supported by Cuban troops. The southeastern quarter is controlled by the National Union for the Total Liberation of Angola

(UNITA), an anti-communist movement led by Jonas Savimbi. In the grey areas between the two jurisdictions, civil war is fought as Savimbi's guerrillas try to expand the UNITA area and as the government and the Cubans fight back and launch occasional offensives.

The Portuguese colonies in Africa were not immune to the wave of independence which swept that continent following World War II. In what was then known as Portuguese West Africa, in February of 1961 the Marxist-oriented Popular Movement for the Liberation of Angola (MPLA) launched a revolt against the colonial government headquartered in the capital of Luanda. About a month later, additional anti-government guerrilla warfare broke out in the northern provinces. This involved the more moderate Union of the Peoples of Angola (UPA).

The rebellion was ruthlessly suppressed by the Portuguese, and it has been estimated that 20,000 black Africans died in the fighting. Nevertheless, the revolt smoldered on as the MPLA shifted its activities to the country's eastern sector, continuing its guerrilla campaign from bases in neighboring Zambia.

In 1966 the UPA split into the pro-western, socialist National Front for the Liberation of Angola (FNLA) and the also pro-western National Union for the Total Independence of Angola (UNITA). UNITA moved its guerrilla operations into the south-central region. The rebels conducted standard guerrilla warfare—ambushes and hit-and-run attacks—and these persistent efforts tied down a sizeable Portuguese force. Estimates are that in the late 1960s half of Portugal's national budget was being spent on its forces in Africa. Campaigns against the Portuguese were also under way in what later became the independent countries of Cape Verde Islands, Guinea-Bissau, and Mozambique.

As often occurs in such cases, young Portuguese officers came to resent the unrelieved bush fighting and the inefficiency of the bureaucracy running the war from Lisbon. For years Portugal had been ruled by a dictator, Antonio de Oliveira Salazar. He died in 1970, but his successors continued the wars. In April 1974, however, young officers toppled the national government and installed a leftist regime that was willing to relinquish Portuguese West Africa (Angola) once an orderly succession rule could be insured.

Twice the three main liberation movements, the MPLA, FNLA, and UNITA, formed coalitions and twice the coalitions collapsed. When the Portuguese finally withdrew in November 1975, they left a country divided by civil war, with UNITA and the FNLA pitted against the MPLA. The MPLA held the capital and its port. Through this port Cuban soldiers and Soviet arms and technicians entered the country in support of the MPLA. This assistance turned the tide in favor of the leftists. Although South African forces and American supplies were sent to aid UNITA and the FNLA, the MPLA and its Cuban-Soviet allies overcame the opposition parties by February 1976.

The first contact between Cuban government officials and the leadership of guerrilla organizations fighting to end Portuguese colonialism in Angola is believed to have taken place in 1965. The renowned Ernesto "Che" Guevara and other Cuban officials met with Agostinho Neto, political leader of the MPLA, and his military commander-in-chief somewhere in present-day Zaire or in the Republic of Congo (Brazzaville).

Within a few months of this meeting Cuban troops began to train MPLA guerrillas both in Cuba and in the Congo. Cuban ships delivered weapons to the MPLA through Brazzaville and continued to do so for over ten years. In 1966 Neto and other MPLA officials visited Cuba and from that time on maintained contact with the Cuban government. Angolan communists were provided a haven in Cuba. Some were given scholarships to attend Cuban schools.

The final assault to take over Angola came after the military *coup d'état* in Portugal in 1974. The new Portuguese government invited the principal guerrilla organizations fighting for the liberation of Angola to participate in the formation of a transition government until the final withdrawal of Portuguese forces from that country.

The three guerrilla organizations clashed, however, in a bloody civil war. Zambia was offering support to UNITA, led by Jonas Savimbi. This group had also received aid from the People's Republic of China. The FNLA, led by Holden Roberto, was receiving aid from Zaire, North Korea, and the People's Republic of China. The FNLA was also receiving assistance from the United States. It had managed to take a large territory in the northeast and set up a capital at Carmona.

South African troops had entered the southern part of Angola in August 1975 and were giving assistance to UNITA and the FNLA. They supplied weapons and assisted in the organization of a military force headed by Daniel Chipenda, a former member of the MPLA who had defected to the FNLA.

Cuban *Comandante* Flavio Bravo and Agostinho Neto met in Brazzaville in May 1975 and worked out plans for substantial Cuban military assistance to the MPLA. The MPLA needed help from the Cubans in order to be able to capture power after the departure of the Portuguese. A second meeting is said to have taken place in August of 1976 between *Comandante* Raúl Arguello and Neto in Luanda. The struggle for power between the different guerrilla organizations had put the MPLA on the run. The MPLA requested Cuban military assistance as soon as possible. Meanwhile, the Soviets were waiting until the departure of the Portuguese before they intervened directly to provide assistance to their friends in the MPLA.

According to a press report, United States and Cuban officials held high-level talks in 1974 and 1975 in Washington and New York about the situation in Angola. Assistant Secretary of State William Rogers made it clear to Cuban officials at a meeting that took place in November of 1975 that the United States firmly opposed Cuban military involvement in Angola. The meeting did not have any noticeable effect. The Cuban government was already in the process of sending military advisors and training personnel. The Cubans set up four training bases for MPLA troops at Benguela, Saurimo, Cabinda, and Delatando. The Cubans were supporting the MPLA effort to capture power upon the departure of the Portuguese, which had been scheduled for 11 November.

Three Cuban ships with men and an assortment of weapons and other equipment arrived in Angola in early October. The Cuban merchant ship *Viet Nam Heroico* arrived on 4 October, and two more ships arrived within a week. But before the Cubans could establish their camps and train a large force of MPLA troops, the military situation grew worse for Cuba's allies. South African troops began to advance north toward the capital and the FNLA closed in from the north toward MPLA-held territory.

The Cuban government then decided to send a battalion of special forces (650 men) to Angola by air to support the MPLA and the Cuban troops that had arrived in October. The battalion was transported by air in 13 days, starting on 7 November 1975. The Cubans used old Bristol Britannia turbo-prop airplanes, making refueling stops in Barbados, Guinea-Bissau, and the Congo before landing in Luanda. Preparations began for sending thousands of additional troops by sea and air. These would include at least one artillery regiment and a battalion of motorized troops.

The troops were carried in Cuban merchant ships, fishing boats, and an assortment of airplanes. The logistics, although fairly primitive, were effective enough to transfer large quantities of men and materials. Commercial airplanes and small cargo vessels were often overloaded in the effort to carry large numbers of troops quickly to Angola. Considering that Cuba had never been involved in an operation of this type, this was a creditable operation. But the key to success was the ambivalence and the lack of direction of the United States on the Angolan situation. Cuba would not have been able to intervene in Angola had the United States taken a strong stand and prevented Cuban troops from leaving their home island.

The Cuban forces entered combat almost from the time they arrived. War on several fronts at the same time was not easy. The Cubans suffered several major defeats including one at Catofe, where South African forces surprised them and caused a substantial number of casualties. The months of November and December 1975 were difficult ones. Mistakes were made and the Cuban losses included Raúl Arguello, a veteran of the revolution in Cuba against Fulgencio Batista.

Cuban troop strength continued to increase. Members of the Cuban general staff were replaced by younger, junior officers and were sent to Angola to lead the battle. *Comandantes* Victor Chueng Colas, Leopoldo Cintras Frias, Abelardo Colome Ibarra, Raul Menendez Tomassevich, along with the Casas Regueiro brothers, and others participated in the fighting.

By the end of January 1976 between 6,000 and 7,000 troops were deployed in Angola. Cuban planes used the Azores, particularly Santa Maria Island, between 20 and 30 December 1975 as a refueling stop. Despite objections from the Portuguese government Cuban planes again used the Azores for the same purpose between 10 and 15 January 1976. The troops were transported in Soviet-manufactured IL-62 airplanes.

Cuban troops fought 3 campaigns in less than 12 months against the FNLA and UNITA guerrilla forces in the north and southeast and South African forces in the south. The Cubans also joined MPLA troops in a bloody campaign to defeat the Front for the Liberation of the Cabinda Enclave (FLEC), led by Francisco Xavier Lubota.

In February 1976 the Cubans and the MPLA captured the last major strongholds of UNITA. UNITA fled to neighboring countries where they regrouped. They revived their guerrilla warfare against MPLA. White mercenaries—South African and Portuguese—frequently aided UNITA militarily, and covert U.S. arms assistance was reportedly received as well. In 1977 UNITA initiated a series of guerrilla raids on urban areas in Angola. A rebellion that UNITA supported, however, was crushed.

Even so, the guerrillas gained control of an extensive area in southern Angola. The following year a government offensive against the guerrillas failed to dislodge them from the areas they controlled. Sympathetic to South Africa and vice-versa, UNITA allowed South African forces to maintain bases in its territory for raids against nationalist guerrillas in Namibia, also known as South-West Africa. By the early 1980s UNITA guerrillas had extended their control to central and southeast Angola. This was the area of the Ovimbundu tribe of which UNITA leader Jonas Savimbi is a member. Political and military matters in Africa are often determined along tribal lines. The guerrillas won the support of Great Britain, France, the United States, Saudi Arabia, and a number of African nations, while the MPLA continued to be backed by the Soviet Union and Cuba. The protracted warfare destroyed much of Angola's economy and displaced one-sixth of its people, who were forced to become refugees in neighboring Zaire, Zambia, and the Congo.

Over the past few years there have been offensives—or drives, if one prefers—by all the parties involved in Angola. The South African Defense Force, which in 1975, 1977, 1979, and 1980 had entered Angola, again crossed the Namibian border in August 1981 to strike at SWAPO bases in Angola. SWAPO [South West Africa People's Organization] is the black movement which seeks independence for Namibia. [Namibia became independent in 1990.]

South African aircraft destroyed radar stations and Soviet missile sites, and 3 task forces of motorized troops drove over 90 miles into Angola. Towns were taken; some 1,000 guerrillas and government troops were killed. Substantial quantities of Soviet tanks, weapons, and other equipment were captured. Ten South Africans died in the drive.

UNITA soon launched an offensive of its own. Savimbi's troops struck into Moxico Province, capturing Lupire on 19 September and other towns in later weeks. The rebels were operating 200 miles inside Angola.

In August 1985 the government launched drives against the rebel-held towns of Cazombo in the northeast and Mavinga in the southeast. Four motorized infantry brigades headed for Cazombo; five brigades moved against Mavinga. The offensive was supported by Soviet-made MiGs, helicopters, and fighter-bombers of the Angolan Air Force.

Savimbi knew that he lacked sufficient strength to retain both towns. His forces, therefore, abandoned Cazombo, which they had held for 22 months.

In mid-September South Africa launched another invasion of Angola. The South Africans said they were in pursuit of SWAPO guerrillas again. The Angolan government, however, charged that the South Africans were actually fighting its troops involved in the drives against Savimbi. The government produced the body of a South African orderly killed near Cazombo. The South African Air Force was said to be providing air support for the rebels. On 7 October Savimbi claimed full control of Mavinga and defeat of the government forces, who were now reportedly retreating under counter-attack and in disarray.

The Cuban forces have been successful in keeping the MPLA in power but have been unable to defeat the UNITA guerrillas. Without the support of Cuban troops and military advisers from the Soviet Union and East Germany, the Angolan government would not have been able to retain power. The total number of Cuban combat troops and technical and support personnel has reportedly reached as high as 36,000 at times in the past 10 years. In 1985 Castro stated that to date over 200,000 Cubans had served in Angola. During the Third Congress of the Cuban Communist Party, in February of 1986, several Cuban generals sporting Angolan combat decorations sat among the 1,790 delegates.

Casualties in Angola have been relatively high in relation to the size of the Cuban population. In addition to combat losses, tropical diseases have also taken their toll, not only on the troops serving in Angola but also back in Cuba where previously unheard-of diseases imported from Africa have caused problems in agriculture, animal husbandry, and the general population (i.e., AIDS, dengue, conjunctivitis or red eye, rare strains of VD, and African swine fever, to mention only a few).

Much of the heaviest fighting took place between 1975 and 1978, when the MPLA was able to consolidate its hold over the Angolan capital and most of the national territory with the support of the Cuban troops. By March of 1977 the MPLA and Cuban forces had stabilized their military control enough for Fidel Castro to visit Angola (and several other African countries) and brag about the victory. But 2 months later, in May of 1977, a coup was attempted against Agostinho Neto by Nito Alves and Jose Van Dunem with the support of several army units. The bloody uprising was defeated, with Cuban troops playing an important role. Heavy fighting took place again in Cabinda Province in June 1977 against FLEC guerrillas, who were routed. In July about 4,000 more Cuban troops arrived to provide additional support for the MPLA.

Despite the additional Cuban troops, UNITA was able to launch a military offensive in December 1977 against the government. The next year, in April and June, Cuban-supported military offensives were carried out against UNITA, but the guerrilla units led by Savimbi had by then been able to consolidate their forces in tribal lands of people who supported UNITA.

The relationship of the Cuban Revolutionary Armed Forces (*Fuerzas Armadas Revolucionarias*—FAR) with the MPLA began in the early 1960s. At that time, the FAR provided instructors to the MPLA, which was operating in Brazzaville, Congo.

Later the assistance was expanded to include materiel. In November 1975 the MPLA came to power in Angola. By June of that year, the first 200 Cuban instructors had already been sent there. By February 1976 the number of Cubans in Angola had jumped to 9,000, and this included combat troops. Today the Cubans number 33,200 men, including support troops.

The FAR uses Soviet doctrine in Angola, and has adopted it to local conditions. The structure of command of the Cuban forces in Angola is as follows: The head-quarters is the *Missao Internacionalista de Cubanos en Angola* (MICA). Under the MICA are the Cuban army and air force units and the advisors and instructors. The army is divided into regiments. The advisors and instructors work with the Angolan army, air force, and navy. The Cubans have complete autonomy over their own forces; the Angolans have absolutely nothing to say about them.

The Cuban units in Angola are as follows: 19 motorized infantry regiments—7 of these have tanks; 2 anti-aircraft brigades; and one medium artillery regiment. There are 1,000 advisors and instructors. The instructors are attached to training units. The advisors are attached to combat units and help command them down to the brigade level. The advisors participate in combat. There are 4,000 Cubans in support services. There are 1,000 Cubans in their air force in Angola.

The Cubans in Angola maintain four basic defense lines stretching across the country. The lower one is of course the one bordering on the UNITA free territory. The next one is roughly along the Benguela railway. The third line is around Luanda, and the fourth line is in the north, developed as a result of UNITA guerrilla actions in that area. The first line, which extends eastward to Cuito Cuanavale, has been used three times as the base for offensives. All have failed to dislodge UNITA from its territory.

The training given to the average Cuban is considered by experts to be fair. Much better training is given to the specialized services—air, tanks, and so forth. The Cubans are gaining a great deal of combat experience from Angola. Their adventure in this country is providing them with a number of military advantages. One, they are testing their command and control structures. Two, they are evaluating Soviet equipment. Three, they are gaining experience in counter-revolutionary tactics. Four, they are adapting tactics and doctrines. Five, they are evaluating and practicing air defense. Six, they are obtaining practical experience for their pilots.

The FAR is involved in advisory roles, defensive roles, offensive roles, and social action. Until 1980 the Cubans participated primarily in offensive actions. Since then, however, they have gone more into defensive modes, so that the FAPLA—the Angolan Army—can gain more experience in offensive tactics. The Cubans advise the Angolan forces in combat and logistics. Some Soviet advisors are now working at the brigade level, and indeed in a recent offensive UNITA took out several Russians who were actually in the front lines, manning tanks. The Cubans maintain the more sophisticated equipment. The Cubans give intelligence and propaganda advice.

Today 18,500 Cubans are in defensive roles. They protect key infrastructures: rail lines, oil wells, strategic towns, and important industrial areas such as those in

Luanda. They also maintain the early warning systems and the air defense equipment and missiles. In the oil-rich Cabinda enclave there are 6,000 Cubans. The number was recently increased from 3,500 men. The Cubans serve as escorts on logistic routes, and in the area of Luanda and other main urban areas they fulfill counter-insurgency roles. In their offensive roles they do reconnaissance. They have a reaction force along the southern defense line, the line that borders on the UNITA territory. The Cubans conduct counter-insurgency operations against UNITA, they provide close air support for the Angolan air force, FAPA. The Cuban artillery and tank units support the FAPLA.

Since 1985 the Cubans have become more involved in directly countering UNITA. This apparently is because the FAPLA has failed to do a good job. Another reason is that the Cubans, in defensive roles day in and day out, month after month, face a horrendous morale problem, and certainly their officers would rather see at least some combat.

The social work done by the Cuban troops includes medical aid, construction of bridges and roads, and emergency assistance in famine areas. There are 7,000 Cuban civilians in Angola who teach, construct, do health work, help with forestry, the sugar crop, and other agriculture, and are also involved in communications.

There has been friction between the MPLA and the Cubans. The Angolan army resents the Cubans having better food—even better than the population, portions of which often are close to starving. In addition, the Cubans are taking diamonds and wood without payment. Some top MPLA people, according to intelligence reports, have become fed up with the Cubans.

Captain Antonio Luis Francisco Mango of the general staff of the FAPLA's 16th Brigade, who recently deserted, stated:

> Concerning the presence of the Cubans in Angola, the Angolan people feel oppressed. They feel oppressed because of the role the Cubans play in Angola. Initially we thought they were coming here under the banner of proletarian internationalism, but over time we discovered that their mission has nothing to do with helping the Angolan people. Their mission is to occupy our country.

In addition to military advantages, the benefits to the Cubans are several. First, maintaining a relatively large force in Angola keeps unemployment low in Cuba. Second, the Soviets pay the logistical cost of stationing the Cubans there. In addition, according to intelligence sources, the Cubans in Angola receive more advanced arms from the Soviet Union than even the weapons sent by Moscow directly to Cuba. (Angola also reportedly gives some $43 million monthly to help pay for the Cubans.)

As mentioned, keeping the troops occupied is a morale problem. Cubans are restricted from any contact with the local population. They are rarely, if ever, allowed to go outside Luanda on their own. In areas where UNITA has operated, there is serious friction between the locals and the Cubans, as the locals tend to support UNITA.

The Cubans mistrust the FAPLA for several reasons. The FAPLA performs poorly.

Second, the Cubans suspect, and apparently rightly so, that the FAPLA—or at least some people in it—sympathizes with UNITA.

If there have been advantages for Cuba in its intervention in Angola, there have also been perhaps even greater disadvantages. Cuba involved itself in Angola during the heyday of Cuban dictator Fidel Castro's interventionism in Latin America and Africa. It may well be that the Soviet Union encouraged the Cuban role. Today, 12 years later, Cuba is still heavily involved in Angola, and Angola has sometimes been referred to as Cuba's Vietnam. Cuban youths do not want to serve there, and evidently the officers are not too happy about going there either. Youths fleeing Cuba in rafts and small boats say when they reach the United States that they did not want to serve overseas. Cuban General Rafael del Pino, who in the mid-1970s commanded Cuba's air force in Angola and who defected to the United States in May 1987, stated:

The people do not want to go to Angola. The people, the officers resist going to Angola. This is not only because ... we have converted ourselves into a mercenary army ... but it is that our officers see that the problem is that neither the sons of the members of the Politburo or the sons of the principal leaders of the government go to Angola, do not go into military service.

Del Pino said that Cuban casualties in Angola (missing, wounded, and dead) totalled approximately 10,000. He reported that during 3 years, 56,000 deserters from the Cuban armed forces had been "captured" (including repeaters).

There is an increasing Russian presence in Angola. This may be because the Cubans, like the Angolans, have not done well. The Russians are in advisory or command positions and have even participated in combat.

Brigadier Isidoro Huambo Chindondo, chief of military intelligence for UNITA, states:

The Cubans are responsible for atrocities against the local population. They are raping the women in Angola. They are destroying the food and the facilities for the local population. They are conducting roundup operations to get Angolan youngsters and to send them to the Island of Youth in Cuba. They are stealing in industrial factories in Angola, like the big machines in factories. They are putting these in Antonovs and then flying them back to Havana. Cattle are also being flown to Havana. They are also putting the wood in Antonovs and flying it to Havana.

Intelligence Chief Huambo provided information on the organization of the military arm of the MPLA, the FAPLA (Popular Armed Forces for the Liberation of Angola). At the top of the military structure is the Internationalist Committee. This is composed of two groups: one is made up of all military personnel, basically Cubans and Russians, and the second is made up of military representatives of the MPLA. Below it functions the National Council for Defense and Security, which is composed of representatives of the armed forces, the government, and the MPLA. Then there is the commander-in-chief and the Defense Ministry. Underneath these function the general staff, which has representatives of the army, air force, and navy. There are 10 military regions, each governed by a regional military council.

The basic unit of the FAPLA is the brigade. Each consists of between 600 and 700 men. There are two types of brigades: light infantry and mechanized. The strength of the FAPLA is approximately 80,000 men. There is a militia (ODP) of about 60,000 men. There are some 2,500 men in the navy (MGPA) and 1,500 in the air force (FAPA). There are also lesser numbers in Special Forces. The navy is equipped primarily with Soviet-made patrol and fast attack craft. The air force has Soviet-made Antonov transport planes, MiG-17, -21, and -23 fighter planes, and Mi-8, -17, and -25 helicopters.

According to Brigadier Huambo, apart from the Cubans, there are the following foreign military personnel in Angola: 2,500 Soviets, 2,500 East Germans, 2,500 North Koreans, 3,500 men from Portugal. The Portuguese are said to be "communists and mercenaries coming for money." (Other intelligence sources in the region place non-Angolan, non-Cuban military personnel at a lower figure: 3,250.) The commander of the Portuguese is Colonel Leitao Fernandez. The Soviet commander is identified as General Constantine Chacknovich. The East German commander is known only as General Von Status, and the Cuban commander is General Gustavo Freitas Ramirez.

Huambo stated that in Angola there are also guerrillas from other areas of Africa. He identified these as 1,200 members of South Africa's African National Congress, 1,400 Katangese (Zaire) and 7,000 SWAPO guerrillas.

Facing the combined Angolan-Cuban-Soviet forces are the troops of UNITA. The military arm of the organization is FALA (Armed Forces for the Liberation of Angola). At the top is the high commander, General Jonas Savimbi. Below him functions the Strategic Operational Command (COPE), in charge of general strategic planning. Below the COPE is the EMG, the general staff, and under this function divisions and services.

Divisions include ground artillery units, anti-aircraft artillery, demolition units, and communications units. The services include the SIMI (military intelligence), the military police, health units, logistic units, personnel units, and training units.

The UNITA military organization is divided into seven military-political fronts plus the liberated territory. The fronts are divided into zones. UNITA has a spectrum of military forces ranging from local defense units to regular battalions. The defense forces are organized to protect villages. They are trained and armed and the protection of these villages is their sole responsibility. There are six battalions of these local defense groups. Each has about 300 men.

With additional training, these men are formed into mobile guerrilla units. There are 15 to 50 men in each unit.

After they are given further training, they become companies of what are called "compact guerrilla units." There are 150 men per unit. Brigadier Huambo said:

These are units that can cut off the logistic lines of the enemy, can surround deep targets, and can support local people when they transport material for the guerrillas.

The next step up is what UNITA calls semi-conventional forces. These consist of semi-regular battalions of about 600 men per unit. UNITA has 44 such battalions.

The battalions are spread over the country and support the guerrillas.

There are four regular battalions and these are used only to protect the liberated territory. The battalions receive about 6 months of training. There are about 600 men in a regular battalion. The battalions have land rovers and other means of transportation as well as anti-aircraft and anti-tank weapons. UNITA also has 16 platoons of Special Commandoes.

The UNITA forces total 65,000 men, of which 28,000 are regular and 37,000 are guerrillas.

The charismatic leader of UNITA—party and military—is Jonas Malheiro Savimbi. Savimbi was born 3 August 1934 in Munhango, a small town on the Benguela railway. His father worked on the railway and it was from his father, Loth, that he inherited the faculties of determination and perseverance which would shape his own future and that of his country. Loth rose in 20 years from being a low-grade clerk on the railway to the first black station master.

It was from his grandfather that Jonas inherited his dislike of the Portuguese. Jonas once said, "My grandfather told me that although he had a big soul, it was in great pain because of the humiliation imposed upon him by the Portuguese." His grandfather at one time had fought the Portuguese. It was also from his grandfather that Savimbi inherited and learned the use of the Ovimbundu language which stood him in good stead in the years ahead when he led the Ovimbundu in wars against the Portuguese and the Luanda government and its Cuban allies.

Savimbi received his secondary education at a missionary school. Later he studied at a government fee school and earned his keep by working in the headmaster's kitchen and watching his dog. In 1958 he graduated at the top of his class from a senior secondary class in southwest Angola. To embark upon a medical career, he took a boat to Portugal for advanced studies. A sailor gave him books on Marxism and on Marcus Garvy, the early American black consciousness leader. Savimbi said, "After I read them I was really burning to join a freedom movement. On the ship I already knew that my studies would be a secondary matter for me."

In the years that followed, Savimbi mixed plotting against the Portuguese with his studies. Savimbi travelled to Spain, France, and Switzerland. After his tour of Europe, he returned to Africa to attend an international student gathering in Kampala, Uganda. There were two small Angolan liberation movements operating in exile outside of that country: the MPLA, with its roots among the slum dwellers, intellectuals, and the Kinbundu people of the capital's hinterland; and the Union of the Angolan People (UPA), the forerunner of the FALPA, whose roots were among the northern Kikongu. Savimbi decided to join the UPA.

In February 1961 there was an uprising in Luanda in which UPA members participated. Africans armed with clubs and knives attacked the capital's jails in an attempt to release political prisoners. Fourteen Portuguese were killed but the colonial authorities bore down heavily on the rebels. In March of that year Savimbi returned to Switzerland to prepare for examinations. By July, however, he decided to give up his medical studies. Savimbi alternated between Switzerland with his studies and Africa on political work. He was now studying law and international politics. He founded an Angolan student movement, the National Union of Angolan Students (UNEA), which was funded by the UPA. He established youth and trade union wings and a medical service.

By 1963 nearly 30 countries had become independent in Africa. The Organization of African Union (OAU) was created in Addis Ababa 22-25 of May 1963. Savimbi attended and was given an influential position as chairman of a group of liberation movement representatives who advised on the formation of a committee which would coordinate fund-raising to support nationalist movements in those countries still under colonialist rule.

In 1964 Savimbi travelled to the Soviet Union, Czechoslovakia, Bulgaria, Hungary, North Korea, North Vietnam, and China in search of support. The Eastern Europeans displayed little interest in helping him. The Chinese were more receptive and promised to train some of Savimbi's men and to distribute $1,000 from the Chinese embassy of Brazzaville to those of his supporters who were there. Savimbi continued his studies in Switzerland and returned again in 1965 to China to receive guerrilla training and to arrange for instruction for his first recruits. The Chinese gave Savimbi $15,000—the first donation received by UNITA for its party funds.

In July of 1965 Savimbi completed final examinations in Lausanne for his degree in legal and political sciences. He returned to China for additional training and he also welcomed there a group of 11 men chosen as UNITA's first guerrilla commanders. Savimbi knew the fight had to be fought right in Angola. He wrote, "George Washington could not have freed the British colonies of America by fighting from a base of exile against an army superior in numbers and equipment."

In March 1966 UNITA was born at a meeting in the town of Muangai, 250 kilometers inside Angola from the border with Zambia. Attending the meeting were 67 village chiefs and other delegates. A constitution was adopted which called upon UNITA to educate "all Angolans living outside the country to the idea that real independence for Angola will only be achieved through an armed struggle waged against the Portuguese colonial power inside the country." Savimbi, who was still abroad, had had a hand in writing the constitution.

In October 1966 Savimbi crossed into Angola, setting foot on his native soil for the first time since he had set sail for Portugal 8 years earlier. There were 50,000 Portuguese soldiers in Angola. Savimbi and what were called his Chinese Eleven had only knives, machete-like *pangas*, and one Soviet pistol. The first attack by UNITA was launched on 4 December 1966 against Cassamba, a small outpost protected by several hundred Portuguese soldiers. Savimbi later admitted that the attack was "a failure, it was a disaster." He said:

> It was the first time we had come under real fire, and the bullets had several colors—red, yellow, blue. We were really in a mess. One of our men was killed and we had to leave

him. Two were wounded. We took them with us. We were all lying flat and had to crawl
out through the (barbed) wire.

The war was on and would continue until the Portuguese were finally driven from Angola.

Savimbi had been taught Maoist guerrilla warfare tactics in China. He learned in Angola, however, that every guerrilla commander must adapt tactics to the conditions in the country in which he is fighting. Of what he had been taught in China, Savimbi later said: "Real war is very different. It was just luck that UNITA did not die in that first attack, because half the commanders trained in China took part in it."

Savimbi had studied Mao Tse–Tung's *Selected Military Writings.* He also on one occasion engaged in an argument with Ernesto "Che" Guevara on guerrilla tactics. The two warriors met in January 1964 at a conference on African liberation movements held in Dar–es–Salaam, Tanganyika. Guevara argued in a speech that the Congo, huge and rich in minerals and agricultural products, was the key to revolution in central and southern Africa. It would be a major breakthrough if the Congo could be removed from imperialist control by a combined effort of African nationalists, Guevara stated. Savimbi responded that it would be a big mistake if the liberation movements were crushed while making a joint endeavor in the Congo. Who would be left to continue the struggle?

Savimbi and Guevara met privately and exchanged ideas for 5 hours. Savimbi argued against one of the principles that Guevara had expounded during the conference: establishment by guerrillas of fixed base camps. This was contrary to Mao's principle of avoiding set bases. Savimbi also disagreed with Guevara's thesis that the working class had to be the vanguard of any liberation struggle. In Angola, the people who mattered were the peasants, 90 percent of the population.

Guevara, in his major contribution to guerrilla literature, the book *Guerrilla Warfare,* had written, "There must always be preserved a strong base of operations and the strengthening of it must continue during the course of the war." This is precisely what Savimbi has done. He has established the Free Territory and over the years expanded it. It is, fundamentally, his base of operations.

Savimbi's guerrillas have moved out of the Free Territory, and as the enemy has pulled back, or limited his operations, the liberated territory has grown. Savimbi told this writer:

The tactics that we use are general, classic guerrilla tactics. We may change them here and there, but also this type of war is a combination of a military war, a political war, information, economic war, and so forth. So it is not one-side tactics.

The territory, because of its size, has become much more than merely a base for military operations. Within it functions a social and governmental system. There are elementary and upper-grade schools, first-aid stations, and hospitals. There are machine shops that do military and civilian work. There is a rudimentary postal system. No money, however, of any kind is used. Food and consumer goods are distributed according to necessity. An UNITA officer comments: "Fighting the war is only one aspect of the struggle. Victory will go to those who prove they are best capable of ruling Angola."

To help maintain the Free Territory, UNITA has received some assistance from the United States. Most important are the surface-to-air Stinger missiles, a fine equalizer in view of the fact that UNITA has no air power. South Africa, too, provides assistance, although the extent and nature of this is largely wrapped in military secrecy. There appears little doubt that South Africa, as in the past, would not permit the Angolans-Cubans-Russians to overrun the Free Territory.

Because of its geographical location and accidents of history, Angola is now of considerable strategic importance on the stage of world conflicts. Angola has over 1,000 miles of coastline on the South Atlantic, and running into the ports are several cross-country railroads. This makes Angola a significant outlet for the raw materials of Central African nations, including minerals, diamonds, and agricultural products. Recently NATO extended southward its contingency planning to a line running west from Luanda.

The United States has refused to grant diplomatic recognition to Angola as long as Cuban troops remain in that country. Nevertheless, the United States has over the years participated a number of times in negotiations aimed at removal of those forces.

In June 1978 the deputy chief of the U.S. mission to the United Nations, David McHenry, traveled to Angola for discussions. The U.S. Assistant Secretary of State for African Affairs, Chester Crocker, visited Angola in April 1981. In September of the same year, U.S. Secretary of State Alexander Haig conferred in New York with Angolan Foreign Minister Paulo Jorge, and additional talks were held at the United Nations between the two countries. Chester Crocker and Paulo Jorge met in Paris in February 1982. Further talks were held that year in Paris and Luanda between United States and Angolan officials. Twice in 1987 Crocker visited Luanda, and he also had talks with Angolan officials in Washington, Brazzaville, and Brussels.

On 28 September 1978 the United Nations Security Council adopted Resolution 435 calling for "the withdrawal of South Africa's illegal administration from Namibia and the transfer of power to the people of Namibia ..." Angolan leader Jose Eduardo dos Santos, who had succeeded Neto after his death in 1979, indicated willingness to negotiate withdrawal of the Cubans once Resolution 435 was implemented. Ever since, there has been an Angolan-Namibian linkage in all negotiations.

In a speech in Harare, Zimbabwe in September 1986 at a summit conference of the Non-Aligned nations, Cuba's Fidel Castro tossed in a new issue. He stated that Cuban troops would not leave Angola until apartheid was ended in South Africa. This statement apparently surprised the Angolans, and it does not now appear to be a serious issue in negotiations.

Angola won its independence from Portugal; in the subsequent internal struggles a Marxist party gained control. The Cubans and Russians provided support, and the door was opened for Angola to be thrust into the East-West conflict. The emergence of white-controlled South Africa as a regional power and its rule over Namibia added another dimension to the struggle for Angola.

Angola is today one of three places in the world where U.S.-supported forces are at war with Soviet-supported forces. Savimbi states:

> ... *If the Russians do control and consolidate in Angola, they will have an ideal base from where to operate—to control central Africa, which is Zambia, Zaire; eastern Africa: Mozambique, Tanzania, Malawi; (then) move to Namibia and South Africa.*

Since World War II, the communists have in various parts of the world utilized guerrilla warfare as a means to try to seize power. Now, in Angola, Nicaragua, and Afghanistan, this type of warfare is being used against them.

Says Savimbi:

> ... *What we want for our country, first, a true independence. And we fought for that. We fought for 15 years against Portuguese colonialists to get a true independence ... (We want) a country which will decide whom will be our friend, and not have imposed upon us a friendship, as it is today. And more than that, we believe that our people have suffered a lot, during colonial domination, during this war against the Russians, the Cubans. The Angolans, they need to rest. They need to rest in order to look after their own interests. Our people work very well on agriculture. They need only peace. They need only seeds. They need only tools. And they will produce food for themselves, and it is our priority number one.*

[By the late years of the 1980s the Cold War was coming to an end. There was no reason for the United States or the Soviet Union to continue investing resources in the surrogate wars in Nicaragua, Afghanistan, and Angola. A series of negotiatory meetings were held over a period of several years involving, directly or indirectly, the parties involved in Angola: the Luanda government, UNITA, Cuba, South Africa, the United States, and the Soviet Union. Under pressure from the major powers, agreements were hammered out. The South Africans withdrew their forces, and then the Cubans did, too. On 31 May 1991 a peace agreement between Luanda and UNITA was signed in the Portuguese city of Estoril. Under international supervision, parliamentary and presidential elections were held in September 1992 with both the MPLA and UNITA participating. The MPLA won 129 seats in the parliament, UNITA won 70. In the presidential race the incumbent (Luanda) President, the MPLA's Jose Eduardo dos Santos, won 49.5% of the votes, UNITA's Savimbi 40.07% Because neither received the majority required by law for victory, there was to be a runoff to determine the winner. Savimbi, however, charged that the vote had been rigged. Within weeks Angolans were again fighting their civil war. By July 1993 press dispatches reported that UNITA had won control of some 75% of the country's territory.]

chapter eleven
ESPIONAGE DIRECTORATE

Orlando Castro Hidalgo (no relation to Fidel) defected in 1969 from Cuba's General Directorate of Intelligence (DGI), the country's primary intelligence service. Castro Hidalgo and his wife were spirited out of Paris, where he was serving at the Cuban embassy, by the U.S. government. He took with him hundreds of embassy documents. The information that Castro Hidalgo provided the CIA was a mother lode of intelligence on the operations and personnel of DGI. For his safety Castro Hidalgo was maintained in concealment. Nevertheless, he had a series of meetings at a Washington, D.C. motel with Mallin. Mallin interviewed him and was also given copies of the embassy documents. He then ghost-wrote *Spy for Fidel* in 1970, the first public revelation of the inner workings of the Cuban intelligence service. The following chapters are taken from the book.

Intelligence

Section III was the "illegal section" of the DGI. Its basic duty was to carry out espionage and counterespionage in the United States, Canada, and Mexico. A major function was spying on the CIA and Cuban exile organizations engaged in anti-Castro activities. The offices of Section III were located in a gray, three-story house on Línea Street in the Vedado suburb of Havana. Nothing indicated the nature of the work conducted inside the building. In order to camouflage its activities, the section had a sign across the front of the building which proclaimed, *Prevención de Incendios* (Prevention of Fires). There was no fire-fighting equipment to be seen, however.

The subsection located in the upper portion of the building was in charge of operations at the Intelligence centers in Mexico, Canada, and the United Nations. It also handled the training of *oficiales* assigned to serve at these centers. The grounds and first floors were occupied by the *Buró CIA y Contrarevolución.* Technically one bureau, in actuality there were two separate units, and eventually DGI did split them into two distinct bureaus. The *Buró CIA y Contrarevolución* was headed by "Demetrio," a one-time teacher, who had formerly worked in a section of G-2 which kept watch on the foreign embassies in Havana. Under him was "Menéndez," who also acted as chief of the counter-CIA section. Another official, "Cándido," headed the contrarevolución section, which spied on the activities of Cuban exiles.

The work within the various sections often overlapped, and at times there was also involvement with G-2, whose task was to uncover and eliminate anti-regime activities inside Cuba. Liaison was maintained with G-2, and when G-2 caught someone who had been infiltrated into Cuba, or had knowledge of infiltrations, copies of the tapes and transcripts of the interrogations carried out by G-2 were turned over to DGI. If DGI wanted particular information from a prisoner, a request was made to G-2, which would then try to elicit the data required. Of special interest were details about the operations of a vessel named the *Rex*, which was known to bring infiltrators to Cuba. Through information that had been gathered, DGI had been able to build up a description of this vessel, which during the daytime appeared to be a commercial ship, but at night became a well-armed warship. Small, fast boats were believed used to carry infiltrators from the *Rex* to the Cuban shore.

DGI also on occasion sought the cooperation of the *Comites de Defensa de la Revolución*, neighborhood vigilance committees which keep watch on the citizenry. If DGI needed information about a certain person—perhaps someone who had lived in Cuba but was now involved in exile activities in the States—an *oficial* would question members of the CDR in the place where that person had resided. A small problem was presented by the fact the DGI was—and still is—virtually unknown in Cuba, and the security-conscious CDR members cooperated only with G-2. CDR offices had lists of G-2 agents to whom they were authorized to facilitate any requested information. When DGI needed data, the tactic was adopted, therefore, of having an official go to the CDR, tell them he was new at G-2, and ask them to check with G-2 headquarters. G-2 would already have been advised by DGI that one of its men was going to see the CDR, and so when the check was made, G-2 would vouch for the individual. The *comites* did not know that in reality they were dealing with the Intelligence service.

Upon leaving the DGI school, I was assigned to work in the *contrarevolución* unit of Section III. My tasks amounted to counterespionage by remote control. The unit was concerned with infiltrating and spying on exile organizations operating out of Miami. I was given the *expedientes* (dossiers) of a number of key exile figures, and my task was to build up information about these persons with the view of finding a way to place a DGI informer close to them. As a case officer, I had to delve into the background and relationships of not only the target individual, but also his relatives, friends, co-workers, and acquaintances. As this detailed information was gathered, I watched for possible opportunities which DGI could exploit (a friend of the target individual known to be in need of funds and perhaps susceptible to bribery, a coworker with a relative still in Cuba and therefore subject to coercion, and so on).

The most important of my *expedientes* was that of Eloy Gutíerrez Menoyo. Menoyo had been one of the leaders of a sizable guerrilla organization that had fought the Batista regime during the Revolution. Once the rebels had won, the organization was dissolved. Subsequently, Menoyo assisted in uncovering a major conspiracy aimed at toppling Castro, but later turned against Castro and fled to the United States. He helped set up an exile organization named Alpha 66, which became known for its raids against shipping off Cuba.

DGI believed that Menoyo was in the process of bringing weapons to isolated spots on the Cuban coast and concealing them there, to be picked up and used at a future date. Reports received from Miami indicated that Menoyo himself planned to infiltrate into Cuba, and therefore DGI and G-2 were conducting an investigation to ascertain which of Menoyo's friends in Cuba might be making preparations to assist his eventual arrival. It was felt that Menoyo would need the help of a "reception team" of local fishermen in order to be able to come ashore without being detected by the authorities, and likely fishermen were also being investigated.

I did not work in this section of DGI long enough to see completion of the Menoyo *expediente*. Menoyo did infiltrate into Cuba in an effort to launch a new guerrilla campaign, and he was captured and imprisoned. By this time, however, I had been transferred to another department.

Another file which I handled was that of Andres Nazario Sargen, also a top figure in Alpha 66. The Sargen family was from Matanzas Province, and an investigation was under way to determine whether a connection could be found with any fishermen in that area. DGI and G-2 were seeking to ascertain who might be serving, or might in the future serve, on "reception teams" for Alpha infiltrators or for weapons that were being buried on cays and near beaches. The investigators were also trying to find out whether Sargen was in contact with any friends inside Cuba. The file was being built up, and eventually a plan would be prepared for consideration by the chief of DGI, Manuel Piñeiro. This plan would suggest methods by which it might be possible to penetrate Alpha, perhaps to place a spy or informer close to Sargen.

A third case on which I worked was that of a doctor, an orthopedist, who had participated in anti-Castro activities in Cuba and had been found out, but had managed to escape to the United States. In Miami the doctor was again active in the anti-Castro movement. As was the usual procedure, a detailed study was undertaken of relatives and friends of the doctor who were still in Cuba, and out of this study two possible approaches were being developed. A brother of the doctor was serving a prison term, and consideration was given to offering his release in return for cooperation by the doctor with DGI. If he would secretly supply Intelligence with information about exile activities, his brother would eventually be released—or so he would be told. The second approach would involve another relative who had applied for permission to leave Cuba. The permission would be granted—provided the man agreed to spy on the doctor for DGI. What if the man acceded and then reneged once he was in the States? This presented no problem: DGI would simply keep his wife and children in Cuba as hostages. And if the man were to decide that, under the circumstances, he did not wish to go to the States, after all? That was no problem, either: he would be confronted with evidence that he had been involved in clandestine activities and told that he would be brought to trial unless he did cooperate. Thus does a police state "recruit" unwilling agents.

I handled four cases in the short time I served in Section III. The fourth file was that of Miguel Díaz Isalgué, a veritable Scarlet Pimpernel who was believed to have made numerous secret trips in and out of Cuba. Isalgué was well-experienced in this type of work: while in Miami during the Batista dictatorship he had run weapons into Cuba for the Castro rebels. Later he had turned against Castro, as had Menoyo, and begun working against Castro's regime. Isalgué had succeeded in setting up a clandestine network in Cuba, and had even recruited an Army *comandante* as a member. DGI and G-2 knew that Isalgué had reception teams composed of fishermen in Matanzas Province, and possibly Las Villas Province also. An effort was under way to infiltrate agents into these teams.

It was learned that Isalgué had utilized his mother's home in Havana as a secret meeting place with his contacts in the area. The home was placed under close surveillance: all correspondence was opened and checked, the telephone was tapped, phone calls to and from the States were tape-recorded. Isalgué's friends were being investigated to see whether any were working with him. Despite the extensive effort made by the authorities, however, they did not succeed in capturing the elusive Isalgué.

In the course of gathering information for my various files, I had occasion to talk with a Cuban woman who had worked as a spy in Miami for the Cuban government. Marta A. González, a divorcée with a fair face and figure, in her thirties, had been trained by "Menéndez" in intelligence work and had been sent to the States. She had entered the country as a refugee in April of 1962. Becoming a part of the exile milieu, she presumably dispatched such information as she could gather about the activities of the anti-Castro organizations. About a year and a half after her arrival, she returned to Cuba. There she published a book, *Baja Palabra* (Under Oath), a caustic account of the life of Cuban exiles in the States. The book said nothing about the authoress being an Intelligence agent.

In her book, Marta González indicated that disillusionment with the United States was the cause of her return to Cuba. She told me a different story, however. She had been working under orders from Chafik Homero Saker Zenni, chief of the Intelligence Center within the Cuban delegation to the United Nations. Although travel of Cuban diplomats was restricted by the U.S. government to New York, Saker came to her one day and told her she had to leave, evidently because he suspected that the U.S. authorities were on to her activities and might be about to arrest her. He took her in his car and drove to Texas, where, posing as an American, she crossed into Mexico, from there to return to Cuba. (In her book, Mrs. González said that she went from the United States to Canada, and from there returned to Cuba.)

I was in Section III for 2 months. Subsequently I was transferred to the personnel selection department, where my work was not much different than it had been in the CIA and counterrevolution bureau. My function was to put together reports of men who had been chosen as possible members of the DGI. The selection was made by party and governmental organizations which had been requested to submit the names of their best men. All the information that could be obtained about these candidates was put together, and this was studied to see whether the men were suitable material for DGI. My job was to gather the various reports on each individual, and then to write an account summarizing what I had found regarding the individual's good and bad points. Final selection was made by the departmental chief.

I worked in the personnel section for only two and a half months. I was then transferred to Section II-2. My chief had asked me if I would like to change positions, and I had replied, yes, I would prefer to be engaged in intelligence work than the desk job I was now doing. Section II-2 had been set up as a result of the breaking of diplomatic relations with Cuba by all of the Latin American countries except Mexico. Cuba then established Intelligence centers in France, Spain, England, and Italy whose function was not only to handle espionage activities in Europe, but also to serve as a liaison between Havana and its agents in Latin America.

At Section II-2 I learned that I was to be sent to Paris, a fact which thoroughly delighted both my wife and me.

Headquarters for Section II-2 was located in what had once been the large, two-story home of a private family in the city of Marianao, adjoining Havana. The building was also where *oficiales* received their final training before being sent to European posts. By having headquarters and school in the same building, students were enabled to study the actual operations of the centers to which they were being assigned. Thus, I had access to messages sent to and from the Paris Center, and in this way became acquainted with the work carried out there.

Chief of Section II-2 at this time was Alberto Boza-Hidalgo Gato, an affable individual whom I had first met when Boza-Hidalgo had made occasional trips to the Intelligence school. Boza-Hidalgo's career in DGI followed a rocky road. After I went abroad to serve in France, I heard that Boza-Hidalgo had suffered disciplinary action, evidently because of a lack of sufficient enthusiasm for his work, and perhaps also because he was not as ideologically militant as was deemed desirable. Despite these failings, Boza-Hidalgo managed to reinstate himself in the good graces of his superiors and was sent to serve in the Intelligence Center within Cuba's United Nations delegation. There he became involved in espionage against the United States, and as a result, upon taking a trip to Cuba, he was barred by the U.S. government from reentering this country.

Part of the training I underwent in Section II-2 amounted to a refresher course on what I had learned at the Intelligence school. Studied again were such matters as how to arrange a clandestine meeting with another person, how to pass messages from one person to another, how to spot and evade anyone who might be following you. A large portion of my instruction, however, was directly related to the position and work I would assume in Paris. I was briefed on diplomatic rules, behavior, and protocol, and I delved into the French language, French politics, French economy, and information in general about Paris and the country. At night I attended classes on the arts at the National Council of Culture. Since I could not identify myself as being with the Intelligence service, my "cover" was that I belonged to the Foreign Commission of the Communist Party.

I was told that all friendships I might make in Paris had to be reported to the *jefe* of the *Centro*. In the Intelligence viewpoint, one did not have private friends abroad: acquaintances were supposed to have some bearing on the Intelligence work one was doing. Conversely, people who approached Intelligence personnel with a view to establishing a relationship were viewed with suspicion: they might be planted by the local counterintelligence service. The *jefe* had to be informed of any approach that was made, who had made it, how it was made, and the apparent intentions of the person involved.

The trainees were warned to beware constantly of counterintelligence services. We were told that every diplomat was an object of interest to counterintelligence, and for an Intelligence official everything outside of the *Centro* was a potential threat, a possible trap. We were especially warned about relationships with women, no matter how casual those associations might be, since the women might be working for counterintelligence.

Practical training at II-2 consisted mainly of planning and carrying out contact work on the streets of Havana. Two students would prepare a plan for meeting at a specified place at a certain hour. They were supposed to do this without being seen by anyone who might be following either of them. To make this practice highly realistic, actual surveillance was carried out by agents of G-2. We would work out a contact plan and then submit it to our chief, who would usually inform G-2. G-2 was not always told, but we did not know when it was or wasn't. As part of the exercise, we were required to report later whether we had been under surveillance, and if so, to provide details about the men and the vehicles that had followed us. On one occasion a trainee reported that he had spotted five G-2 cars. Later, to his chagrin, he learned that that day G-2 had not followed him at all.

Ordinarily, an *oficial* had to undergo about one year's practical training before being sent abroad, but in my case this was cut to 3 months. The Paris *Centro* was shorthanded and in need of a new official. One phase of my training that was eliminated was a period of work at the Ministry of Foreign Relations, where I would have learned at firsthand the functioning of Cuban diplomacy. The purpose would have been to enable me to pose more knowledgeably as a diplomat while abroad.

Before leaving for Paris, I went before the Party Commission within DGI, composed of Communist Party members in DGI. All officials going abroad had to be investigated—"processed" was the preferred word—by the commission. Approval by this group amounted to granting membership in the Communist Party. It was felt that only persons acceptable for Party membership were fit to serve Cuba abroad. I was subjected to several days of interrogation. Questions ranged from my knowledge of Marxism and views on Viet Nam to my role in the Revolution and the political positions of my relatives and friends. I was asked about my wife's opinions regarding the Revolution. I was careful not to reveal that a few years earlier, before we were married, she had applied for permission to leave Cuba and go to the United States. Although this was an official record, apparently no one in DGI had checked back and discovered this.

I won approval from the commission. Actually, this "processing" was little more than a formality, since the commission members knew that for a person to have come this far, he must already have been well-investigated and able to prove his worth. I was further aided by the presence on the commission of two men who had studied with me at Intelligence school.

Official papers from the Ministry of Foreign Relations, a last chat with the section chief, and a farewell dinner at the Mandarin Chinese Restaurant (which served Cuban food; Chinese food, like many other things, was lacking in Cuba), and I was ready to take up my post in Paris.

A Brief History of DGI

In the preceding chapters I have told the story of my career with the Dirección General de Inteligencia. *The espionage system built up by the government of Cuba, with guidance and assistance from the Soviet Union, has become one of the most sophisticated in the world. Little has ever been written about the DGI. The following, therefore, is an account of some of its operations and personnel.*

Fidel Castro's intelligence service had its genesis in the mountains of eastern Cuba. The rebel movement, in 1957 and 1958, was engaged in guerrilla warfare against the forces of Dictator Fulgencio Batista. *Campesinos*—peasants—moved back and forth between the government and rebel zones, and some of these rural folk kept the guerrillas posted on the movements of the government's troops. In the nearby city of Santiago and extending across the island there was a clandestine rebel apparatus that served as a support organizations for the guerrillas, funneling funds, recruits, and supplies into the hills. The underground also waged urban warfare— terrorism, sabotage, propaganda—and this attrition eventually so weakened the regime that the guerrilla forces were able to come down out of the hills and take over the country and the government.

With the victory of the rebel cause and the establishment of the Castro government, Castro set his sights on a larger target, the Caribbean and then the entire Southern Hemisphere. The first attempts at subversion were crude. Filibustering expeditions were dispatched to a number of countries, but were quickly wrapped up by the defense forces of these countries. Cuba turned to more sophisticated methods of subversion, and its intelligence operations were concerned mainly with supporting these efforts. The primary function of Cuban intelligence was, and has remained through the years, the support of subversion and guerrilla warfare in target countries, countries which have ranged geographically from Canada to Argentina, from the United States to Zanzibar. Cuban intelligence operations and subversion projects have usually been so interwoven that they have been virtually indistinguishable.

Cuban intelligence functions were originally the responsibility of G-2, a department of the Ministry of Interior. (Subsequently this section was named the *Departamento de Seguridad del Estado*, although it is still popularly known as "G-2.") In late 1961, owing to Cuba's increasing interest in foreign affairs, the *Dirección General de Inteligencia* (General Directorate of Intelligence) was created as a separate entity within the Interior Ministry. The DGI is headed by Major Manuel Piñeiro Losada, who is First Vice-Minister and Technical Vice-Minister of the Ministry, the latter capacity giving him authority over DGI. Piñeiro's high rank attests to the importance attached by Castro to his espionage service. Piñeiro had been one of the guerrilla officers serving under Raúl Castro during the Revolution. At one time a student at Columbia University in New York, Piñeiro evidently met there the American girl who was to become his wife. Sporting a red beard, Piñeiro is sometimes known as *Barba Roja*, which, when one thinks about it, seems quite appropriate for the chief of Fidel Castro's Communist spy service.

One of the first functions of DGI was the running of special schools for the training of Latin Americans in guerrilla warfare and subversive techniques. At one time, in the early sixties, as many as 1,500 men a year were being brought to Cuba for training. Once a major air and sea hub for travel in the hemisphere, Cuba's virtual exclusion from the hemispheric political system sharply cut down transportation means to and from the island. Nevertheless, flights have continued between Havana and Mexico City and Madrid, and there are also flights to and from Iron Curtain cities via Algeria. These circuitous routes were utilized to bring Latin Americans to Cuba, and use was also made of clandestine methods: communist freighters and Cuban fishing boats.

Once in Havana, the trainees were grouped by nationality. Usually there were 15 to 25 men in each group, although there might be as few as 3. The various nationalities were generally kept apart, for security reasons as well as because the courses given to the different groups varied. Venezuelans concentrated on guerrilla operations and sabotage techniques. Chileans, coming from a country with a strong Communist Party, were coached on furthering the communist cause through political methods. In special cases, emphasis was placed on techniques of agitation and propaganda in particular fields in which the trainees were involved in their homelands: unions, universities, intellectual organizations, or such.

Guerrilla warfare courses lasted 3 to 6 months, but occasionally as long as a year. Trainees showing particular promise were sometimes given additional training to become intelligence agents when they returned to their home countries. Appearing before an investigating committee of the Organization of American States in June

1967, a Venezuelan, Manuel Celestino Marcano Carrasquel, detailed the subversive preparation he had received in Cuba. Marcano testified:

> I took courses in guerrilla and counter-guerrilla tactics, theory and practice; assembling and disassembling short and long weapons, automatic and semi-automatic weapons, especially some of the ones that were easiest to acquire, especially "Springfield," "Garand," "Fals," "M-1," "Mendoza" machine guns, as well as the Mexican, the .30 and .50 caliber; theory and practice of firing long and short weapons; security measures; then rapid firing, which they call "Mexican defense." In explosives I was given a course that covered homemade bombs using chlorate, grenades, booby traps, "Molotov cocktails" of various kinds—including wickless, detonating wicks, blasting caps, calculation of charge. They put a great deal of emphasis on blowing up oil pipelines.... Then in topography: I took a course in map-making and map-reading, including reading of tactical maps, contour lines, intersection, reception, scientific orientation and practice with the compass.

There were a relatively large number of people in Marcano's original group, but most were eventually weeded out. He reported:

> We began with 150 persons. After 3 months we numbered 50. Later the number was 10. Apparently they [the instructors] made a series of observations with regard to the ability and ductility of each individual.

The group was also given instruction in a range of intelligence and clandestine fields. This included:

> Checks and counterchecks ... Hiding places for making indirect contacts; places where it would have been possible to leave explosives, arms, money; the international post boxes for indirect correspondence on the basis of cryptography ... Underground organization and structure at various levels. Photography ... Infiltration ... The falsification of documents, make-up, tailoring, simulation of dialects, phonetics, etc. This with regard to [false] identity.

Never before had so ambitious a program of subversion been launched by a small country. North Viet Nam has tried to subvert South Viet Nam; Cuba was aiming at subverting an entire continent. The Castro-Guevara program was one of the most systematized subversive schemes in the annals of the Cold War. The tentacles reached out from Havana to every corner of the continent.

"Che" Guevara, the fervent advocate of guerrilla warfare, was the mastermind behind Cuba's vast subversive program. Violence, directed and fueled by Havana, touched virtually every country in Latin America, and in some places it reached dangerous proportions. Nevertheless, the end result that was sought—the establishment of other communist governments—was not achieved. Guevara's myrmidons approached, but never quite grasped, victory. At some point Guevara decided to relinquish his managerial role, leave Cuba, and go into the field as a guerrilla commander once again. Guevara had always been a restless individual, and perhaps he had found prolonged residence in one country, Cuba, too confining. Perhaps he had tired of playing second fiddle to Fidel Castro. The continued failures of Cuba's subversive efforts may have convinced him that his personal leadership was required if a guerrilla movement were to succeed.

The disappearance and clandestine travels of Guevara were one of the intelligence feats of the Cold War. Guevara was the top man in Cuba after the Castro brothers, he was a prominent figure in the ranks of international communism, and he was recognized around the world as a guerrilla chieftain and theoretician. For a person of this stature to drop completely out of sight was a unique and bizarre occurrence in modern times. Rumors cropped up that Guevara had appeared in this or that place around the world, but none of these were confirmed, and some experts on Cuban affairs became convinced that Guevara was dead, the victim of either illness or assassination.

Although some of Guevara's travels and activities during the period 1965-1966 remain in mystery, it has now become possible to reconstruct a portion of his wanderings. Evidently disguised as a priest, Guevara secretly slipped out of Cuba and made his way to the Congo, there to lead a guerrilla operation which included a number of Cubans. Guevara had chosen Africa because he believed that, since it was more distant from the United States, a rebel movement there would have a greater chance of success than one in Latin America. In the Congo, at a place called Baraca, Guevara's forces battled troops led by famed mercenary leader Michael Hoare. Years later, in an interview, Hoare described what happened:

> When we arrived at Baraca, which ... was an amphibious operation, the first thing that impressed itself upon me was the extent of the firepower which was being directed upon us, which was fantastic.
>
> Congolese rebels' tactics would be normally to get drunk on, say, marijuana or something of that nature and to gather in thousands and to come on you in their thousands, overwhelming. But this we didn't experience at Baraca. Here we had troops responding to whistle signals, wearing equipment, carrying out maneuvers, and this went on for 4 or 5 days.

Despite the fine combativeness displayed by his men, at least on this occasion, Guevara's African adventure ended disastrously. [The Cubans had a falling out with their allies and had to flee.]

For months afterward the story of Guevara remains a blank. At some point he obtained two Uruguayan passports, made out to false identities. Although these passports were evidently genuine, the information and signatures in one, possibly both, were false, and so it has not been possible to ascertain whether Guevara obtained these in Uruguay, or possibly France (one of the passports may have been sent to the Uruguayan Embassy in Paris), or whether they were obtained by DGI for his use, without his having been in Uruguay or France. At any rate, Guevara eventually returned secretly to Cuba, and there began preparations to launch a guerrilla movement in Bolivia. Guevara's ambitions were still great: his long-range plan was aimed not so much at the Bolivian government as at the entire continent of South America. The Bolivian movement was to serve as a spawning ground for additional guerrilla operations in adjoining countries, and particularly Argentina.

The mounting of the Bolivian movement required extensive intelligence work, in which DGI played a major role. A Bolivian communist purchased a farm in a hinterland area which was to serve as the guerrillas' base. Guevara, still in disguise, traveled to Spain and Brazil, and slipped into Bolivia early in November 1966. Sixteen Cubans, including high-ranking officers, also traveled to Bolivia, at least one of them passing through the United States. In France, DGI recruited Régis Debray to join and report on Guevara's guerrillas. In Argentina, a man associated with a guerrilla group was summoned to Bolivia, where Guevara gave him detailed instructions on laying the groundwork for a rebel movement in their mutual homeland. For the same purpose, a communist leader was brought from Peru to confer with Guevara. A DGI official who used the code name "Ivan" served as a liaison between Guevara and Havana. Another DGI official, René Martínez Tamayo (code name: "Arturo"), was Guevara's radio and explosives expert and died with him in Bolivia.

For, despite all the planning and preparations, Guevara's hopes came to naught. After 11 months of ambushes and skirmishes, Guevara was captured and executed by the Bolivian army. The Bolivian adventure had been far more successful as an intelligence operation than as a guerrilla rebellion. For DGI it had been a project carried out on an international scale, and DGI's role in the affair did not terminate with "Che's" death. [DGI helped Cubans who had been with Guevara but managed to escape.]

That DGI was able to carry out its tasks on so wide a scale was an indication of how large and effective Fidel Castro's espionage service had grown since "Section M" of the Department of State Security became the nucleus of a new intelligence organization. Following are details of the structure and personnel of DGI.

The headquarters in Havana is known as the *Centro Principal.* The major staffs are called "sections," and these in turn are divided into desks. The Principal Center is divided into ten sections, five of which handle operations, while the other five are of a support nature. The operational sections, and their areas of responsibility, are:

Section II-1	*Latin America*
Section II-2	*Western Europe*
Section III	*Offices in Moscow, Prague,*
	East Germany, Canada, Mexico,
	the United Nations
Section III-1	*Illegals*
Section V	*Africa and the Middle East*

The support sections are:

Section III-2	*Contacts*
Section IV	*Personnel*
Section M-1	*Technical services*
Documentation Center	
Logistics	

The work and personnel of the ten sections are as follows:

SECTIONS II-1 and **II-2**. The overall chief is "Armando." He was the official at the Principal Center who was in charge of DGI activities related to Guevara's Bolivian operation.

SECTION II-1. "Ariel" is chief of this section under "Armando." "Ariel" is responsible for the six branches into which Latin America is divided. The six branches, and their branch chiefs, are:

Colombia/Venezuela/Ecuador .... *"Arana"*
Brazil/Uruguay .... *"Fermin"*
Argentina/Chile/Peru .... *"José Luis"*
Dominican Republic/Haiti/Jamaica...................... *"Jesus"*
Guatemala/Central America .... *"Noel"*
Bolivia.. *"Lino"*

Chiefs of country desks within the Section II-1 branches include "Gary," chief of the Uruguayan desk, and "Jordan," chief of the Peruvian desk. "Gary" uses as his cover a position with the Cuban Institute of Friendship with Peoples (ICAP). Among the personnel attached to Section II-1 is "Renan," who as "Ivan" served as a liaison between DGI and Guevara in Bolivia. "Renan" bears a strong resemblance to movie actor Kirk Douglas.

Section II-1 maintains centers only in those hemisphere countries with which Cuba has diplomatic relations: Mexico, Jamaica, and Chile. Some of Section II-1's activities are handled through the Intelligence Center in Paris. The Paris Center takes care of agents traveling through that city en route to or from Havana, and it establishes letter drops used by revolutionaries under the jurisdiction of II-1, forwarding their correspondence to Havana.

On occasion, Section II-1 officers travel abroad. In October 1967 the chief of the Dominican branch, "Jesus," traveled to Paris to meet the Dominican leader, Francisco Alberto Caamaño [Deno]. In November 1968 "Noel," the chief of the Guatemala/Central America branch, went to Paris to meet Ricardo Ramírez de Leon, a leader of a Guatemalan revolutionary organization.

SECTION II-2. "Julio" is the chief of this section. He personally supervises French, Austrian, Swiss, Portuguese, and possibly Spanish matters. His deputy is "José." Section II-2 has seven country desks, each with five to eight officials. The desks: Austria, France/Belgium, Italy, Portugal, Spain, Switzerland, and the United Kingdom. Each desk is responsible for supporting its respective overseas center. Chief of the Italian desk is either "David," former head of the DGI center in Rome, or Roberto Alvarez Barrera ("Remigio"). Alvarez was formerly assigned to Paris, where his cover position was that of Second Secretary of the Cuban Mission to UNESCO. In 1968 he was in charge of organizing participation of French youths in summer work and indoctrination camps in Cuba. "Orestes" is chief of the Spanish desk. He was formerly First Secretary of the Cuban Embassy in Madrid. Chief of the

French/Belgian desk is "Janio." Among the personnel in Section II-2 are: "Leyda," wife of section chief "Julio" and a member of the Cuban delegation to the General Assembly of UNESCO, a specialist in diplomatic affairs and business management procedures; "Magaly," who is responsible for counter-intelligence and for contacts with journalists; "Manolo," who was trained in the Soviet Union; "Taimara," also trained in the Soviet Union; and "Isnoel," responsible for scientific and technical matters.

The overseas centers of Section II-2 are located within the Cuban diplomatic posts in Geneva, Lisbon, London, Madrid, Paris, Rome, and Vienna. The *Centro* in Vienna is the newest, having been opened in the spring of 1968. There are no centers in Scandinavia, although it is believed DGI plans to open one in Stockholm. Cuba closed its diplomatic mission in Athens in 1968 and Cuban interests in Greece are handled by the Cuban Embassy in Rome. Presumably any intelligence matters related to Greece are managed by the DGI center in Rome. In Belgium, DGI affairs were handled by a collaborator, Luis Palacios Rodríguez, who was Second Secretary of the Cuban Embassy in Brussels. In The Hague, DGI was represented by Aldo Rodríguez Camps ("Aldo"), who was the Commercial Counselor of the Cuban Mission.

Among the DGI personnel in Europe are/were the following:

Center	Names and other data	Position
Geneva	Santiago Díaz Pas ("Rodrigo")	Chief
	Has cover position with UN office in Geneva	
Lisbon	Mario García Vázquez ("Daniel")	Chief
London	Cristobal Fajardo Rabassa ("Abel")	Chief
Madrid	Aristides Díaz Rovirosa ("Domingo")	Chief
	Orlando Kautzman Torres	Official
	His wife may also work for DGI.	
Paris	Armando López Orta ("Arquimides")	Chief
	Was recalled as a result of Orlando Castro [Hidalgo]'s defection.	
Rome	Adalberto Marrero Rodríguez	Chief
	Was formerly Chief of Logistics at Principal Center. Wife is also believed to be DGI official.	
	"Oneido"	Official
	Trained in Soviet Union.	
Vienna	"Armando"	Chief
	Trained in Soviet Union.	

SECTION III. This section in divided into nine subsections: Central Intelligence Agency (CIA), Counter-Revolution, United Nations, Mexico, Canada, Soviet Union, Czechoslovakia, East Germany, and a false documents unit. Head of Section III is "Demetrio," who came to DGI from the Department of State Security (DSE) in August 1966. In DSE he had been chief of "Section L," which was charged with surveillance of foreign diplomatic missions in Havana.

In the mid-sixties an office of Section III called the CIA and Counter-Revolution Bureau had as its objective to penetrate CIA and Cuban exile activities directed against the Castro regime. In August 1966 "Jacobo" was placed in charge of the CIA group. He was a former officer of DSE's "Section L." "Candido," also a former DSE officer, was put in charge of the Counter-Revolution unit. In 1967 the Bureau was split, and the men remained as chiefs of the now separate desks.

The United Nations desk supports the activities of the DGI *Centro* within the Cuban Mission to the United Nations. Most of the mission officials work for DGI. The UN Center maintains contact with subversive organizations in the United States, serves as a funnel for Cuban propaganda to enter this country, and through its agents, particularly in the Miami area, keeps track of the activities of Cuban exile organizations. It is Castro's espionage outpost within the United States.

The unit responsible for false documents is called "Diosdado's Group." The formal name of the unit is not known. This is the name by which it is always called, because it is headed by an official who uses the code name "Diosdado." It acquires the seals, stamps, and stationery of foreign embassies, as well as different types of paper from foreign countries. It secures maps, train schedules, photographs of airports, information about frontiers, and in general all types of information that may be useful to DGI officials traveling abroad, including details on how foreign borders may be crossed illegally.

The DGI center in Mexico City is responsible for supporting clandestine operations in that country as well as in the rest of Latin America, particularly Central America. Since Mexico City is one of the few places which still maintains a regular air route with Havana, the Mexico *Centro* assists the comings and goings of agents and subversive figures. The Centro also arranges for agents to be slipped across the border into the United States. Because of the variety of tasks carried out by this key office, its staff members probably are under the jurisdiction of more than one of the DGI sections, although basically it functions as a part of Section III.

DGI officials now or recently assigned to Mexico City include the following:

Name	Cover position at Embassy, Consulate
Felix Luna Mederos	First Secretary ("Filiberto"), chief of Centro
Rafael Mirabel Fernández Vice Consul,	Attaché
Edgardo Obulio Valdés Suarez	Commercial Attaché
Enrique Micuel Cicard Labrada	Consul General, Third Secretary
Lineo Fernando Salazar Chia	Consul
Juan Astorga Frometa	Employee
Luis Ismael Cruz Arce	Consul
Jesus Cruz González	Second Secretary

The Section III center in Prague arranges for the travel, housing, and documentation of leftist revolutionaries en route to Cuba for training or consultation. Antonio Perez Caneiro ("Nico") is the chief of the center. His cover position is that of First

Secretary of the Cuban Embassy. His brother, Ricardo Perez Caneiro, is also a DGI official and also holds the position of First Secretary.

The centers in the Soviet Union and East Germany serve as liaisons with the intelligence services of those countries. The Moscow *Centro* handles Cuban personnel sent to that country for intelligence training.

The DGI center in Canada serves as an outlet for propaganda, handles agents slipping into or out of the United States, and is in touch with subversive separatist movements. For months in 1963 the city of Quebec was troubled by terrorists who were setting fires and placing bombs in public buildings. After intensive investigations, the police arrested 17 members of an organization called *Front de Libération Québecois.* Among the leaders who were jailed was a former University of Montreal student, Georges Schoeters, who had met Castro during a trip the latter made to Montreal. Subsequently, Schoeters took two trips to Cuba, on of them of several months' duration, during which time he is believed to have been given instruction in subversive techniques.

SECTION III-1. Sometime between mid-1967 and early 1968 Section III (Illegals) was divided into two separate entities: Section III and Section III-1, which became the "illegal" section. Section III retained most of the operational units of the former section, as described above. Section III-1 is engaged in such activities as recruitment, training, and infiltration. It is headed by "Lucio." A subsection, referred to by the code name of its chief, "Dario," is believed to have some responsibility for activities in other Communist countries.

SECTION III-2. This section, called *Enlaces,* provides DGI officials abroad with mail drops, safe houses, meeting sites, and accommodation addresses. It also handles liaison with other organizations of the Cuban government, including DSE. "Quero" is the chief of the section. His deputy is Adalberto Quintana Suarez ("Sexto"),1 who is also Vice-Director of the Cuban Institute of Friendship with Peoples. Section III-2 maintains a file on clandestine contact facilities throughout the world, available for any DGI operation.

SECTION IV. Called *Cuadros,* this section is responsible for the recruitment and training of all DGI staff personnel. It also selects personnel for the diplomatic courier service. The chief is believed to be "Pelayo." Another high official is Ramiro Rodríguez Gomez, who was the chief of the DGI Centro in Rio de Janeiro from 1961 until Brazil severed relations with Cuba in 1964.

SECTION M-1. This section supplies clandestine communications systems to DGI personnel, as well as any technical support that may be needed. The section's facilities include an audio unit, a photographic unit, a concealment devices unit, and a codes and secret-writing unit.

DOCUMENTATION CENTER. This office takes care of official documents used by DGI personnel in their travels. The chief is "Facundo."

LOGISTICS SECTION. This section handles the food, clothing, and housing needs of officials coming to Havana, as well as the logistic and administrative needs of the various departments in the Principal Center.

Cuba's interests in Africa and increasing interest in the Middle East has augmented the importance of Section V, which is responsible for both areas. Armando Ulises Estrada Fernández ("Ulises") is the chief of Section V. He works closely with his military counterpart, Major Victor Emiliano Dreke Cruz, an official of the Ministry of the Revolutionary Armed Forces, of which Raúl Castro is chief. Dreke is in charge of Cuban army operations in Africa (there are Cuban military units stationed in Brazzaville), as well as of Cuban guerrilla activities in that continent.

Estrada traveled to the Middle East in early 1969 and visited camps of the Al Fatah Arab guerrilla organization. He accompanied Arab raiders on an incursion into Israeli-occupied territory.

The *escuelas especiales* (special schools) which had been run by DGI for the guerrilla training of foreign nationals was transferred to the Armed Forces Ministry in February 1967. DGI and the ministry coordinate in this enterprise, and it is believed that Estrada may head a school which has given training to members of Al Fatah. Abu al-Hasan, an official of Al Fatah, stated in April 1970:

> Some time ago a group of our combatants was graduated from the Havana military college. We were the first Asian group admitted to this college. At the graduation the college commandant, who happened to have spent some time with us in the Jordan Valley, said: "I present to you today a class of legendary guerrilla fighters from Asia—Al Asifah fighters."

(Al Asifah is the military wing of Al Fatah [Al Fatah is the dominant faction of the Palestine Liberation Organization].)

The geographical extensiveness of DGI's operations attests to the importance attached to its work by the Castro government. DGI is an expanding organization. In addition to its own structure, it has virtually taken over the *Prensa Latina* news agency and the Cuban Institute for Friendship with Peoples (ICAP). The latter is in charge of the many foreigners who visit Cuba for one reason or another. DGI officials have moved into Cuba's diplomatic corps to such an extent that this has become hardly more than an arm of the intelligence service. In Africa and the Middle East, where Cuba's diplomatic aims and intelligence designs are one and the same, most Cuban ambassadors are DGI and double as chiefs of *centros*.

The United States itself has not been beyond the reach of Castro's intelligence organization. It has, in fact, long been an area of primary interest. When Castro was still a guerrilla in the Sierra Maestra mountains, his agents in the States carried out propaganda activities and arranged for the shipment of weapons to the rebels. Following Castro's rise to power, his agents have continued highly active in this country.

In 1959 two of his agents attempted to bribe two Florida police officers and an FBI agent pretending to be a local officer to arrange the kidnapping of a man wanted by the Cuban government. In a reverse operation, two American flyers in a small plane were shot down over Cuba in March 1960 as they participated in a scheme to make it appear that the United States was involved in helping "war criminals" escape from Cuba. (Their being shot down was apparently due to an accident.) The Americans had been bribed by a Castro agent in the United States.

This same agent—a naturalized American citizen—kept Havana informed of the activities of the Cuban exiles in Florida and was believed responsible for the capture in Cuba of a number of exiles who participated in clandestine missions to that country. This agent circulated freely in the exile community, and was particularly well-informed about missions to Cuba because of his work on small boats in the Miami area. To transmit information to Havana, he sent coded messages by telephone and commercial cable, and he was also in contact with the Cuban Intelligence Center at the United Nations. This agent still lives in Miami; because his activities have not directly involved espionage against the United States, charges have not been brought against him.

Cuba has never had any real difficulty in infiltrating agents into the United States. When one considers that more than 900 Cuban refugees enter the country every week, it is understandable that DGI is able to get personnel into this country. Most of the refugees arrive via the daily Varadero-Miami airlift; others come in small boats. Still others are flown in from the Guantánamo Naval Base, having jumped over the fence there and asked for asylum. And still more eventually make their way to the States after having flown from Havana to Spain or Mexico. Refugees are screened by U.S. officials, but there is no sure way of weeding out all the men and women who may be working for DGI.

In the fall of 1965, when Castro permitted flotillas of small boats to leave Cuba filled with refugees heading for the States, a DGI official began recruiting large numbers of the refugees to work for the Intelligence service once they arrived north. Rather than endanger their hopes of leaving, the refugees agreed to the official's demands. Some of them evidently took seriously their promise to help: DGI began receiving reports from a number of them. The official had failed, however, to instruct his recruits on how to identify themselves when sending their reports, and when these began arriving, DGI was unable to determine who was sending them. The reports were virtually useless.

Groups of leftist American students have visited Cuba over the years. Radical black leaders, such as Stokely Carmichael and Robert Williams, have also been in Cuba. The Castro government encourages subversive movements in the States by radio broadcasts, by playing host to these visitors, and probably by giving some of them basic training in subversive techniques.

Among pro-Castro "front" groups established in the United States have been the Medical Aid for Cuba Committee and the Fair Play for Cuba Committee. The latter organization was spotlighted when a person associated with it, Lee Harvey Oswald, assassinated President John F. Kennedy in November 1963. Although there has been no indication that Castro had any hand in the assassination, it is not inconceivable that he had an inkling it might be attempted. Oswald was in Mexico from 26 September until 3 October of 1963, and during that time he visited the Cuban

Embassy in Mexico City, ostensibly seeking a visa to enter Cuba. A few weeks earlier, Castro had warned that if American leaders were involved in plans against his regime, "they themselves will not be safe."

Because the United States and Cuba do not maintain diplomatic relations, and therefore there is no Cuban diplomatic mission accredited to this country, the Intelligence Centro at the United Nations serves as headquarters for Cuban-directed subversive and espionage activities in the United States. There have been a number of cases in which the United States has had to take action against Cuban United Nations officials because of their intelligence activities.

In November 1962 the FBI arrested three Cubans in New York and seized a cache of explosives and incendiary devices. The Cubans were charged with attempting to gather information about U.S. military installations and with stockpiling the explosives "for the purpose of injuring and destroying national defense materials, premises, and utilities." Among the contemplated targets were retail stores, oil refineries, and the New York subway system. The detainees included Roberto Santiestebán Casanova, an *attaché* at the Cuban Mission. Because he had arrived recently, his official papers were being processed and the U.S. government asserted he still did not enjoy diplomatic immunity. A Cuban couple, José Gómez Abad and his wife Elisa Montero de Gómez Abad, were charged with complicity in the affair and ordered to leave the country. Both were *attachés* at the Mission, and as such did have diplomatic immunity from arrest.

In January 1968 Chafik Homero Saker Zenni (who also used the name Rolo Martínez; code name "Rolo"), First Secretary of the Cuban Mission, was barred from reentering the United States. In February 1969 Jesus Jimenez Escobar, Counselor of the Mission, was also refused reentry. Both men had been providing guidance and financial assistance to black extremist groups in the States.

In August 1969 Lázaro Eddy Espinosa Bonet, Third Secretary of the Mission, was ordered expelled because he had attempted to recruit several Cuban refugees for the purpose—the United States said succinctly—of gathering information about "the security of the office of the President." The fact was that, meeting clandestinely with Espinosa in New York, the refugees had been instructed to obtain all the information they could about President Nixon's home on Key Biscayne in Miami: photographs, floor plans, details of security, itineraries, and modes of travel used by the President when arriving and leaving. It is not known why DGI wanted this information.

At the same time that Espinosa was expelled, the United States also barred Alberto Boza-Hidalgo Gato (code name "Zabo"), who was in Cuba at the time, from reentering the country. Boza-Hidalgo, First Secretary of the Cuban UN Mission, was charged with attempting to recruit refugees for the purpose of gathering "material of an intelligence value" about a U.S. military installation.

In October 1970 another espionage case involving Cuba's UN mission was revealed. Orlando Gutiérrez, First Secretary of the Mission, and Rogelio Rodríguez

Lopez ("José"), Counselor of the Mission, were given 48 hours to leave the United States by the U.S. government. They had been using the services of a young secretary employed at the Washington embassy of the Republic of South Africa. The secretary's access to embassies and cocktail parties had been useful to the Cubans, whose diplomatic activities are officially limited to the New York area.

These are cases that have been partially brought to view. Other operations continue in the gray world of espionage. DGI, in the United States as well as elsewhere in the world, relentlessly pursues its goal of attempting to subvert other nations to the communist standard. As DGI grows larger, its operations become more sophisticated, its tentacles extend farther and farther abroad, and it steadily becomes a more deadly instrument.

chapter twelve
AMERICA DEPARTMENT

In 1974 Cuba established the America Department, an espionage organization that would operate in the Western Hemisphere. The DGI had already been functioning for years, but there were reasons why the Castro brothers wanted an additional service. For one thing, DGI, as the result of a Soviet crackdown on a rebellious Castro, had come under virtual KGB control. Secondly, the Castros wanted an organization under their direct authority which could conduct subversive operations. In this respect, the America Department was unique: unlike other national intelligence services it was dedicated not to gathering intelligence but to subversive operations aimed at extending Cuban power. It scored a success in Nicaragua, helping the Sandinistas to win a civil war. It almost succeeded in Grenada and Suriname. The following account is from the *Washington Times*, which in a five-part series by Mallin in 1983 revealed details about the America Department for the first time.

How Cuban Agents Deliver Arms to Leftist Guerrillas in El Salvador
22 August 1983

Fidel Castro's attempts to export his brand of communist revolution throughout the western hemisphere and, indeed, anywhere he perceives an opportunity to de-stabilize governments and push their people toward the Soviet-Cuban block, are detailed in a five-part series beginning today by veteran Latin American correspondent Jay Mallin, who has just joined the staff of the Washington Times. *Today, Mallin tells how Cuba sends arms to leftist guerrillas in El Salvador and outlines the structure and operations of Castro's intelligence-gathering and subversion-spreading organizations operating beyond Cuba's borders.*

Soon after dusk, a small Nicaraguan freighter pulls out of the port of Estero Padre Ramos on the northwest coast of Nicaragua. It carries a cargo of M-16 rifles, other weapons, ammunition, and field equipment.

The vessel heads straight out to sea and into international waters. Forty or so miles from shore, it slows its speed. A light flickers nearby. Soon three speedboats pull up and are lashed alongside.

The weapons are loaded aboard the small craft, and they pull away, heading northwest to El Salvador's Bay of Jiquilisco, an isolated area of swamps, waterways, and river tributaries.

The speedboats anchor, canoes pull up, and the weapons are again transferred. The canoes now take the arms to depots hidden among the swamps. From there, they will be transported by pack animals, or in concealed compartments of vehicles, to the leftist guerrillas fighting in El Salvador.

The operation described is one of the ways that weapons have been and are being sent by Cuba to the Salvadoran guerrillas. There are other operations by sea, as well as by air and land. Today, approximately 70 percent of the weapons obtained by the guerrillas come from abroad.

All these operations are masterminded and run by an intelligence arm of the Cuban government—the America Department. Of the major intelligence agencies in the world, it is one of the smallest, most dangerous, and least known. This espionage organization is the main instrument that Cuban dictator Fidel Castro utilizes to conduct subversive activities throughout the Western Hemisphere.

Intelligence-gathering and subversion-spreading have long been highly important to the Cuban government. They are so important, in fact, that Castro has no less than five separate organizations conducting operations abroad.

These are:

DIRECCION GENERAL DE INTELIGENCIA, headed by Brigadier General Jose Joaquin Mendez Cominches, a member of the Central Committee of the Cuban Communist Party. The DGI is a unit within the Ministry of the Interior. The minister of the interior is Ramiro Valdes Menendez, who in the early days of the Castro regime headed G-2, at the time the country's internal security apparatus.

The DGI is the primary intelligence-collection service abroad of the Cuban government, as distinct from the Communist Party. The DGI functions throughout the world and maintains close liaison with the Soviet Union's KGB.

DEPARTAMENTO DE SEGURIDAD DEL ESTADO, headed by Division General Jose Abrahantes Fernandez (in his capacity as first vice minister and vice minister for security of the Ministry of the Interior). The DSE is a part of the Ministry of the Interior. [For Abrahantes' eventual fate, see chapter 16.]

Having early in the Castro regime replaced what was called G-2, the DSE has primary responsibility for internal security. This includes not only watching for dissent and conspiracies but also counter-espionage.

The latter is specifically aimed at countering infiltration and intelligence operations of the U.S. Central Intelligence Agency.

Because the activities of Cuban exiles, particularly in the south Florida area, sometimes have a direct bearing on Cuban internal security, the DSE maintains covert agents abroad. One responsibility the DSE has been given is the setting up of cover businesses abroad. One such company, Moonex, was involved in smuggling weapons into Jamaica. Another, Cimex, SA, a Mexican firm, tries to circumvent the U.S. embargo on trade with Cuba by making purchases in the United States through other companies.

Two DSE agents, Carlos Alfonso Gonzalez and Charles Romeo, were involved in setting up Havanatur in Miami. Havanatur served as a "travel agency" that arranged for Cuban exiles to visit Cuba in the late '70s.

DIRECCION DE OPERACIONES ESPECIALES, commanded by Brigadier General Pascual Martinez Gil, member of the Central Committee and vice minister of the interior. The DOE is a military unit within the Ministry of the Interior. An elite detachment, it is somewhat akin to the U.S. Special Forces.

The DOE helped to train Nicaraguan Sandinistas and then accompanied the rebels as advisers during the Nicaraguan civil war. The DOE continues to train militants from other countries, particularly Central America, and is involved in the clandestine transportation of men and materials. In Africa, DOE troops were the first Cuban force into Angola.

DEPARTAMENTO GENERAL DE RELACIONES EXTERIORES, headed by Jesus Montane Oropesa, alternate member of the Politburo and member of the Central Committee. Following the Soviet model, the DGRE is a department of the Central Committee. It serves as the party's intelligence organization for those parts of the world in which it operates. It has sections for Europe, Asia, Africa-Middle East, and the communist bloc countries.

The DGRE maintains contact with Communist parties and other leftist organizations. In the Soviet Union and its satellites, it has liaison with equivalent party departments.

DEPARTAMENTO AMERICA, headed by Manuel Piñeiro Losada, member of the Central Committee. Theoretically, the DA is a section of the DGRE; in actuality, because of its importance, it is an independent service. It functions directly under the Central Committee and is the party's intelligence and operational unit for the Western Hemisphere.

The DA conducts subversive activities, including support of *fidelista*-line guerrilla groups, but it also maintains contact with Communist parties and other leftist organizations.

How Cuba Turned to Spying and Terror
August 23, 1983

In the second of five articles on Fidel Castro's ambitious program of international subversion, reporter Jay Mallin describes the beginnings of Castro's intelligence services and details how he turned his island into a training camp for terrorism to export his destabilization efforts to far-flung points, including Africa.

Various reasons have impelled Cuba to build its extensive intelligence structure.

For one thing, Cuba has had to keep track of the activities of exiled militants who sporadically have launched commando raids and infiltration attempts against the island.

For another, Cuba has had to counter the longtime efforts of the CIA, endeavors which have ranged from the Bay of Pigs invasion to securing the defection of Cuban officials to plots to assassinate Castro.

Intelligence collection and other covert activities have been an intrinsic part of Castro's own campaign of almost 25 years to extend Cuban influence and hegemony in various parts of the world.

Beginning with a seaborne expedition against Panama in April 1959 and right through the clandestine shipment of weapons to guerrillas in Central America today, Castro has never ceased in his efforts to export the Cuban revolution. The Cuban intelligence services have played key roles in that campaign.

The services had their genesis in the mountains of eastern Cuba during the revolution of 1956-58. The rebels were engaged in guerrilla warfare against the forces of dictator Fulgencio Batista. Campesinos moved back and forth between the areas controlled by the government and the rebels and some of these campesinos kept the guerrillas posted on the location, numbers, and movements of army troops.

In the nearby city of Santiago and extending across the island to the capital of Havana, there was a clandestine rebel apparatus that served as a support organization for the guerrillas, funneling funds, recruits, and supplies into the hills.

The underground also waged urban warfare—terrorism, sabotage, propaganda—and this attrition eventually so weakened the regime that the guerrilla forces were able to come down out of the hills and take control of the country and the government. Castro led one of the major rebel groups and it became the dominant force in Cuba.

With the rebel victory and the establishment of the Castro government, Castro set his sights on larger targets, the Caribbean and then the entire southern portion of the hemisphere. The first attempts at subversion were crude. Exiles from Latin American countries flooded into Cuba seeking support, and from their ranks expeditions were organized and dispatched against several countries. All those inept filibustering efforts failed.

Cuba turned to more sophisticated methods of subversion, including use of propaganda and expenditure of funds to encourage and support individuals and groups sympathetic to *fidelismo*. These were intelligence functions, and so often Cuban diplomats doubled as intelligence operatives. As Castro reached out farther and farther, the work of his agents extended to target countries ranging geographically from Canada to Argentina, from the United States to Zanzibar.

Cuban intelligence functions were initially the responsibility of G-2, a section within the Ministry of the Interior. Later this unit was named the *Departamento de Seguridad del Estado*. Late in 1961, due to Cuba's increasing involvement in foreign espionage, the *Direccion General de Inteligencia* was organized (from what had been

"Section M") within the Interior Ministry. The DGI was headed by *Comandante* Manuel Piñeiro Losada in his position as first vice minister and technical vice minister.

The son of a bar owner in Matanzas Province, Piñeiro at one time studied at Columbia University in New York. It was evidently there that he met the American girl, Lorna Nell Burdsall, who became his first wife. Lorna was a ballet dancer, and years later, as intelligence boss of Cuba, Piñeiro would run for his men films of his wife dancing. (Even spies like to show home movies.)

During the Cuban civil war, Piñeiro served as an officer directly under Raúl Castro in the guerrilla forces.

Piñeiro apparently divorced Lorna, who is believed to be still in Cuba, and he is now living with a Chilean woman. They may be married. Piñeiro occasionally travels abroad, and was among the mourners at the funeral of Panamanian strongman Omar Torrijos in 1981. Tall and slim, Piñeiro has a hard, raucous voice. A red beard, now white-rimmed, long ago earned him the nickname *Barba Roja*. He is audacious and smart. Always close to Fidel Castro, he has survived in the top hierarchy of the Cuban regime since it began. He reports directly to Fidel and takes his orders from him, or Raúl, as the particular case may be. For more than 20 years Piñeiro has been Cuba's No. 1 spymaster.

One of the first responsibilities of DGI was the running of special schools for the training of Latin Americans in guerrilla warfare and subversive techniques.

During the early 1960s as many as 1,500 men were brought to Cuba every year for training. Cuba's ostracism by other hemisphere countries had almost isolated the island, but flights continued between Havana and Madrid and Mexico City, as well as between Havana and cities in communist countries, and these routes were used to bring guerrilla recruits to Cuba.

Also utilized were freighters from communist countries and Cuban fishing boats, the latter making clandestine trips to and from Caribbean and Central American shores.

Once in Cuba, the trainees were grouped by nationalities. Usually there were 15 to 25 men in each group, although there might be as few as 3. The various nationalities were kept separate for security reasons as well as because training was not uniform.

Venezuelans concentrated on guerrilla operations and sabotage techniques. Chileans, in whose country a strong communist party openly functioned, were coached on how to further the communist cause through political activism. Emphasis was placed on techniques of propaganda and agitation in particular fields in which specific trainees were involved in their homelands: unions, universities, intellectual organizations, and such.

Guerrilla training lasted 3 to 6 months—occasionally as long as a year. Trainees who displayed exceptional talents were sometimes given additional instruction so they could be agents for the DGI when they returned home.

Africa also became the target of a prominent figure in the Castro government: Ernesto "Che" Guevara. An Argentinean adventurer who had joined Castro in Mexico and come with him on his 1956 expedition to Cuba, Guevara was the most international-minded of the top Cuban leadership. He was the mastermind and director of the vast Cuban intelligence-subversion program.

Violence, fueled by Havana, touched virtually every country in Latin America, sometimes reaching dangerous levels. Nevertheless, the goal of establishing other *fidelista* governments was never achieved. Guevara's troops approached but never quite grasped victory.

Always a restless individual, perhaps tired of playing a subordinate role to the Castro brothers, Guevara decided to take to the field again. His first target was Africa, which he believed ripe for revolution. Possibly disguised as a priest, Guevara slipped out of Cuba and made his way to the Congo. He organized and led a guerrilla operation which included a number of Cubans. The movement failed; Guevara and the Cubans had to flee their erstwhile African allies.

Guevara returned to Cuba, regrouped, and launched a guerrilla campaign in Bolivia. This, too, failed; Guevara was captured and executed.

The mounting and operation of the Bolivian guerrilla movement had required extensive intelligence participation, and DGI played a major role in events. To enable him to travel to Bolivia, Guevara was provided with two evidently genuine Uruguayan passports, giving him false identities. For a disguise, Guevara's famous beard was shaved and so was part of his pate, and he wore eyeglasses.

DGI recruited French writer Régis Debray to join and report on the guerrilla movement. A DGI official who used the code name "Ivan" served as liaison between Guevara and Havana. Another DGI official, Rene Martinez Tamayo, was Guevara's radio and explosives expert.

Cubans Targeted U.S., Canada for Covert Intelligence Efforts
August 24, 1983

Covert operations against the United States and Canada by Cuban intelligence agents are examined by Washington Times *reporter Jay Mallin in the third of a five-part series on Fidel Castro's attempts to export communism and destabilize governments.*

Canada and the United States also have been targets of Cuban intelligence.

The embassy in Ottawa has been used as an outlet for propaganda, to maintain contact with separatist movements, and to handle covert agents slipping in and out of the United States.

For months in 1963 the city of Quebec was troubled by terrorists who were setting fires and placing bombs in public buildings. After intensive investigations the police arrested 17 members of an organization called *Front de Liberation Quebecois*. Among the leaders jailed was one Georges Schoeters, who had met Castro during a trip Castro had made to Montreal and subsequently took two trips to Cuba. He was believed to have been given training in subversive techniques.

The United States has been an operational area for Cuban intelligence since the early days of the Castro regime.

Cuba has never had difficulty in infiltrating agents into the States. At one time in the 1960s 900 Cubans were arriving weekly on Freedom Flights.

Other Cubans have come to the States in small boats, or via Spain and other countries, and by jumping over the fence at the Guantánamo base and requesting asylum.

In 1965 and again in 1980 Castro opened ports and permitted Cubans to flee, and hundreds of thousands did. It has been easy for Cuban intelligence to slip hundreds of agents in among the legitimate refugees.

Every Cuban exile organization in the United States is believed to be penetrated by Castro agents. Exiles going to Cuba on clandestine missions are invariably wrapped up by Cuban security forces.

Over the years, activities of Cuban agents in the States have been exposed a number of times. With the opening of a Cuban interest section in Washington in the late 1970s Cuban intelligence was able to resume more fully its activities there. In February 1981 the United States expelled the second-ranking Cuban diplomat in the country, Ricardo Escartin, first secretary of the interest section. He was accused of intelligence activities and conspiring to violate the embargo on trade with Cuba.

The advent of the age of technology caught the interest of Cuban intelligence. Two more Cuban officials at the United Nations were expelled in July 1982 for "buying, and trying to buy, large quantities of high-technology electronic equipment, much of it subject to strategic trade controls." The Cubans had purchased television satellite monitoring equipment.

Two more Cubans at the United Nations were expelled in April 1983 for conducting "hostile intelligence activities." A U.S. State Department spokesman said what they were doing was of "a very sensitive nature."

Cuban Intelligence Elite Pushes Subversion in Americas
August 25, 1983

In the fourth of five articles tracing the activities of Fidel Castro's intelligence agents abroad, Washington Times *reporter Jay Mallin describes the inner workings of the elite units attempting to undermine the Americas.*

In keeping with the system in effect in the Soviet Union, the Cuban Communist Party established its own intelligence branch in 1974.

This took the form of the *Departamento General de Relaciones Exteriores* (DGRE) and the *Departamento America* (DA). Spymaster Manuel Piñeiro Losada was moved over from the *Direccion General de Inteligencia* (DGI) to the DA.

The DA would handle subversion and contacts with other leftist groups in the Western Hemisphere; the DGRE would have this responsibility for the rest of the world. (Previously these matters had been handled by a "national liberation" section within the DGI.)

Today, the America Department enjoys a primary role among the Cuban intelligence services because of the successes it has achieved, and because of the growing Cuban thrusts into Central America and southward to Grenada and Suriname. Piñeiro today has a role and position within the Cuban hierarchy enjoyed once by "Che" Guevara.

Serving under Piñeiro are two deputies: Jose Antonio Arbesu Fraga and Armando Campos Ginesta. The DA is divided into sections: North America (chief—Alfredo Garcia Almeida, who was formerly with the Cuban mission to the United States); Central America, excluding Costa Rica (chief—Ramiro Jesus Abreau Quintana); Mexico, Costa Rica, and Panama (chief—Roberto Marquez Orozco); Caribbean (chief not identified); South America (chief not identified).

Although the Guyanas are on the South American mainland, at the America Department they are considered part of the Caribbean because Cuban activities in the Guyanas are an extension of East Caribbean operations. Each section is subdivided into desks representing individual nations or groupings of nations in which Cuba's interests are similar. Thus Grenada and other East Caribbean countries have a single desk. The DA also has logistical and other support sections.

The number of personnel in the DA is estimated at 200 to 300. All are carefully chosen; many were in DGI and moved over to DA with Piñeiro when the department was set up.

As far as is known, there never has been a defection from DA. There are two or three AD men or women at every Cuban diplomatic post in the hemisphere, including the United Nations and the Cuban interest section in Washington. At some overseas posts where responsibility extends to several countries, there may be five or six DA agents. At the DA post in Panama, which also has responsibility for Colombia and is a link to Central American operations, there are about half a dozen agents.

Three Cuban ambassadors are DA men: Julian Lopez Diaz in Nicaragua, Osvaldo Cardenas Junquera (and his wife, Ida Borja Paz Escalante de Gomez) in Suriname, and Julian Enrique Rizo in Grenada.

Having DA men as ambassadors attests to the importance of these three countries in the Castro scheme of conquest.

Other DA men holding high diplomatic positions: Damian Arteaga Hernandez, first secretary at the Cuban Embassy in Buenos Aires; Jose Francisco Ross Paz, *chargé d'affaires* in Quito; Pedro Silvio Gonzalez Perez, minister counselor in Georgetown; Jorge Luis Joa Campos, consul general in Mexico City.

Piñeiro has approval authority over all diplomatic appointments in the hemisphere below the rank of minister counselor, and when he sees fit he fills a post with one of his own men. Obviously, in key countries he picks the ambassadors, as well.

The DA has its own codes and communications systems. DA personnel at Cuban diplomatic posts utilize these to communicate with Havana, and they can do this independently of ambassadors or anyone else. They do not have to clear their activities or messages with the ambassadors, and this causes occasional friction.

The America Department has both overt and covert responsibilities.

On the overt side, DA operatives will identify themselves thus: "I represent the Communist Party of Cuba." If pressed, on occasion they will even admit working for the DA. They engage in propaganda activities and maintain contact with individuals and political groups that are or could become friendly to Cuba.

The DA helps members of clandestine organizations that are in exile in Cuba. When Colombian M-19 leader Rosenberg Pabon Pabon and some of his people flew to Cuba in April 1980 after having seized the Dominican Embassy in Bogota, they were greeted by Piñeiro himself.

In Washington, DA members engage in lobbying activities, seeking Puerto Rican independence and an end to U.S. trade restrictions with Cuba. The DA had a Lear jet (for which it overpaid $5.3 million) which made occasional trips to the States until it was seized in Fort Lauderdale, Florida, by the FBI in September 1980. Three Cubans carrying Nicaraguan passports were arrested.

DA covert activities include manipulation and then control of foreign individuals and groups that fall within the DA net. The DA conducts agent-of-influence operations, utilizing influential persons recruited by bribery, blackmail, or ideology, to further the Cuban cause.

Members of the media are a particular target of the DA, which engages in covert as well as overt propaganda work. The DA also operates through front groups.

A major responsibility of the DA is to facilitate military and sabotage training for *pro-fidelista* clandestine and guerrilla groups.

The DA brings members of these organizations to Cuba and then gets them back home. It provides them with weapons, explosives, and other materials. Actual transportation and training may not be done by the DA but by troops of the Special Operations Directorate.

Although the DA's responsibilities are supposed to encompass only this hemisphere, it is believed there are DA agents in Europe and elsewhere. These operate primarily where there are substantial numbers of Latinos.

Because of its proximity to Cuba, its deep social ills, and its penchant for strongman governments, Central America has been a tempting target for Castro since the first days of his regime.

The first overt move by Cuba was the launching of an expeditionary group against Panama in April 1959. Early in 1959 Nicaraguan exiles were trained in Cuba, and in May of that year a Cuban air force plane ferried weapons to Nicaraguan guerrillas.

The early Cuban subversive efforts failed, but with the establishment of the America Department, Central America was again targeted. The Cuban view was expressed by Piñeiro in a speech to Latin American leftists in Havana in 1982. Piñeiro stated: "In those countries where the extreme right rules, using forms of armed fighting (by the left) ... is a virtually inescapable imperative."

Cuban Unit Fans Flames in Latin America
August 26, 1983

Washington Times *reporter Jay Mallin, in the last of five articles on Fidel Castro's attempts to undermine foreign governments, details the fall of Nicaragua and Cuba's growing influence elsewhere.*

Nicaraguan dictator Anastasio Somoza, whose family had ruled Nicaragua for decades, was long seen by Fidel Castro of Cuba as a vulnerable target and, in addition, Castro never forgot that Nicaragua served as a staging area for the 1961 Bay of Pigs invasion of Cuba.

Cuba provided training and weapons for members of the rebel Sandinista National Liberation Front (FSLN) in the early 1960s, but after that Cuban support consisted mainly of propaganda and giving safe haven to militants.

In 1977, however, Cuba decided to pay greater attention to Nicaragua. Opposition to Somoza was strong, and it was fueled further by the killing in 1978 of Pedro Joaquin Chamorro, a newspaper publisher outspoken in his antipathy toward Somoza.

The FSLN was split into three major factions but Armando Ulises Estrada Fernandez, No. 2 man at Cuba's America Department (DA), began meeting secretly outside Cuba with the faction leaders. Cuban assistance was contingent on the groups' uniting, and Ulises Estrada helped them work toward this unity. In July 1978 Cuba announced the unification of the FSLN and asked leftist movements in other Latin American countries to support it.

Nicaragua was plunged into civil war and the DA played a major role. Ulises Estrada put together a network for the channeling of weapons and other supplies to the guerrilla forces. Arms were flown from Cuba to Panama, and then sent on smaller aircraft to Costa Rica, where they were distributed to FSLN guerrillas based in the northern part of that country.

Later, as the conflict progressed favorably for the rebels, weapons were flown directly from Cuba to the town of Liberia in Costa Rica. To manage its support work, the DA set up a secret operations center in San Jose, the capital of Costa Rica. This was headed by Julian Lopez Diaz, who after the rebel victory became Cuba's ambassador to Nicaragua. One of his assistants, Andres Barahona, also from the DA, later organized the Nicaraguan security service and is its actual, although not titular, chief. Barahona was given Nicaraguan citizenship (it wouldn't look good for a foreigner to be running a country's security organization).

The overthrow of Somoza in July 1979 was almost as much a victory for the America Department as it was for the Nicaraguan revolutionaries. The Cubans had united, trained, equipped, and advised the rebels in the field, and Castro, after 2 decades of striving, had achieved his first triumph in Latin America.

Not only did Cuba now have a friendly, allied country in Central America, it could enjoy other dividends as well. Nicaragua under the Sandinistas provided Castro a strategic base from which Cuba could conduct operations throughout the region.

The America Department turned its attention to El Salvador, where social and economic inequities seemed to hold promise for *fidelista*-supported revolution. Prior to 1979 Cuban assistance to Salvadoran leftists consisted mainly of providing a little financial aid and training small numbers of guerrillas. As had been the case in Nicaragua, the left of El Salvador was fragmented. The DA set about uniting the various factions. Again, it had a powerful inducement: Cuban aid depended on the groups' uniting. The DA efforts were successful and the Unified Revolutionary Directorate (DRU) was established.

While working to unify the Salvadoran guerrillas, the America Department also was developing a clandestine network through which weapons could be funneled to them. Part of this network consisted of the same mechanisms and channels that had been utilized during the Nicaraguan conflict. Arms coming from Cuba would go to Costa Rica and Nicaragua, and then would be sent by sea, or secretly through Honduras, to the rebels in El Salvador. The weapons did not come from Cuba's own stocks—those would be traceable and blame could be placed on Castro. Rather, Cuba coordinated the acquisition of weapons from Vietnam (which had plenty of captured U.S. materiel), Ethiopia, and Eastern Europe.

In addition, the number of Salvadoran guerrillas receiving training in Cuba was increased significantly. Reports that groups up to battalion size (250 to 500 men) were given instruction indicated that the Cubans were training integral units.

With a full-blown civil war under way in El Salvador, Cuba is using a variety of methods to smuggle weapons into that country (as well as neighboring nations). Weapons are brought from Cuba to the Nicaraguan ports of Corinto and El Bluff by Soviet-bloc ships. The material ranges from U.S. automatic arms captured in Vietnam to Soviet tanks. A portion of the material is for the Sandinista forces themselves. The rest goes to guerrillas.

Some is carried by coastal vessels, as previously described. Other arms have been transported across the Gulf of Fonseca, between Nicaragua and El Salvador, aboard fishing boats with false bottoms, and even on dugout canoes. Weapons also have been smuggled directly across the Nicaraguan-Honduras border, particularly near the town of El Guasaule, and then on into El Salvador. Also utilized has been a longer sea route from Nicaragua to points on the Caribbean coast of Honduras. From there they have been taken in trucks and other vehicles across Honduras and into El Salvador.

Honduran and Salvadoran land and sea patrols try to stop the flow, and electronic equipment aboard U.S. vessels and aircraft seeks to spot the smugglers, but only a few shipments have been intercepted. Nevertheless, because of increased vigilance, greater use is being made of small, low-flying aircraft that drop weapons by parachute or land on tiny airstrips or even roads. The planes are unloaded in less than 5 minutes and quickly take off for Nicaragua again.

Lesser flows of weapons originate in Mexico and Belize. Some are transported by air or land across Guatemala to El Salvador; the rest remain in Guatemala for the *fidelista* guerrillas there.

The running of this huge arms operation, as well as other support and advisory tasks, is in the hands of the America Department. Lopez Diaz, as top DA operative, was in charge of the support given the Sandinistas during the Nicaraguan conflict. Today, as Cuban ambassador to Nicaragua, he continues to have a major role in Cuba's subversive campaign, although his responsibilities now are mainly in the political sphere.

Operations are conducted from a house in Managua; it is a secret meeting and planning place for DA agents and Salvadoran guerrilla leaders. The DA operational chief is Luis Hernandez Ojeda, who during the Nicaraguan war was stationed in Panama and ran support operations for the Sandinistas in that country. Hernandez is in daily communication with spymaster Manuel Piñeiro Losada in Havana. He reports to Piñeiro, discusses matters with him, takes instructions. The broad range of these communications—covering matters not only in Nicaragua and El Salvador but all of the region—indicates that Hernandez is now the No. 1 Cuban agent in Central America.

Guatemala is to be Cuba's next target after El Salvador. Already the America Department has brought together various guerrilla groups. A unity agreement was signed in Managua in November 1980, which established the National Revolutionary Union (URN). Present at the signing ceremony were Piñeiro and the head of DA's Central American section, Ramiro Jesus Quintana.

Cuba stepped up the sending of weapons and the training of guerrillas. In June 1981 Paulino Castillo, a captured guerrilla, told newspapermen that he had been part of a 23-man group of Guatemalans that had undergone 7 months of training in Cuba. He had traveled by bus from Guatemala to Costa Rica, had been given a Panamanian passport so he could enter Panama, and in Panama had been provided a Cuban passport so he could continue to Cuba.

After being trained, he had returned via Nicaragua to the guerrillas in Guatemala, where he later surrendered to an army patrol. A large percentage of the 2,000 or more guerrillas in Guatemala are believed to have received training in Cuba, have been transported to and from the island through the extensive network set up by the America Department.

The DA has been busy in other countries, too:

GRENADA—Grenada is already a Cuban satellite. Cuban advisers function in all departments of the Grenadian government and with the Grenadian military. A 9,000-foot airfield is being built which will extend the operational range of Cuban military aircraft. Including workers at the airfield, there are some 600 Cubans on the tiny island. All Cuban activity is directed by an agent of the DA, Ambassador Julian Torres Rizo. The No. 2 man at the Cuban Embassy is also from the America Department. He is Gaston Diaz Gonzalez, formerly chief of the DA's Caribbean section. By inviting receptive individuals from nearby islands, by possibly providing insurgency training for militants, the DA is seeking to make Grenada into a base for subversion, much like Nicaragua.

SURINAME—This country on the South American mainland is moving rapidly into the Cuban sphere. Surinamese soldiers have been sent to Cuba for indoctrination and training, and some six agreements are in the works which will bind Suriname to Cuba. A key factor is the Cuban ambassador, Osvaldo Cardenas Junquera, who is highly influential with Surinamese dictator Desi Bouterse. Cardenas is a longtime intelligence operative. Born in February 1943, he was recruited out of the University of Havana in 1962 by the Ministry of the Interior. He worked in the "national liberation" section of the *Direccion General de Inteligencia* (DGI). Around 1963, as a young agent, Cardenas was assigned to a Cuban trade mission in British Guiana. His responsibility evidently was a covert operation aimed at infiltration of Venezuela, and for this task he was given a considerable amount of money by Havana. Cardenas went with Piñeiro when the America Department was established. He served as Caribbean section chief until being named ambassador to Suriname in September 1982.

JAMAICA—The Peoples' National Party, led by Michael Manley, came to power through elections in 1973. Manley developed a close relationship with Castro. Cubans trained Jamaican security personnel, including a unit which functioned directly under Manley. Jamaican youths were sent to Cuba for political indoctrination and military training. Ulises Estrada, fresh from his work supporting the Nicaraguan Sandinistas, was sent to Jamaica as ambassador in July 1979. Elections were to be held in 1980 and in a troubled period prior to the voting weapons were smuggled to Manley followers. Despite this, Manley lost the elections, and the new government broke relations with Cuba. Ulises Estrada is now ambassador to the People's Republic of Yemen, having presumably been switched from the America Department to the General Department of Foreign Relations. The Peoples' Party still sends members to Cuba and is believed to receive clandestine funds.

DOMINICAN REPUBLIC—Repeatedly over the years Cuba has dispatched infiltrators and expeditions to the Dominican Republic. All efforts have failed, although it took U.S./OAS intervention to prevent a *fidelista* takeover in 1965. Cuba today continues to provide political and military instruction for Dominican extremists; some organizations receive financial assistance. The America Department has urged different factions to unite. Omar Cordoba Rivas, chief of the DA's Dominican desk, has visited the island to press the unification effort.

COLOMBIA—The America Department has provided training for members of the April 19 Movement (usually called "M-19"). In mid-1980, the DA arranged a meeting of representatives of guerrilla and other extremist groups in an effort to forge unity. It was not achieved, although cooperation did increase among the groups. One hundred to 200 armed M-19 guerrillas, trained by Cuba, returned to Colombia in a boat from Panama in February 1981. Colombian forces broke up the operations and Colombia severed relations with Cuba. The Cuban ambassador at the time, Fernando Ravelo-Renedo, was an America Department agent. It was during his tenure that Cuba began to assist Colombian traffickers to smuggle cocaine into the United States.

An intelligence source who knows the America Department well qualified it as "dangerous." This is not because it kills people, but rather because it is highly effective.

America Department agents are busy from Washington to tiny islands in the eastern Caribbean to Bolivia high in the Andes. The DA is small but it is an elite organization, and it has proved that it is a tiger with a powerful bite.

Spreading Castro's brand of virulent subversion, it has caused much trouble for the United States and other nations in the hemisphere. In all likelihood, Manuel Piñeiro and his men will cause a great deal more.

chapter thirteen

W ithin the strategic aspects of the Cold War, Cuba became a base for Soviet land, air, and sea forces, as well as the site of a highly important electronic listening post. It was an unsinkable aircraft carrier not far off the shores of the United States, a gift to Moscow from the Castro brothers. The following article, titled "The Russian Knife at America's Throat," was co-written by Ralph Kinney Bennett and Mallin and was published in the *Reader's Digest* in 1982.

Day in, day out, Soviet ships cruise into the bustling harbor of Mariel. Part of the multibillion-dollar lifeline to the perpetually sinking Cuban economy, the ships sometimes unload refined flour, grain, or the frozen catch from the Russian fishing fleet. But, more often than not, it is the food of war that the cranes hoist onto the Mariel docks: Soviet-made MiG-23 fighter-bombers, tanks, missiles, machine guns—the stuff to feed an immense complex of airfields, radar sites, and other military installations on this island 90 miles from the United States.

The flow of Soviet military equipment into Cuba has reached a level unseen since the days preceding the Cuban missile crisis of 1962. Then, President Kennedy, wielding clear U.S. strategic superiority, faced down Soviet Premier Nikita Khrushchev, forcing him to withdraw the intercontinental ballistic missiles aimed at the United States. Since that time, however, as the Soviets have equaled, and in some cases surpassed, the United States in strategic muscle, they have quietly and deliberately developed their Cuban client state into a vital military asset.

Nowhere else in the world, outside the East Bloc, have the Soviets spent so much treasure (they're pouring $3 billion a year into Cuba, 5 times U.S. aid to all Latin America) or installed so many military resources. The result is a grotesque military anomaly in the Caribbean. This island nation, with a population of about 10 million, fields an army of 225,000 men, twice the size of Mexico's, population 70 million. Such military growth in a country with virtually no economic growth suggests that Cuba is simply an expensive military convenience for the Soviet Union.

So far, the payoff to the Russians has been well worth the outlay. Using Cuba as a surrogate, the Soviets have been projecting power to distant points of the globe, exploiting world trouble spots without directly involving their own troops. But while Soviet-backed Cuban activities in such nations as Angola and Nicaragua have captured headlines, the potentially greater danger of Cuba has been largely ignored. It is a knife—in Russian hands—held at America's throat. This direct threat manifests itself in three ways:

1. *Extensive Soviet facilities on the island provide a picture-window look into America's national-security apparatus.*

2. *Cuba puts the Soviets directly astride the most important air and sea lanes connecting the United States and its European allies.*

3. *The combined Soviet-Cuban military strength on the island is now so great that it would divert an increasing portion of American military forces that may be needed elsewhere in a crisis.*

South of Havana, near the tiny village of Lourdes, is a collection of about 50 buildings packed with sophisticated electronics equipment, open to no Cubans and only a few of the 10,000 Russians on the island. It is one of the most important Soviet installations outside of Russia—a super-secret electronic-surveillance complex aimed mainly at the United States.

When U.S. B-52 bombers make low-level practice runs from Florida to Louisiana or Virginia, the Soviets record the unique electronic signatures of the planes to aid Soviet air-defense forces in the event of war. When troops on maneuvers at Fort Benning, Georgia, talk on their radios, the Russians gain insight into American battlefield tactics. Radio traffic from the Atlantic Fleet headquarters, radar emissions from U.S. aircraft carriers off the East Coast, all are filtered through Lourdes. When generals in the Pentagon talk via satellite to bases in the Pacific or Europe, the Russians listen.

In the United States itself, Soviet and Cuban "diplomats" routinely record thousands of American microwave-transmitted telephone calls at a time, speed up the recordings, and radio them to Cuba in unintelligible "bursts." At Lourdes, Soviet technicians use computers to sort the calls out by telephone numbers or key words, and zero in on those most likely to have an intelligence payoff. Although they have the capability to listen in on millions of American phone calls, they pay particular attention to those of the defense industries, the State Department, the Pentagon, and Congress. Is an Air Force sergeant in the Pentagon getting calls because he's behind on house or car payments? Maybe he's ripe to sell secrets. Perhaps a congressional aide's idle talk will put the final piece in a puzzle involving naval weapons procurement.

From San Antonio de los Baños air base southwest of Havana, giant Tu-95 reconnaissance planes of the Soviet air force conduct flights to monitor communications along the U.S. East Coast and to spy on ships of the Atlantic Fleet. Such missions once required tiresome flights over the Pole from Murmansk. But now Cuban basing allows rested crews to stay longer over the Atlantic and make quick responses to U.S. military activity. The reason for these quick surveillance flights lies in the crowded Gulf, Caribbean, and Atlantic sea lanes. These SLOCs (sea lanes of communication), as the Navy calls them, are America's lifeline to Europe. In time of war, half of U.S. supplies for NATO forces would leave from Gulf of Mexico ports. Right now, 45 percent of all foreign tonnage coming into the United States and 66 percent of Europe's crude oil must pass through the Caribbean or along South Atlantic SLOCs.

For this reason, Cuba's little navy looms large. Its two Soviet-built "Foxtrot" diesel-powered submarines, with a submerged cruising range of 11,000 miles, are notably silent when running under the surface. "One of these subs loose in the Caribbean or the Gulf could play hell with tankers and cargo ships," says a U.S. Navy captain.

Cuba also has a Soviet-delivered frigate armed with ship-to-ship missiles, and 25 Soviet attack boats that carry guided missiles. Cuba's MiG-23s, some equipped with laser designators and precision-guided munitions, have a range of 600 miles, making them formidable weapons for ship attacks.

The Cuban navy will not be all the United States has to deal with in an emergency. Last year's visit of a Soviet cruiser, accompanied by two guided-missile frigates, to Cuban ports typified Russia's growing naval presence in waters once considered solely the U.S. Navy's. In 1970 Soviet warships spent 200 ship days in the South Atlantic. By 1980 they were spending 2600 ship days there.

For some time now, American intelligence officials have watched the photographic evidence pile up of the building of an immense naval facility at the harbor of Cienfuegos, on Cuba's southern coast. The ambitious complex is far beyond the needs of Cuba's 117-ship, 11,500-man navy. Say U.S. intelligence sources: Either the Soviets intend to vastly increase the size of Cuba's navy, or they intend to open their first base in the Americas there.

When Admiral Harry D. Train II, commander of the U.S. Atlantic Fleet, went before the Senate Armed Services Committee last spring, he made a sobering observation: "There is a major chink in our strategic armor—the rapidly growing military capability of Cuba, supported by the Soviet Union." He went on to explain an increasing concern of the Defense Department—Cuba represents a major threat to U.S. freedom of action in the event of a crisis, such as a war in Europe, requiring movement of U.S. forces overseas.

Dealing with that threat will not be easy. The Soviets have seen to it that their Cuban vassal is protected by one of the most formidable air defenses in the world. Along the northern coast of the island, the Soviets operate a string of early-warning radars that can detect aircraft as far as 300 miles out. They would direct Cuba's 200 MiG fighters to meet incoming aircraft over the Straits of Florida, the Gulf of Mexico, and the Bahamas. Backing up this system are about 100 surface-to-air missile sites and hundreds of anti-aircraft gun emplacements.

In the perspective of overwhelming U.S. naval power, Cuban forces may seem insignificant. But they would buy time, time when U.S. forces might be sorely needed elsewhere, to close the Greenland-Iceland-Norway gap, for instance, to prevent the bulk of the Soviet fleet from breaking out into the Atlantic to strike our European-bound convoys.

The Russians maintain an elite 2600-man combat brigade in Cuba. Some of its men are quartered in Havana, the rest at a camp near Lourdes. This formidable unit's purpose is not known (some believe it is a Praetorian Guard for Castro). But it remains a sign of Moscow's deep commitment to its Cuban military investment.

The clear threat of a Sovietized Cuba has brought suggested solutions ranging from trade sanctions against Russia (Soviet grain shipped to Cuba may have included grain bought from the United States) to a tightening of the existing trade embargo against Castro. But one plain and prudent step could be taken now: *Draw a high-water mark in the Caribbean—this much and no more.* Havana and the Kremlin should be made to understand that further increases in quality or quantity of the Soviet or Cuban military establishments on the island will be unacceptable. U.S. responses might include stationing more weaponry—such as cruise missiles in Florida—to effectively neutralize the Cuban threat, or establishment of a corollary threat against the Soviet Union. This might involve placing additional U.S. naval forces north of Norway, in the Indian Ocean, or in the northern Pacific.

Whatever the options, drawing the line on the Cuban-Soviet buildup is a minimal step for the protection and peace of the hemisphere.

After Castro came to power in 1959, relations between the United States and Cuba rapidly deteriorated. Because U.S. economic and other assistance was withdrawn, Castro needed to find support elsewhere. Raúl Castro and "Che" Guevara opened domestic doors to local communists, and Fidel Castro joined them in paving the way into Cuba for the Soviets, too. For Moscow, Cuba was a long-sought beachhead in the Western Hemisphere, and a strategic base in the Caribbean, close to the United States and to the Panama Canal. For Castro, the alliance with the U.S.S.R. meant that he was protected from the United States and could proceed with his plans to become the *Líder de las Américas*. The old-time Cuban communists, riding high, thought that they, and not Castro, should become dominant in the government. Castro decided otherwise.

A highly significant event occurred in downtown Havana on 5 February 1960. It happened as the Castro government was beginning to move into the Soviet orbit.

Soviet Deputy Premier Anastas Mikoyan flew into Havana 4 February ostensibly to inaugurate a Soviet industrial and commercial exposition. He was accompanied by 75 officials, far more than were necessary for a ceremonial visit.

On the 5th, Mikoyan was scheduled to lay a wreath at a statue of José Martí, leader of Cuba's wars for independence from Spain. As a correspondent for *Time,* I had received a tip that there might be a disturbance during the wreath-laying.

The morning of the 5th I waited near the statue, accompanied by a photographer. The following description of what happened is based on a file I subsequently cabled to *Time.*

Mikoyan was due to place the wreath at 11:30 in the morning. The statue is in Central Park, two blocks from the site of the Soviet exposition. Mikoyan arrived early, however, and neither the wreath nor the honor guard were there yet. While onlookers pushed against him, Mikoyan stood sourly waiting (he usually looked as if he were sucking a lemon, anyway). Finally the wreath came and Mikoyan started toward the statue (the honor guard arrived still later). Mikoyan put the wreath in place and said a few words in Russian. The floral design consisted of a white and blue globe surmounted by a red star and covered by a yellow hammer and sickle. On an attached ribbon were the words in Spanish, "To the apostle of Cuban liberties." After Mikoyan had spoken he and his retinue headed toward their limousines to go to the exposition, the official inauguration of which was slated for noon.

The photographer and I remained in the park. Only a few passersby came up to look at the wreath. Two green-uniformed policemen stood guard.

Small groups of young men and women gathered on the fringe of the park.

Precisely at noon a young man and several young women (the women wore the uniform of a Catholic school) appeared carrying a wreath representing the Cuban flag. Attached was a ribbon which said, "Vindication for the visit of the assassin Mikoyan."

The group gathered around the wreath and moved toward the statue. The police who were on guard tried to wave them away. Someone shouted, "If he can place a wreath, why can't we?" The men and women pushed against the police, attempting to place the wreath.

A sizeable number of onlookers had gathered by now and suddenly they broke into applause, cheering the students on. The scuffling increased as additional uniformed police and plainclothesmen ran up. The police at the statue became desperate as they were pushed back. They pulled out their guns and began firing into the air. Other police in the area also fired their weapons.

Magically, placards appeared throughout the crowd: "Out with the communists," "Down with Mikoyan," "We don't want the Iron Curtain here." There was even one *"Viva Fidel"* sign.

The students continued pushing forward, and the police were trying to force them back. More police rushed up, firing as they came. Despite the heavy shooting, the students held their ground. Only a few flopped on the ground and crawled behind bushes and wooden stands where an art exhibit was on display.

The students kept yelling, *"¡La universidad, la universidad!"* One tall police officer, to his credit, tried to reason with them, but to no avail.

As the melée continued, soldiers began to rush on the scene. Probably they had been on guard at the Soviet exhibition and in its environs. Some standing, some on their knees, the soldiers discharged their Belgian-made rifles into the air, compounding the general noise and confusion. A hard core of students still stood their ground.

During all this I was shooting pictures. About 30 feet away, the photographer was also working. We were both within 20 yards of the Martí statue. The cops were at first too busy with the students to bother with us.

Then several cops surrounded the photographer and took away his camera and photo equipment bag. He argued with the police. Elsewhere the cops and soldiers were herding the remaining students into a circle.

I began edging away. A cop spotted my camera. It was hanging at my side and I assured him it contained no film. He let me go.

Firing continued sporadically. I started across the road to get away from the park. Suddenly a cop ran up behind me and grabbed me. Other police also converged on me. They yanked away my camera and forcibly pushed me back toward the park. A long-haired soldier ran along behind me, waving his rifle. Raging, he kept yelling and cursing, "*¡Te voy a matar! ¡Te voy a matar!*" (I'm going to kill you!). The fact that I was in the hands of the police quite possibly saved my life.

I was pushed toward the circle of captive students. Again heavy firing broke out. The cops loosened their grips on me, and I took advantage of this lapse to scoot away. (The following day I went to the local police station and was able to retrieve my camera and film. Full repression had not yet been inflicted on Cuba.)

I noted in my dispatch:

> *The demonstration was significant far beyond that of the usual student protest. It was the first demonstration which, by implication, was directed against the Castro regime. It was the first clash between Castro's forces and a section of 'the people' he is always talking about. It was the first public and physical protest against communist ascendancy in Cuba, the first real sign of discontent over communist advances. It was also the first indication of discontent within the Catholic Church, and a willingness to do something about this.*

The incident was significant on the obverse side of the coin, too: the Mikoyan visit accelerated the communization of Cuba and its alignment with the Soviet Union. And Castro demonstrated his willingness to use force to suppress any protest against the ideological direction he was taking.

The Cuban-Soviet alliance lasted for over 30 years. It is now coming apart.

This transoceanic *entente* defied the Monroe Doctrine and enabled the Soviet Union to establish a military, naval, and air base—in effect, a very large "aircraft carrier"—in the western hemisphere, and at one point it took the world to the brink of nuclear war.

Why did Fidel Castro turn to communism and the Soviet Union? The answer lies in Castro's personality. Castro has never been guided ideologically in a true manner; he is impelled by his emotions, his desires, his vision of what his role is in Cuba and the world. As *Washington Post* correspondent Lee Hockstader stated in a dispatch from Havana in October 1991: Castro's "bottom line has never been ideology, but power and survival."

Castro did not lead the Cuban revolution. He survived, and in surviving he became the leader of Cuba. Castro has always been a survivor. He has survived the enmity of and even attacks by the powerful United States. His relationship with Moscow on several occasions has turned mighty sour, but he is still there (the same cannot be said of the Soviet Union).

Castro came out of the Sierra Maestra a charismatic figure who had captured the imagination of the American and world press and the Cuban people, and to some extent of the American public. He was Robin Hood incarnate.

Castro's revolutionary organization, the 26th of July Movement, was one of two major guerrilla forces, each with its supporting underground network. The other was the Second Front of the Escambray, an arm of the university students' *Directorio Revolucionario.* Even within the 26th of July Castro was outshone as a military leader by his brother Raúl, the Argentinean Ernesto "Che" Guevara, and the popular Camilo Cienfuegos. All three displayed daring by leading groups of rebels out of the Sierra and establishing new guerrilla fronts at other points on the island.

The basic backbone of the revolution was the country's middle class, fed up with the repressive tactics of the regime of Fulgencio Batista. These were the people who supplied much of the manpower and all the funds that kept the revolution going, not only in the mountains but also in the cities. Urban clandestine organizations staged strikes and engaged in sabotage and terrorism, eventually helping the guerrillas to bring the government and the country to paralysis and forcing Batista to flee.

Castro came down from the hills, and already the rebel soldiers were saying the Dominican Republic was next—it was the fiefdom of another dictator, Rafael Leónidas Trujillo. Castro boasted, "The Caribbean is ours," and he also said the Andes would be the Sierra Maestra of the Americas. Signs and followers called Castro *"El Líder de las Américas."*

Castro was a hero in the United States, but the United States was not interested in supporting his hemispheric aspirations. Relations cooled, and became decidedly cold when Castro, unaccustomed to criticism from Americans and the American press, was assailed because of the kangaroo courts and firing squads that continued taking a heavy toll of *Batistianos.*

Even as this was occurring, the communists were seizing their opportunity, important doors being opened to them by Raúl Castro and "Che" Guevara. Raúl was probably not a card-carrying Communist; in fact, he had volunteered to fight with the American forces in Korea. But Raúl is a realist; he saw that relations with Washington were bad and Cuba would need help from another quarter. Cuba has never been able to support itself economically. Guevara was not a communist either, but he was definitely anti-American. It is believed he once had an unpleasant incident with a U.S. sailor. And in 1954 he was working for the leftist government of Guatemala when U.S.-supported invaders overthrew the regime.

For the Soviet Union, a move into Cuba would be of enormous strategic value, positioning Soviet forces virtually off the coast of the United States and providing a base for political and subversive activities throughout the hemisphere. The Soviet military would be in the backyard of the United States.

The Cuban Communist Party (called the *Partido Socialista Popular*) had long been a potent political force in Cuba. When Castro began his operations in the Sierra

Maestra, the party disdained him, feeling that he was nothing more than an adventurer. When it became apparent that the revolution would be successful, the communists warmed to him. Raúl and Guevara made the going easy. The communization of Cuba began. The Soviets—surely much to their surprise—were handed their aircraft carrier, as well as a major political and psychological gambit in the Cold War.

Was there no resistance to this within Castro's inner circle? Yes, Cienfuegos evidently did not go along with it, at least not happily. When newspapermen pointed out to Cienfuegos, who was now commander of the army, that military vehicles were painted with red stars similar to those of the Soviet Army, he ordered the stars removed. But the well-liked officer mysteriously disappeared on a flight inside Cuba; there will always be the suspicion that he was done away with.

The Soviet Union poured military advisors, weapons, and equipment into Cuba. Under Raúl's command Cuba's armed forces became among the most powerful in Latin America, rivaling, and perhaps exceeding in strength, those of the larger countries. Eventually air and naval installations were opened for the Soviets and a Soviet combat brigade was brought into Cuba. The Soviets built an electronic monitoring station near Havana that could eavesdrop on or watch U.S. military maneuvers, commercial shipping, air traffic, and all radio messages and telephone calls transmitted by satellite in the southeastern United States.

The United States had long supported the Cuban economy by paying an inflated price for Cuba's sugar, the country's prime product. When this assistance was cut off the Soviet Union picked up the slack, providing credit equivalent to above-world prices. This was done through a barter arrangement by which Soviet petroleum was shipped to Cuba in exchange for the sugar. Cuba's debt to the Soviet Union—credits for economic assistance and the purchase of military equipment above the "prices" the Soviets paid for the products received from Cuba—has been estimated at over $5 billion—a cheap price for an aircraft carrier which suffered little wear and tear, other than from an occasional hurricane.

The road between Havana and Moscow has not always been a smooth one; in fact, it has been a very rocky road at times, with grave problems arising between the two governments. There have been questions of who-is-in-charge?, and finally, the enormous distress to Castro of the breakup of the Soviet empire and the disintegration of the Soviet Union.

In the beginning the professional, old-line communists seemed to have Castro and the Cuban situation well in hand. Then, in August 1961 Blas Roca, secretary-general of the Cuban Communist Party and an experienced party stalwart, flew to Moscow and spent 3 months there. It was already quite apparent that Castro was unstable, expensive, and in other ways not an ideal figure for the world communist movement. The early attempts by his armed bands to invade other Latin American countries had alienated their governments. Furthermore, at a time when Soviet leader Nikita Khrushchev was easing police controls in the U.S.S.R., there was no relaxation of the police state in Cuba. There were frequent arbitrary arrests, and long prison terms and death sentences were still being meted out by the incompetent, impassioned "Revolutionary Tribunals." Hundreds of thousands of Cubans were fleeing the island and telling stories about their fear-driven lives.

Administrative mismanagement was rampant in Cuba, the economy was steadily deteriorating, and there were shortages of everything from food and clothes to vehicles and industrial equipment.

The Castro regime was giving communism a bad (or worse than it already had?) name precisely when Khrushchev was attempting to improve its image.

Blas Roca and the Kremlin planners decided the time had come to downgrade Castro and establish their own central discipline. The Bay of Pigs attempt to free Cuba had failed and there appeared little prospect of another overt American move against the island. Internal resistance inside Cuba had been crushed in the wake of the failed invasion. The communists, unpopular though they might be among the general populace, nevertheless felt they could gather all the reins of power in their own hands. Dedicated communists already held positions in all sectors of the government and all phases of public life. And Cuba was almost entirely dependent on Iron Curtain trade and assistance. It was a matter of bringing Castro to heel.

Roca returned to Havana, and the communist takeover got under way. Previously, old-line communists like Roca had shunned publicity. Now they emulated Castro by going on television and making speeches across the island. Roca appeared before the national convention, in November, of the Confederation of Cuban Workers and told the delegates:

> *The revolutionary government is a government that carries out the historic tasks of the working class. Some could say that among the majority [of the members] of the Council of Ministers there are no workers, but the President of the Republic [and] our Premier, even though they came originally from other social levels, have fused themselves with the working class, have completely embraced the working class, have entered the ranks of the working class, and today are representatives of the will of the working class of the country.*

Premier Castro accepted this role as an honorary member of the proletariat—or appeared to do so. Whereas early in 1959 he had declared, "I am not communist," now, within a week of Roca's speech, he asserted, "I am a Marxist-Leninist and I will be a Marxist-Leninist until the last day of my life." He rapturously praised Marxism: "We believed in Marxism, we believed it was the only correct theory, the most scientific, the only true theory, the only truly revolutionary theory." Furthermore, said Castro, "I believe in collective leadership, I believe in leadership by a vanguard political party."

The communists rapidly moved in. Lazaro Peña, an old-time, hard-core communist, took control of the Labor Confederation. Another old-liner, Juan Marinello, was named Executive Rector of the University of Havana. At the same time, the downgrading of Castro began. He lost one of the three posts he held in the government. He had once declared, "The agrarian reform is the great battle of the revolution," and he had been head of the powerful *Instituto Nacional de Reforma Agraria*.

Now, however, he was suddenly replaced by a communist economist, Carlos Rafael Rodríguez.

Castro still held two posts, Premier and Secretary-General of the *Organizaciónes Revolucionarias Integradas* (United Revolutionary Organizations), the country's only official political party. The ORI was being set up to bring together the three major pro-government political organizations: the 26th of July Movement, the *Partido Socialista Popular*, and the *Directorio Revolucionario*. There would be a single party, and the communists plainly aimed to dominate it. Castro was the chief but his leadership soon appeared to be little more than titular. He called one of his beloved mass rallies to respond to an Organization of American States conference on Cuba at Punta del Este in Uruguay—and twice the communists postponed the event. When the rally was finally held Castro delivered a brief speech—totally atypical—and then was reduced to reading a lengthy statement drawn up by the communists.

Roca subtly, but not too subtly, pointed out in public the error of Castro's ways. Once a staunch Stalinist, Roca took a hard swing at Castro's own personality cult. In typical communist fashion Roca did this by indirection: he talked about Rubén Martínez Villena, a Cuban communist leader who had died in 1934. Roca's message was plain as he said of Villena:

> He had a sense of responsibility.... Rubén would accept neither lies nor deceit nor exaggeration.... Rubén was intransigent with indiscipline. He himself gave constant proofs, despite his enormous authority, despite his leading position within the Party—he gave constant evidence of abiding by the rules, of strictly submitting himself to the discipline of obeying agreements and all dispositions. He never trusted his own decisions alone.... He constantly consulted the committee, the organization, and constantly demanded respect for internal democracy within the Party, which is the basis of collective leadership, of the ability of the revolutionary organization to carry forward the revolutionary tasks.

All of which was the antithesis of Castro and his leadership style. "Discipline," "abiding by the rules," never trusting "his own decisions alone"—there could scarcely have been a more accurate description of the things Castro *didn't* do. Now he was expected to reverse his course, to submit to wiser heads than his. The severity of Roca's reproof was a measure of the self-confidence of the communists.

During the course of this speech Roca made a direct reference to Castro—and the audience at once broke into cheers. Roca listened and then snapped:

> The applause is good, the vivas are good, but if these are not followed tomorrow by resulting action in the house, in the school, in the shop, if there is not resulting revolutionary action every hour and every minute, the applause is converted into deceit and the viva is converted into charlatanry and does not help the revolution.

One would hardly have expected anyone in Cuba publicly to administer such a sharp slap at Castro and his love of cheering, adulating crowds.

Roca's boldness indicated the communists believed they had successfully lassoed Fidel Castro, the maverick Marxist. They had underestimated him, however, as badly as his enemies had on previous occasions (and would in the future). Castro's reaction took a bizarre form. He went on an extended and highly public drinking bout. Reports circulated in Havana that in frequent appearances at local restaurants he loudly assailed the communists and charged that they had betrayed him. The drinking may have been an expression of the frustration of an unstable personality, or it may have been a cunning, deliberate warning to the communists. In any case, they were worried. Castro's popularity was such that he was necessary to them—as he well knew. The Communist daily newspaper, *Hoy*, tried on 16 February to soothe him, declaring:

> *Blas Roca, like all the Cuban revolutionaries, from the highest to the lowest, admires, likes, and respects Fidel Castro as our national hero and our proved and capable leader.*

A series of incidents now occurred. Raúl Castro shot and seriously wounded an important local communist in Santiago de Cuba. Rumors were that the communist, Juan Taquechel, had tried to exercise increased authority and infringe on Raúl's position as part of the plan to reduce the Castros' role. When Fidel Castro sent a routine message to the Soviet Union, a Havana radio station reported that "the independent foreign policy of Cuba is expressed with great force in the Cuban communique" (the significant word was "independent"). Raúl Castro delivered a speech in Havana and pointedly referred to "our socialist revolution led by *Compañero* Fidel."

The outcome of Castro's resistance was not long in doubt. The National Directorate of the ORI was announced 9 March 1962, and of the 25 persons named only 10 were old-line communists. Fidel Castro himself was First Secretary of the party and Raúl was appointed Second Secretary and Vice Premier of the government, thus continuing the line of succession established by Fidel in 1959. The ORI Secretariat, a sort of executive board within the National Directorate, had the following members: the two Castros, Guevara, President Osvaldo Dorticós, Emilio Aragones (former Coordinator General of the 26th of July Movement)—and only one old-time communist, Blas Roca.

For 5 weeks Castro had refrained from delivering speeches, a most unusual state of affairs. When Roca had returned from Moscow with the new communist line, Castro had appeared at first to swallow it. It may have been that Castro felt he had to accept his reduced role as the price for Soviet support and assistance. The situation was not unlike that in the early weeks of 1959, after the rebel victory, when Castro, in the interests of democracy, seemed amenable to a subordinate position within the new provincial government. Castro, however, despite his lip service first to democracy and then to collective leadership, was congenitally incapable of assuming a role inferior to that of any other person or any organization. As the communist takeover progressed, he fretted. He saw himself being downgraded. He realized that his political control was diminishing. Perhaps some day the communists would get rid of him altogether. The remnants of the 26th of July Movement remaining in the Army and the government were being shunted aside. His followers complained to him and urged him to stop the communists.

While Castro drank in public, he maneuvered behind the scenes. He saw to it that the communists were a minority on the ORI Directorate. He conferred with his brother Raúl, who had flown to Havana from Santiago, where he maintained his residence and from where he controlled the country's military establishment. (For security reasons the Castros lived at opposite ends of the island.)

Finally Castro made his move, and when he did he used the same potent weapon that he had utilized in 1959 when he wanted to rid himself of President Manuel Urrutia: a televised speech to the nation. In a 3-hour address on 17 March on TV and radio, he delivered broadside after broadside against the communist apparatus and the communists themselves. Castro, who had crushed the conservative elements that stood in his path in 1959, now struck at the communists who had been trying to push him aside.

Assailing the "fearful sectarianism" of "old Marxist militancy," Castro charged:

> Sectarianism creates the belief that the only revolutionaries, the only compañeros who are trustworthy, the only ones who can be given a position on a state farm, on a cooperative, any place, must be old Marxist militants.

The best jobs were going to communists, said Castro indignantly, and he lashed at "the folly, the idiocy, the negativeness, and the stupidity of such a policy." The communists were given jobs "which they had no ability to do." They thought, gibed Castro, that "they had obtained the revolution in a raffle."

Castro turned his attention to the ORI and asked:

> The Party was being formed.... But were we making a truly Marxist party? Were we setting up a true vanguard of the working class? Were we really integrating the revolutionary forces? We were not integrating the revolutionary forces. We were not organizing a party. We were organizing a yoke ... a straitjacket.... We were nor furthering a free association of revolutionaries, but an army of domesticated and coached revolutionaries.

Castro continued, "When we took a look, all was sacred garbage." He charged that the ORI had become "a nest of privileges, of tolerance, of benefits in a system of gifts and favors of all kinds"—an accusation which in Cuba, afflicted with corrupt government for generations, was especially apt to be believed and was particularly infuriating to the populace.

Castro was angered primarily by the communist attempt to seize power, but his lengthy talk added up to a stinging indictment of the Marxist system in terms worthy of a staunch anti-communist. Castro bluntly stated:

> The communists ... err. Because the communists are men. The communists have erred many times. The history of the national communist movement itself ... had great errors.

For those who believed Castro had become a deep-dyed communist, obediently taking orders from the Party and the Kremlin, he was making it plain that he was a communist only on his own terms. He would be the one to decide the "correct application" of Marxism. He would decide matters of leadership. Said Castro: "I sincerely and firmly believe in the principles of collective leadership, but no one imposed that on me. Rather it was my own profound conviction." The communists had raised the matter of collective leadership, but, said Castro disdainfully, this was not a Cuban problem. It was "a problem of the U.S.S.R."

After that night's telecast there was to be no question as to who was in charge. Castro was the *"Maximo Líder."*

Hardly had Castro finished speaking when massive alterations were launched in the country's political structure and among the political personnel. Cuban communists hurriedly backpedaled and their newspaper *Hoy* piously led off its story on Castro's speech saying:

> There is no breach but rather more union for all, declared the First Secretary of ORI, Compañero *Fidel Castro, in his transcendental appearance last night on radio and television.*

A top-to-bottom purge was begun immediately within the ORI, and it even swept away Blas Roca's brother, who had been the ORI boss in Matanzas Province. Soon ORI itself was disappearing as a name and a structure, and another political apparatus was abuilding, the *Partido Unido de la Revolución Socialista* (United Party of the Socialist Revolution). Moscow recalled its ambassador, Sergei Kudriavtsev, and a new one, Alexander Alexeyev, was named to replace him. Kudriavtsev (who had been head of a spy ring exposed in Canada in 1945) had been too closely associated with the communist effort against Castro to remain in Cuba. The Soviets evidently felt that Alexeyev, a KGB official who had been in Cuba under a number of guises since 1959, including as a Tass correspondent, would be able to get along with Castro. The ambassadorial change was a clear indication of a backdown by the Kremlin.

Castro had won this round. There would be others.

chapter fifteen

ROCKY ROAD II: MISSILE MENACE

The Soviet leadership underestimated the United States' determination to protect its own security. Washington had permitted Cuba to go communist, and it had not blocked the development of military ties between Cuba and the U.S.S.R. The time had come, it seemed to Soviet strategists, to outflank the United States strategically by emplacing intercontinental ballistic missiles in Cuba. This move brought the United States and the Soviet Union close to nuclear war. There were negotiations, however, and the Soviets backed down, although the United States gave ground, too, notably in agreeing not to invade Cuba. A few years later Moscow put pressure on Castro in an effort to control its maverick ally.

On the morning of August 24, 1992, those of us in South Dade, Florida, had spent a night of deadly, screaming winds as Hurricane Andrew swept through the region. Dawn and the departure of the winds, which had exceeded 160 miles per hour, revealed the terrible devastation. Mile after mile of homes were damaged or destroyed. Downed trees and power lines blocked all roads. Large edifices had collapsed. Office buildings had gaping holes as if struck by artillery fire. Hotels had their windows blown in, or out.

The National Guardsmen came, moving in convoys, taking up guard posts. They were on a massive errand of mercy and security.

Except for the lack of radiation, South Dade had been hit as if by a nuclear blast. There was levelling and severe damage over an area of more than 160 square miles.

For Dade County, there was historical irony here. Just 30 years earlier, short 2 months, the scene might well have been nuclear indeed. I was on Islamorada Island in the Florida Keys with my family. I received word that a crisis of undetermined nature was in the wind. We rushed back to Miami, passing military convoys heading south.

The United States and the Soviet Union were about to go eyeball-to-eyeball in the world's first—and so far, only—nuclear crisis.

It also brought new turbulence between Havana and Moscow, although some of the disagreements did not come to light until decades later.

Soviet military strategists saw in Cuba a golden opportunity to outflank the United States, to place intercontinental ballistic missiles right up against the American underbelly. If the ICBMs were ever launched from Cuba, there would be virtually no practical warning time before they struck their targets just about anywhere in the United States. Ballistic missiles in Cuba would drastically alter the strategic equation between the United States and the Soviet Union. Incredibly, the Soviets thought they could get the missiles into Cuba without the Americans finding out about them, as Nikita Khrushchev later revealed in his memoirs.

Letters from people in Cuba to relatives in Miami told of the presence of Soviet soldiers and missiles on the island. Usually the missiles were spotted being trucked on roads. The reports became so convincing that I wrote a story for the *Miami News* about the Soviet military being in Cuba, one of the first such articles on the Moscow move (published 16 August 1962). This was followed by an account I did for *Time* magazine.

Other publications were now reporting what the Soviets were doing in Cuba. From Washington, however, came only denials. McGeorge Bundy, national security advisor to the President, stated on a television program:

> *... I think there is no present likelihood that the Cubans and the Cuban government and the Soviet government would in combination attempt to install a major offensive capability.*

The U.S. intelligence community, or at least some members of it, uneasy at the Kennedy Administration's lack of concern over the situation, leaked to Hal Hendrix, a *Miami News* reporter, information that U.S. spy planes had photographed the Soviets preparing hard sites for the ICBMs in Cuba. The story Hendrix broke won him a Pulitzer Prize.

There is little doubt that the missile move was a Soviet initiative. In *Spy for Fidel*, Cuban defector Orlando Castro Hidalgo recalled:

> *Raúl [Castro] had ... been in Moscow conferring with Khrushchev, and had requested weapons assistance from the Soviet Union. During the conversation Khrushchev suddenly hit the table with his fist and declared, "What is more, I am going to give you offensive weapons also, because if you are attacked, then you have a right to attack and defend yourselves." Cuba, according to Raúl, had not requested offensive weapons. Khrushchev had offered them, stipulating only that they remain under Soviet control.*

In his memoirs, *Khrushchev Remembers: The Glasnost Tapes*, Khrushchev stated that he "was haunted by the knowledge that the Americans could not stomach having Castro's Cuba right next to them." Khrushchev was concerned that the United States "would do something." Said the former Soviet Premier:

> *It was against this background that the idea arose of placing our missile units in Cuba. The development of the operation was assigned to Comrade [Defense Minister Marshal*

> *Rodion Y.] Malinovsky and only a narrow circle of people were given access to the plan. We made an inventory of our resources and came to the conclusion that we could send 42 missiles, each with a warhead of one megaton. The range of most of the missiles was 2,000 kilometers, but 4 or 5 missiles had a range of 4,000 kilometers. We looked at a map and selected the launch sites. Then we picked targets to inflict the maximum damage. We saw that our weapons could inspire terror.*

> *We decided to send a few thousand men to guard the missiles. We also brought the latest antiaircraft weapons—surface-to-air missiles (SAMs)—coastal defense missiles, and tank units to defend against an invasion. All in all, it was several tens of thousands of troops. We needed to establish a headquarters, and Malinovsky recommended General [Issa Alexandrovich] Pliyev as the commander. We sent our military delegation to Cuba with the task of informing Fidel about our proposals and to get his consent.*

> *Castro gave his approval. The whole thing cost us a lot, but we thought it would be justified if we could maintain the new social order in Cuba.*

Castro's agreement, however, was not obtained quite that easily. In an earlier volume of memoirs, *Khrushchev Remembers: The Last Testament*, the former Soviet leader stated that he and Castro had "argued and argued." In the foreword to the later volume, Strobe Talbott, who had translated and edited the earlier memoirs, tells of "gaps" in the tapes which were used to write that book. He then says:

> *In some cases, it was possible to deduce what Khrushchev might have revealed in the missing sections. For example, recalling the Cuban missile crisis, Khrushchev said, "When Castro and I talked about the problem, we argued and argued." At that point there was an interruption, then the statement, "Our argument was very heated. But in the end, Fidel agreed with me." We could only conjecture that they had argued over who would control the missiles.*

The thought of ICBMs under the control of Castro and his brother Raúl is little short of horrifying. A few years earlier Raúl had spoken of his wish to drop atomic bombs on New York City.

President Kennedy went on the air to explain to the nation the crisis that had developed. A blockade was imposed on Cuba. Messages flashed back and forth between Moscow and Havana. There were behind-the-scenes diplomatic meetings. A spy for the United States highly placed in the Soviet military establishment, Oleg Penkovsky, provided information on Soviet military intentions, as requested by Kennedy, and was caught and later executed.

Finally, the Soviet Union acceded. Ships bearing additional missiles turned around on the high seas; the missiles already in Cuba would be withdrawn. Despite a veneer of victory placed over the matter by the Kennedy Administration, the solution was more the result of secret agreements. The United States soon withdrew its own missiles from Italy and Turkey. And, most important, the United States abjured invading Cuba. Khrushchev claimed that it was not U.S. power that forced him to back down; rather, "We removed our missiles in exchange for the American promise not to invade Cuba."

Journalist Georgie Anne Geyer, in her biography of Castro, *Guerrilla Prince*, described his reaction to the Soviet pullout:

> *As the missiles were leaving the island, Castro's tongue exploded with every scatological and cursing word he could grasp for. He railed at Khrushchev to the editors of [the official daily]* Revolución, *screaming, "Son of a bitch! Bastard! Asshole!" Later he would call Khrushchev a "maricón," or homosexual. Then, as Castro swore still more, he swung around and violently kicked the huge mirror that hung on the wall. A veritable shower of glass rained down on the office.*

As part of the U.S.-U.S.S.R. agreements Moscow was willing to permit United Nations inspection of Cuban soil to verify the removal of the missiles. Further fueling Castro's fury was the fact that Khrushchev had accepted the American demands. Going on television, as usual, Castro overruled the Soviet acceptance of on-site inspection in Cuba: "We positively reject any attempt at supervision, any attempt at inspection. No one is going to inspect our country." And no one did.

Castro remained disgruntled over what he perceived as a retreat by the Soviet Union. Khrushchev recounted a later meeting with him: "We discussed the past from hindsight and conducted an analysis of the events in a calm atmosphere. I saw that he still did not understand." The Soviet Premier told Castro that the Cuban armed forces could not have withstood a major attack by the United States. Khrushchev recalled:

> *I actually asked our minister of defense, "What do you think? Knowing the arms, the numbers, and the strength of Cuba's armed forces, how long would it take the United States to deal with Cuba's forces and crush them?" Malinovsky thought and then answered, "Something on the order of 2 days." When I told this to Fidel, he was bitter and tried to prove to me that Malinovsky was mistaken, that it was a faulty evaluation. "We wouldn't let that happen," said Fidel.*

> *"Well, I said, "that's what Malinovsky says, and I agree with Malinovsky. I think he's right."*

> *I didn't tell Castro that Kennedy promised to remove missiles from Turkey and Italy, since that agreement was just between the two of us. Kennedy asked me to keep it secret. He believed that if it became known to the American public it might bring unpleasant consequences.*

A bizarre and ominous incident occurred during the Missile Crisis. This became known years later. Fidel Castro's wild streak had blazed fiercely and he attempted to get Khrushchev to plunge the world into nuclear holocaust.

Castro informed the Soviet ambassador in Havana that "we have incontrovertible information" that the United States was about to strike Cuba militarily. The ambassador relayed the information to Khrushchev, who had similar information from Soviet intelligence agents. In his memoirs the former Soviet leader recalled:

> *Castro suggested that in order to prevent our nuclear missiles from being destroyed, we should launch a preemptive strike against the United States. He concluded that an attack was unavoidable and that this attack had to be preempted. In other words, we needed to*

immediately deliver a nuclear missile strike against the United States. When we read this I, and all the others, looked at each other, and it became clear to us that Fidel totally failed to understand our purposes. Only then did I realize that our friend Castro, whom I respect for his honesty and directness, had failed to understand us correctly. We had installed the missiles not for the purpose of attacking the United States, but to keep the United States from attacking Cuba. What does it mean to make a preemptive strike? We could deliver the first blow, but there would immediately be a counterblow—both against Cuba and against our own country.

Cuban officials have denied that Castro asked for a nuclear strike by the Soviet Union. Castro himself evidently later chose to disbelieve he had tried to spark a nuclear conflict. Again according to Khrushchev:

I told Castro [at a meeting of the two men], "There is another aspect to this business. You wanted to start a war with the United States. If the war had begun we would somehow have survived, but Cuba no doubt would have ceased to exist. It would have been crushed into powder. Yet you suggested a nuclear strike!"

"No. I did not suggest that," replied Castro.

"How can you say that?" I asked Fidel.

The interpreter added, "Fidel, Fidel, you yourself told me that."

"No!" insisted Fidel.

Then we checked the documents. It was fortunate that Fidel did not tell us this orally, but sent us a message. The interpreter read the document and asked, "How shall I translate this? Here is the word 'war,' here is the word 'blow.'"

Fidel was embarrassed. At that time he was a very hot-tempered person. We understood that he failed to think through the obvious consequences of a proposal that placed the planet on the brink of extinction. The experience taught him a good lesson, and he later began to consider his behavior more thoroughly.

During the crisis an additional problem arose between Havana and Moscow. On 27 October an American U-2 aircraft, piloted by Major Rudolf Anderson Jr., was shot down while flying reconnaissance over Cuba. One account that has circulated among Cubans has it that Castro personally pushed the button that fired the Soviet anti-aircraft missile that hit the plane. (Anderson was killed, the only "combat" casualty of the crisis.) Khrushchev provided a different version, stating that Castro ordered the Soviet military to shoot down the U-2. Said Khrushchev:

There was another uproar. This time we feared that America's patience would be exhausted and war would break out. We ordered [General] Pliyev to obey only orders from Moscow. However, in case of an invasion our troops should coordinate with the Cuban forces and be subordinate to Castro.

Although the Soviet Union pulled its missiles out of Cuba, Castro was a winner. The possibility that the United States would invade Cuba, at least in the foreseeable future, was now virtually non-existent. Khrushchev sent Deputy Premier Mikoyan back to the island to patch things up with Castro, and later Castro was given red-carpet treatment during two visits to the Soviet Union. Dependent on the Soviets for economic support, Castro was too shrewd to loosen ties with them or do anything but profess friendship for the Soviet government. Angry he might be, but for Castro it has always been survival before pride.

There was to be another *contretemps* between Castro and Moscow in this period. Years later, in an interview with Castro by Gillian Gunn, of the Carnegie Endowment for International Peace, Castro stated that the Soviet brigade was placed in Cuba following the 1962 missile crisis, presumably as a tripwire in the event of a U.S. attack on Cuba (the Americans would be forced to fight Soviet troops). In 1979, said Castro, Moscow, seeking to placate the United States during delicate arms negotiations, renamed the brigade a "training school." Wrote Gunn, "Castro said he was consulted by Moscow, expressed opposition to the idea and was unpleasantly surprised when Moscow went ahead and 'unilaterally' announced the name change." Gunn's article on Castro appeared 15 December 1991 in the *Washington Post*.

The old-line communists had been delivered a hard blow by Castro in the early sixties when they attempted to wrest control of government and country from him. It was a setback but the communists did not give up. This time they engaged in conspiracy rather than open politicking. Quite likely there was encouragement from Moscow; at minimum the Soviets were in touch with the old-liners and knew what was going on.

But DGI, Castro's spy/police agency, also knew what was going on and maintained surveillance of the conspirators, including when they met with officials of the Soviet embassy. The key figure was Anibal Escalante, who had been a top official in ORI and had been sent packing to the Soviet Union when Castro cracked down on that organization. In 1964 he was allowed to return to Cuba.

Escalante and companions were arrested in 1968, accused of conspiring against the government. They became known as the *"microfacción"*—perhaps as an effort to exculpate the communist organization as a whole from blame. Castro delivered an 8-hour harangue before the Central Committee of the new Communist Party (it replaced the United Party in 1965). Castro charged that Escalante was a "mistaken" leader and said that he had been clandestinely passing documents and information to the Soviets. Escalante and his collaborators were brought to trial. It was largely conducted in secrecy. The plotters were found guilty and were given lengthy prison sentences.

At issue was not only the question of political control, but a larger question resulting from a divergence between Havana and Moscow over policy toward Latin America. A few years earlier, when the Castro star had been in the ascendancy, the Soviet Union had had little choice but to go along with his plans, policies and postures. A vast program of subversion and guerrilla warfare was prepared in Cuba and set in motion, causing considerable trouble for Latin America. But this also forced latino armies to convert from barrack-and-parade ground coup-makers to hardened, mountain-climbing counter-insurgents. The subversive efforts spawned by Cuba repeatedly failed, and as the years went by, it became apparent that Castro's grandiose overall policy was a failure, too. *Fidelismo* was unable to conquer a single country.

Castro lost much of his lustre; his program had done little more than further isolate Cuba from the rest of Latin America. The Soviet Union returned to its former policy of vía pacífica, seeking friendly relations with the Latin American countries, establishing diplomatic ties wherever the latinos were willing to do so. Those communist parties dominated by Moscow would substitute politicking for subversion.

Nikita Khrushchev had been deposed in October 1964 and the men who now ruled the Soviet Union were ill-disposed to tolerate the antic insubordination of the maverick Marxist of the Caribbean. Moscow slowed the flow of raw materials and other supplies to Cuba. A number of Cuban factories had to close. Most important was a slowdown in the shipment of petroleum, ordinarily transported in a steady stream of tankers. There was not enough fuel to keep vehicles, factories, and sugar mills running. In a desperate move Raúl Castro, as head of the armed forces, allocated about one-third of military fuel stockpiles to civilian use. The Cuban economy was in serious trouble.

Castro buckled, although his humiliation was not made public. Castro Hidalgo revealed in *Spy for Fidel* what had happened:

> *In February 1969 the chief of the Cuban Intelligence Center in Paris, Armando López, summoned his oficiales to a meeting. He was just back from a trip to Havana, where he had conferred with DGI chief [Manuel] Piñeiro [Losada]. López gravely announced, "Somos más soviéticos" (We are more Sovietic). The Castro government had bowed under the Russian pressure, and a secret agreement had been reached between the two governments. López ... cautioned us that we were not to tell even our wives about the agreement.*

General terms of the accord were provided by Castro Hidalgo. Cuba would not criticize—as it had been doing—Soviet policy toward Latin America. Castro would cease assailing the old-line Communist Parties of Latin America that did not go along with his program of subversion. Moscow would be able to pursue its own policies, free of criticism and interference from Castro.

In return for this—and to place Cuba even more under Moscow's thumb—the Soviet Union would provide the island with the economic aid it required. That assistance would amount, at that time, to about one-third of a billion dollars worth of petroleum and other supplies annually. Moscow promised to increase the quantity of raw materials and agricultural machinery it was sending to Cuba, as well as to expand its importation of Cuban products.

As relations between Havana and Moscow had deteriorated, Moscow pulled out many of its technicians who had been helping the Cubans. Now the Soviet Union would send some 5,000 specialists. They would work in the mining, fishing, agricultural, and nuclear energy fields, as well as with the Cuban military and intelligence services. The Soviets especially wanted to expand the island's production of nickel, a metal they needed. The Soviet Union would provide Cuba with a nuclear power plant (by September 1993 construction was at a standstill due to Cuba's economic woes).

In the intelligence field new advisors would be assigned to the DGI. They would also serve as liaison officers between the DGI and the KGB (*Komitet Gosudarstvennoi Bezopasnosti*—Committee for State Security). Under terms of the agreement the operations of the Cuban service would now be more closely coordinated with those of the KGB. DGI became—as was the case with the intelligence services of the East European satellites—virtually an arm of the KGB. This setup was particularly valuable to the Soviet Union in regard to operations in the United States: DGI was utilizing the stream of refugees entering the States as a cover for infiltrating its agents. The Soviet Union had a corps of its own people who spoke perfect Spanish and who, with a little language alteration, could pass for Cubans. These were Spaniards taken from their homeland as children during the civil war in Spain and raised, educated, and indoctrinated in the U.S.S.R.

Manuel Piñeiro Losada, the chief of DGI whose operatives had spied on the old-time communists and Soviet diplomats during the ORI period, was removed from his post. (Years later he would reappear as head of the new America Department, reporting directly to the Castros and engaged in a purely Cuban subversive program for Latin America.)

The Soviet Union had been providing Cuba with most of its weapons and military equipment. Cuba's armed forces were already among the most powerful in Latin America. As a result of the new Havana-Moscow agreement the Soviet Union began re-equipping the Cuban forces with everything from personal gear to new types of surface-to-air guided missiles. These missiles were more accurate and had longer ranges than those previously emplaced on the island. The strategic importance of Cuba to the Soviet Union was emphasized by a visit to Havana in July 1969 of a flotilla of Soviet warships and the visit in November of the same year of Defense Minister Andrei A. Grechko.

The Soviets had secured their Caribbean aircraft carrier. In an interview published in the Soviet newspaper *Izvestia* early in 1970, Raúl Castro humbly said:

> We have learned a lot in the past. We have matured. Therefore, we believe that the possibilities for future friendship and cooperation between Cuba and the Soviet Union are now more positive.

It was almost a plea.

chapter sixteen
ROCKY ROAD III: PULLING THE PLUG

For more than 30 years Castro depended on the Soviet Bloc for economic and military assistance and support in the international arena. But then, surely to his amazement and dismay, the Bloc began to fall apart and the Eastern European satellite nations broke away from the USSR and cast off communism in favor of democracy and free enterprise. And the day came when the mighty Soviet Union itself began to disintegrate, and then was no more, replaced by independent republics. The blows against Castro were harsh. There were little or no replacement parts for weapons and military equipment. There was not enough fuel for aircraft and vehicles, military or civilian. The country's economy deteriorated to near-desparation levels. Fidel Castro faced one of his worst crises. It might well be his last.

When Mikhail Sergeyevich Gorbachev was chosen in 1985 by the Communist Party hierarchy to be leader of the Union of Soviet Socialist Republics, this was the first time that the younger generation was placed in command of the country. Because of his profound impact on Cuba, it is worth looking at the origins and orientations of Gorbachev.

The man who more than any other would change the course of history in the second half of the twentieth century was born 2 March 1931 into a peasant family in the village of Privolnoye, located in the Stavropol area of the Russian republic. The son and grandson of Communist Party members, Gorbachev followed in the family's footsteps. He joined the Komsomol, the Communist Youth League. He was active in the organization during his studies at Moscow State University and afterwards. He and his wife Raisa (they were married during his senior year) returned to the city of Stavropol, capital of the territory, where his first job was as secretary of the local Komsomol. He rose through party posts, eventually being made party secretary of an agricultural unit. This was followed by appointment to be chief of all agricultural production in the territory. Gorbachev was now face to face with the awesome problems of the Soviet economy, and specifically of its farm production. In April 1970 he became party first secretary for the territory, one of the youngest provincial secretaries in the USSR.

Moscow was taking note of the political comer, and in 1971 Gorbachev was given a seat on the Central Committee of the party. He came to the attention of and was befriended by powerful men, including KGB Chief Yuri Andropov and General Secretary Leonid Brezhnev. Gorbachev in 1978 was made agriculture secretary for the entire country. At this time Fidel Castro had already been in power in Cuba for twenty years.

In October 1980 Gorbachev was made a member of the powerful Politburo. He was the youngest member; in fact, he was twenty-one years younger than the average age of the other fourteen members. Brezhnev died in 1982 and was succeeded by Andropov. Gorbachev became Andropov's chief aide. They wanted to reform the deteriorating Soviet system. To do so, they launched an extensive purge of the bureaucracy, ridding it of thousands of corrupt and incompetent officials.

Andropov, however, died in 1984. He was succeeded by Konstantin Chernenko, an ailing and aging (72) party figure. Gorbachev, who was still agriculture secretary, also continued as chief aide to the General Secretary. Chernenko lasted little more than a year; he died 10 March 1985. The next day the Central Committee elected Mikhail Gorbachev General Secretary. Events beyond the foresight of any living being were now set in motion. Certainly the bearded leader in the Caribbean—in power for twenty-six years—could not suspect what the consequences would be for his rule.

Gorbachev knew at first hand the dreadful state of the Soviet economy. Behind a façade of sophisticated military hardware and space technology—a glittering Potemkin's Village of ultramodern MiG-29s and huge space rockets—the Soviet Union's economy was steadily deteriorating. Productivity was low, goods were shoddy, distribution was inadequate and harvests failed to provide sufficient food for the populace. The military establishment was devouring an inordinate share of the national budget. The gap between the Soviet Union and the developed nations of the West rapidly widened. Communism went against basic human qualities; it stifled individual initiative. The Great Fraud would be revealed to the world when the cover of controls was pulled back from over the Soviet Union and its former East European satellites.

Sailing against the winds of historical tradition in Russia/Soviet Union, Gorbachev developed and launched the concepts of *glasnost*—openness—and *perestroika*—restructuring. Whatever political and ideological limitations he may have envisioned for his programs, in actuality he had broken open the dike of centralized command and the resulting flood would be largely uncontrollable. One of the greatest events in the twentieth century was taking place: the disintegration of the communist and monolithic Soviet empire, and later even of the Soviet Union itself.

The world watched in awe and joy as the Berlin Wall was demolished. For over a quarter of a century it had been not only a terrible symbol of the repression of millions of people but also a grim factor in that repression. Scores of people were killed trying to get through or over the wall in desperate efforts to reach freedom.

The people of Prague defied Army tanks and Czechoslovakia threw out communism and proclaimed its independence. Poland, Hungary, Romania and Bulgaria discarded the communist system, disavowed the Warsaw Pact which had long bound them, and declared their independence, too. East Germany was absorbed by democratic, free-market West Germany.

For Castro in far-off Cuba the blows were severe. *Glasnost* and *perestroika* were contrary to the basic precepts of authoritarian Cuba with its police state and government-owned economy. The liberation of East Europe meant that Cuba would no longer receive the economic assistance those countries had previously rendered. Trade had been on the basis of barter; now the newly freed countries demanded payments in hard currency, and Cuba had little hard currency.

The Soviet Union lost its empire and began to come apart itself. It could no longer provide its remaining allies with the amount of assistance of former times. The Soviet Army began its withdrawal from the morass of Afghanistan, leaving the government there to fend for itself. Aid to Cuba would be reduced significantly.

Castro was hit psychologically, ideologically and militarily and, most important of all, in the economic area, where the well-being of the citizenry was at stake. Socialism/communism was discredited. The communist bloc of which Cuba had been a part no longer existed. There would be no more military assistance and support, nor would the shipments of food, petroleum and manufactured products be at anywhere near previous levels.

Castro tightened his hold on power and hunkered down. The government prepared Cubans for the aptly named *"Opción Cero"*—living in little more than a primitive economy, with minimal supplies from abroad.

A personal note: As a journalist I covered the Cuban revolutionary movement in the cities and in the mountains. I saw the rebels achieve victory against a powerful dictatorship, truly a triumph of the human spirit. I accompanied Fidel Castro during much of his trip across Cuba. I saw the new government take control; its ranks included good friends of mine. Then came the cooling relations with the United States and the swerve toward communism and alliance with the Soviet Union and the other Iron Curtain countries.

That alliance suffered hard strains, but it was always there to support Castro. The communist bloc was an immense and threatening geopolitical structure—until suddenly, to the astonishment of the entire world, it simply crumbled, vanished, was no more.

I was at the time director of news of the Radio Martí Program of the Voice of America. This was a station set up to broadcast accurate news and information to the people of Cuba, deprived of these by their government. In 1990 I set out to do what would have been inconceivable two years earlier. I traveled to Budapest, Prague and

Warsaw to recruit correspondents for Radio Martí, and then even to Moscow for the same purpose. I also walked into East Berlin from West Berlin.

This was an awesome experience for a journalist who had covered Cuba through much of his professional life. I visited the Habana Restaurant in East Berlin, watched Cuban military men check into a hotel in Prague, and in Moscow discussed with Andrei Kortunov, of the U.S.-Canadian Institute, ways Moscow might change or even oust Castro.

To gaze at the Danube River in Budapest, which "again goes unvexed to the sea," as Lincoln said of the Mississippi after the capture of Vicksburg; to stare at the ring of candles on Wenceslas Square in Prague, honoring martyrs in the struggle against communism; to look up at the huge, brooding Palace of Culture and Science in Warsaw, an ugly relic of the Stalin era; to chip away at the Berlin Wall with a rented hammer—to be able to do these things in what had been Iron Curtain territory was, to one journalist, a mind-boggling exposition of how tremendously the world had changed.

On 3 April 1989 Mikhail Gorbachev and his wife flew into Havana. He had come to reassure Castro of continued, although reduced, Soviet aid, but also to ask Castro to undertake reforms in Cuba and to support the comprehensive peace effort then under way in Central America. Specifically, in the latter case, Castro would encourage his allies, the Sandinistas who ruled Nicaragua, to continue cooperating with the peace process.

Castro has often been underestimated, and this was to be another occasion for that to occur. In this case Gorbachev underestimated Castro's capacity for incivility. Before the trip was over Castro had used a speech introducing Gorbachev to the National Assembly to chide the USSR for its "errors," had rudely stopped cold a question directed at Gorbachev at a press conference, and had taken the Gorbachevs to the airport in a closed vehicle so they could barely be seen by waiting persons lining the road to wave farewell.

In his introductory speech—which at 45 minutes was almost as long as Gorbachev's—Castro praised the Soviet leader as "a veritable crusader for peace" who was following an "intelligent, bold, and brave policy" of nuclear disarmament. Castro stated that "we don't have any kind of disagreement or discord with the Soviet Union." Castro gave his own interpretation of *perestroika*; to him this was Gorbachev's "determined efforts to make socialism advance in his country—to give impetus to, develop and perfect socialism in his country." Said Castro condescendingly, "It is a country that has made enormous progress ... [but which] could reach even higher levels."

And then an air of superiority as Castro declared:

> *It is not unusual for any revolutionary process to commit errors. From that viewpoint it is undeniable that there were errors in the revolutionary process of the USSR, as the Soviets themselves admit. But we did not have here [in Cuba] the type of phenomena that the USSR had during Stalin's era ... We have not had problems of that type ...*

Castro had a message for the listening Soviet chief:

Today each socialist country attempts to improve socialism starting from its own inter-pretation of the Marxist-Leninist ideas. Each country tries to implement its own ways and formulas. Comrade Gorbachev has supported these principles.

We go our way; you go yours.

Gorbachev began his own address reassuring Castro and the Cubans. He said:

... Soviet-Cuban links have a stable character. They cover practically all the areas of social development; they rely on the principles of equality, are marked by respect for inde-pendence, an understanding of mutual responsibility, and of the need for internation-alist assistance.

In regard to comradely assistance to Cuba, however, Gorbachev made it clear that there had to be changes: "Time presents us with new requirements and this applies in particular to economic links. They must be made more dynamic, more effective. They must do more for both our countries, our peoples." *Señor* Castro, I have to feed and clothe the Soviet people. You have to do more to improve your own lot.

Gorbachev had an additional message for Castro. He stated:

Comrades, we have spoken a great deal in the past few days about the specific problems of the situation today. World civilization is at a crossroads ... One thing is clear. Today only those who are marching in step with the times, who are drawing the necessary con-clusions from the changes resulting from the fact that the world has entered an era of high technology, of intellectual labor, of a decisive role of science, can count on success.

To emphasize his point, and perhaps to irritate Castro further, Gorbachev spoke of changes under way in Nicaragua. He said:

[The Sandinista leadership have] announced elections in the country under interna-tional supervision, the dialogue with the opposition has been resumed, political rights of citizens have been expanded, the amnesty decree has gone into effect, and the reduction of armed forces and of military spending is being considered.

None of these things, of course, was being done in Cuba.

Ingenuously, after the Gorbachevs had departed, Castro explained the closed-car incident to a reporter thus: "... The Soviets asked us, in deference to Gorbachev, that we come in a covered vehicle because the morning is somewhat cool ... They did not want to take the risk that he would catch a cold."

Correspondent Alfonso Chardy reported in the *Miami Herald*: "Soviet President Mikhail Gorbachev left Cuba Wednesday, ending a visit that has subtly, but deeply, altered the relationship between the two allies.

"Between symbols of solidarity—Gorbachev and President Fidel Castro at one point holding up hands like triumphant performers—was an undercurrent of dis-agreement."

As the Soviet empire continued to fall apart Raúl Castro in a speech in mid-June set forth the official Cuban view of events. He declared, in defiance and resigna-tion:

I truly mean it when I say that I am a pro-Soviet, and I will be one until I die. Like Fidel told and taught us on more than one occasion, we can never bite the hand that helped us in the most difficult times. We will never be ungrateful. They can do whatever they want, we will do whatever we want. We must negotiate ... They are going through a process which, in my personal opinion, they needed to go through. It was necessary; but how they do it is their problem. How we do ours is our problem.

This statement by Raúl Castro was contained in a speech which raised the curtain on a surprising and mysterious drama: the arrest of Division General Arnaldo Ochoa Sánchez, as well as other officers and a number of civilians (or military in civilian posts). Ochoa had been the epitome of the "Internationalist Man" so vaunted by the Castro regime. He had fought in the Sierra Maestra and at the Bay of Pigs, served in Latin America, and commanded Cuban forces in Ethiopia and finally in Angola. He had then come home, just as tens of thousands of Cuban troops would when Cuba pulled out of Angola.

The purge in the Cuban government was widespread. Ochoa was accused of drug trafficking. Other officers were similarly charged. Against other accused there were a variety of criminations. Diocles Torralbas, for instance, was dropped as minister of transportation on an accusation of misconduct. José Abrahantes Fernández, the powerful minister of the interior, once close to Fidel Castro, was ousted from office for not having brought to justice the alleged drug traffickers. He was tried and sent to prison, where he died, reportedly of a heart attack.

History does not yet tell us whether in reality the Castros had uncovered and destroyed an extensive plot against them. The government sought to show that the accused were involved in separate cases of criminality, and that none of these involved conspiracy. In charging narcotics trafficking, the Castros were engaging in bald hypocrisy: over the years there has been ample testimony—including that of one-time Colombian drug kingpin Carlos Lehder at the trial of former Panamanian dictator Manuel Noriega in Miami—of official Cuban participation in the drug trade.

Ochoa and fourteen co-defendants faced a show trial reminiscent of those of the Stalin era in the Soviet Union. The men were, not surprisingly in a ruthlessly-controlled police state, found guilty. Ochoa and three other officers were sentenced to death; the rest of the defendants went to prison for long terms.

Ochoa and his three comrades were executed by firing squad 13 July 1989.

Whether Ochoa was truly involved in trafficking, that charge was clearly only a cover for a larger issue. Was it necessary to execute a hero who had long and well served his country, even if he had turned to drug trafficking? It was necessary to do so if that person constituted a threat to Fidel Castro. That danger would persist even if the man were in prison.

Was the threat passive or active? That is, had officers merely been voicing discontent, or was that discontent jelling into conspiracy, or did a well-formed plot exist that was close to fruition? Any of these situations would, in the eyes of the Castros, have been sufficient grounds for the execution of Ochoa.

And another key question: Was there a Soviet role in this affair? Gorbachev had tried—unsuccessfully—to remove hardline communist regimes in East Europe and replace them with what he considered to be reformers (but reformers within the communist system). Did he attempt this in Cuba, too? If so, Ochoa would have been his obvious candidate to replace Castro. Ochoa had studied at the Soviet Union's Frunze and Voroshilov military academies, he spoke Russian well, he had worked with the Soviet military in Angola and probably Ethiopia.

If there was a conspiracy, it is reasonable to assume that Moscow either fostered it or, minimally, knew about it and did not discourage it. Ochoa would have informed his Soviet friends in order to obtain assurances of continued Soviet support for a new government. A Soviet connection with the conspiracy would have been another solid reason for the Castros wanting Arnaldo Ochoa dead. This not only eliminated a threat, but also served as a warning to Moscow not to try anything like that again.

American and other Western publications had long been banned in Cuba. Soviet publications had been available, but early in August 1989 *Granma*, official newspaper of the Cuban Communist Party, announced a ban on the distribution of *Sputnik* and *Moscow News*. They were accused of "justifying bourgeois democracy" and of not corresponding to "our reality or interests," and therefore "are not for us." An article in *Moscow News* in March 1990 noted sarcastically:

> *Revolutionary-minded Cuban women are in no danger of becoming materialistic as long as they continue to receive, as they do today, either one bra or two panties a year (either a bra or a pair of panties of whatever size they have at the stores) with their ration cards. Neither are Cuban men who buy in the "parallel market" a short-sleeved shirt for a third of a worker's monthly wage threatened by materialism.*

The widening breach between Havana and Moscow was not confined to the upper echelons of power. *Wall Street Journal* correspondent José de Cordoba reported from Havana:

> *For many Soviets, Cuba and Cubans for some time have been pariahs. Melba, a 25-year-old Cuban engineer who recently returned home after five years of study in the Soviet Union, says Soviet students sometimes physically attacked their Cuban fellows. The students, she says, blamed aid to Cuba for the Soviet Union's poverty. For them, Mr. Castro was just another dictator.*

The *Miami Herald*, in a dispatch filed from Moscow by correspondent Juan O. Tamayo, reported that a Soviet Foreign Ministry document it had obtained "noted that there is 'a huge gap' between Cuba and the Soviet Union, with Moscow intent upon what it calls 'de-ideologizing' its foreign relations while Havana 'persists in its anti-imperialist policies.'" Said the report, "Cuba is starting to contradict Soviet policy, especially on the issues of human rights, on reductions of the armaments race ... and in its views on regional conflicts."

Following the failure of a coup attempt in Moscow in August by communist hardliners, Boris Yeltsin, President of the Russian Republic, emerged as the most powerful person in the Soviet Union. Yeltsin had held out at his headquarters, defying the conspirators. He climbed aboard a tank and rallied citizens and soldiers alike, and won world attention and respect. Gorbachev was held prisoner by the conspirators, then released, but the situation had vastly changed. The failed coup sped up the disintegration of the Soviet Union; Gorbachev found himself with few powers.

For Castro the new state of affairs was particularly doleful. During a trip to Washington in June 1991 Yeltsin had stated at a press conference: "Considering the fact that 40 percent of our people now live below the official poverty line and also the fact that charity should begin at home, our [Russian parliament] has made a decision to terminate all assistance to foreign countries from this moment on." Within the Russian Republic were a large portion of the Soviet Union's natural resources, including most of its petroleum reserves. If Castro wanted any of this, it would be cash on the barrelhead.

Months earlier, in a speech 7 December 1989, Castro had spoken of "the crisis that erupted in the socialist world" and warned that from this "we can only expect negative economic consequences for our country." He said:

> What is being talked about now in the majority of those countries is not precisely about the imperialist struggle and about the principles of internationalism. Those words are not even mentioned in their press. Such concepts are virtually erased from the political dictionary there. In contrast, capitalist views are gaining unusual strength there. Capitalism means unequal trade with Third World countries, exaltation of individual selfishness and national chauvinism, the empire of irrationality and anarchy in investment and production, and ruthless sacrifice of the peoples to blind economic laws.

Declared Castro: "In Cuba revolution, socialism and national independence are insolubly linked."

When the coup attempt got under way in Moscow in August 1991, Castro's hopes surely soared. He may well have known about the coup in advance; one of the key conspirators, KGB Chief Vladimir Kryuchkov, had visited Cuba earlier in the year. When the coup failed, Havana delayed five days before commenting ("It is no secret that the processes under way in the Soviet Union ... will have a clear impact in our country").

Then, before the end of the month, came the dissolution of the Communist Party of the USSR. *Granma*, almost certainly expressing Castro's thoughts, editorialized, "It is impossible to deny that these are unfortunate and bitter moments, which we would have preferred never to have experienced." But the paper added: "Some hastily write the epitaph of the communist ideal and ridiculously underestimate us and our ability to resist.... We were and are prepared to resist."

If there was to be armed resistance, it would be without the presence of Soviet forces. Still another blow fell. After meeting with U.S. Secretary of State James A. Baker in Moscow, Gorbachev announced (9 September):

> I reaffirmed to the Secretary that we plan to transfer our relations with Cuba to a plane of mutually beneficial trade and economic ties and we will remove the other elements of

that friendship—elements that were born of a different time in a different era. In that context I told the Secretary that we will soon begin discussions with the Cuban leadership about the withdrawal of a Soviet training brigade, which was stationed in Cuba some time ago and is still there.

Gorbachev stated that 11,000 men would be withdrawn, thus indicating that he was referring not only to the 2,800-man brigade but to additional military personnel as well.

The USSR had been urgently seeking economic assistance from the United States. Washington, in turn, was asking for an end to Soviet subsidies to Cuba and to the military ties between the two countries. Gorbachev had acquiesced on both points.

The Cuban government (i.e., Fidel Castro) was furious. It declared that Gorbachev's statement was "not preceded by consultations or any previous advice, which constitutes inappropriate behavior both from the point of view of international norms and of the agreements which exist between the two countries."

The following day, in an effort to pacify the Cubans, Soviet Foreign Minister Boris Pankin called on the United States to take "reciprocal steps," that is, withdraw from its naval base at Guantánamo Bay. Washington said it would not do so.

The diminishing desire of the Soviet Union to assist Cuba, as well as its shrinking ability to do so as the nation disintegrated into independent republics, resulted in a significant tightening of aid and trade for Cuba. Every Cuban was affected, and nowhere more than in his stomach. As supplies dwindled government controls increased. In 1991 each Cuban was given five pounds of rice per month, five eggs per week and a quarter of a chicken every nine days—when these could be found. There was one bread roll per day per person. In September of the previous year ration lists had been expanded to include fish, ham, bacon, sausage, crackers, ketchup, soy sauce and canned meat. It was all part of the "special period in time of peace," a severe austerity program which Castro announced in 1990 and which was more typical of wartime than peacetime.

Correspondent De Cordoba provided a graphic description:

In shabby San Lazaro Street, a few blocks from the magnificent steps of the University of Havana, suddenly the day of the "zero option" looms closer. No one has seen meat here in two months. So when word spreads before dawn one day that meat and fish are to be had, a line of people, mostly elderly women clutching worn cloth shopping bags, forms in front of a dimly-lighted, empty bodega *[store].*

At 9 o'clock, an elderly man in a porkpie hat and guayabera shuffles out of the shop gripping a small paper bag full of little fish. "I've been waiting since four in the morning," says Mario, a retired construction worker, who like most people here is reluctant to offer up his surname for publication. A woman looking on as he pulls a fish from the bag comments: "After you cut off the head and clean it, it won't get you very far. Soon we will be eating dirt."

Poultry had once been plentiful in Cuba. Now a citizen had to wait over a month for a one-chicken ration. There was little feed for poultry, forcing Cuba to import chickens. For this, scarce hard currency had to be spent. There was no money to buy foreign tractors, nor for replacement parts for tractors already on farms. Anyway, there was no fuel to enable them to run. So some 30,000 beef cattle were converted into oxen to replace the tractors. This, in turn, aggravated the already-existing shortage of meat.

Press reports stated that thousands of bureaucrats were shifted from office jobs in Havana to jobs on farms in a desperate attempt to increase food production. It was announced that 20,000 Havana residents would work rotating shifts in agriculture. With the number of taxis being sharply reduced, their drivers were converted into reluctant farmers.

Cuba, almost entirely dependent on petroleum for its energy needs, received about 90% of its oil from the Soviet Union. In 1990 the Soviets cut their petroleum shipments by 24%. This meant that Cuba received 70 million barrels, and in 1991 shipments appeared to have been at the same level, a level considered by analysts to be minimal for preventing economic disaster. The damage to Cuba, however, was even greater than the import figures indicated. In exchange for a metric ton of Cuban sugar the Soviets used to send about 27 barrels of oil. Now the exchange was 18 barrels for a metric ton, as the Soviets brought the trade into line with world prices (that is, ended their subsidy). Furthermore, Cuba had previously earned hard currency by re-selling some Soviet crude. Now it had none to sell.

Factories closed, including one of the island's three nickel-processing plants. Sales of refrigerators and air conditioners were halted. Housewives were urged to cook with wood or charcoal. Street lights were dimmed at night.

In Havana the number of taxis, already low for a population of 2,000.000 people, was halved to 2,000. Horse-drawn carts replaced delivery trucks. Bus and train travel was sharply reduced. Airline flights were cut. The Soviet airline, Aeroflot, shifted its Latin American base from Havana to Miami because of the fuel shortage.

Bicycles became big in Cuba. In less than a year more than 300,000 were sold in Havana. Almost all came from China; Cuba had produced few. Parts were imported and then assembled by students working for token wages. Even soldiers and policemen were mounted on two-wheelers with names like "Phoenix" and "Flying Pigeon." Brides were assured by a magazine that cycling would ease the pain of childbirth. A government official said bicycles "improve your psyche by letting people see the city in a fuller and more beautiful way, not cooped up in a car." Factories were retooled to expand domestic bike production.

Even tobacco, the island's most famous crop, was in short supply. It was a national humiliation that tobacco, too, was rationed: two cigars and four packs of cigarettes per person per month. Castro, once famed for his cigars, did not suffer: he had given up smoking years earlier. Europe was Cuba's major market for cigars, but importers said (October 1991) they were short 30 million cigars, and some complained about the quality of the cigars they did receive.

The Soviet Union was reducing the number of its technicians working in Cuba, involved in everything from agriculture to the construction of a nuclear power plant. Some two-thirds of the technicians on the island were withdrawn, leaving approximately 1,000. And the Soviets were demanding that the remaining specialists be paid in dollars.

For more than 35 years Fidel Castro Ruz, a large man with an even larger ego, had ruled the small island nation of Cuba. At the peak of his power his troops were fighting and his civilian minions were working as far east as Addis Ababa, as far west as Managua. His intelligence services operated on four continents. But Castro, as many dictators are wont to do, went too far. The United States liberated Grenada, and the Castro empire began to crumble. Then the Soviet-dominated Eastern Bloc freed itself from communism, as did the Soviet Union itself soon afterwards. Castro was deprived of his main foreign support.

The Soviet Union and Soviet empire were history.

Would Fidel Castro be far behind?

chapter seventeen

In Miami, Florida, site of the largest overseas colony of Cuban exiles, many optimistic Cubans were figuratively packing their bags for a return to their homeland. But Castro and his cohorts hung on, and three years later they were still in absolute control of the island. This chapter discusses Cuba's current domestic situation and its relations with the two countries whose foreign policies have the greatest impact on it, Russia and the United States. And tomorrow? Set forth are possible scenarios for the future.

The politically astute First Secretary of the United States embassy in Cuba during the 1956-58 civil war, John Topping, commented to this writer, "Castro is a survivor." At the time Castro was leading his band in the Sierra Maestra Mountains, successfully eluding the Cuban army's efforts to capture him.

Topping's statement was far more prophetic than he could have foreseen.

Castro came to power and soon launched his program to alter completely the society, economy, and politics of Cuba. Aided and at least partially guided by his brother Raúl and "Che" Guevara, Castro coddled communists, seized Cuban and American private properties without compensation, executed over a thousand accused "war criminals," imprisoned thousands of counterrevolutionaries, and rid his initial government of moderate figures, including President Manuel Urrutia, Prime Minister Jose Miro Cardona, and Treasury Minister Rufo Lopez Fresquet. Castro was on a fast collision course with the United States, and historically that had been a grave no-no for Cuban leaders. This writer, with great journalistic prescience, gave Castro six months in power.

As of 1 January 1994 Castro will have ruled for 35 years, more than a third of Cuba's history as an independent country. He has survived the bitter hatred of at least the over-one million Cubans who have fled their island, an unknown number of assassination plots and possibly actual assassination attempts, a political-economic quarantine by most Latin American countries for a long period of time, a conflict with the Catholic Church which included the mass deportation of non-Cuban priests, a squabble with the People's Republic of China over commerce, a long and still continuing rocky road with the Soviet Union/Russia, and the Cold War—turned hot war at the Bay of Pigs—with the United States. The growing U.S.-Cuban hostility, after depriving Cuba of the sugar-purchase subsidy which had bolstered the island's economy, then ended all commerce between the two countries. Cuba's new allies, the Soviet Union and the East European countries, were unable to replace fully the U.S. aid and trade, and the Cuban infrastructure, from houses to factories, became frozen in time, and inevitable deterioration proceeded. Moscow provided just enough help to keep Cuba going.

Then came the stunning disintegration of the Soviet empire. Fifteen nations, including three Baltic countries, broke away from the Soviet Union, which returned to its historic identity as "Russia." Five East European nations and Albania cast off Moscow's controls. East Germany was absorbed by West Germany, which again became simply "Germany." Democracy—in varying degrees—replace communist totalitarianism in 23 countries. In Russia Boris Yeltsin replaced Mikhail Gorbachev, and Yeltsin enjoyed an historic distinction: he was the first popularly elected leader the country had ever known. In the 1970s the then-U.S. Secretary of State, Henry Kissinger, had stated that "we face the stark reality that the [communist] challenge is unending." The unthinkable had occurred; the world had rapidly and dramatically been changed—for the better.

In addition to the psychological blow from the disappearance of the vast communist bloc, the effects would be felt in Cuba in the economic and military spheres. Marxism had gone down the tube of history on two continents. Russia and other former allies of Cuba, facing their own immense economic woes, could no longer provide aid at anywhere near former levels, even if they wanted to do so. They were not about to give largess to the far-off Caribbean country to which they no longer had ideological ties. Significant military support was also now out of the question; the new rulers in Moscow were much closer to Washington (from which they desperately needed assistance) than to Havana. The day would come (June 1993) when the last of the Russian troops stationed in Cuba would be withdrawn.

The economy of Cuba, never quite filling the needs of the population since Castro came to power, noticeably worsened as a result of the Soviet alliance and the resulting drastic reduction of aid/trade with Cuba. *Miami Herald* correspondent Tim Johnson reported (in July 1993) from Havana:

> *Except for a few cans of powdered milk, the neighborhood market contained nothing but bare shelves, and the university professor walked out, cranky from an empty stomach.*
>
> *Cubans can't stand much more, he said: "The law of the land these days is survival of the fittest."*
>
> *With no end in sight to Cuba's severe economic cutbacks, the mood is growing ugly. The island is steeped in hopelessness.*

"The daily situation is crushing. It is desperate," said a Roman Catholic Church official . . .

In a bizarre twist to a Marxist revolution that has prided itself on creating physicians and scientists, Cubans today covet the most menial posts that give access to food, or dollar tips with which to buy it. Cooks get to steal from kitchens. Truck drivers take a cut of what they haul. Bellhops, waiters and chauffeurs at hotels catering to foreigners earn tips in dollars.

"Whoever earns $20 a day in tips lives like a millionaire" [said one person] . . .

The *Wall Street Journal's* Jose de Cordoba returned to Havana and reported (July 1993):

Numbers tell the story. Last year, Mr. Castro said Cuba's buying power had fallen to $2.2 billion, from $8.1 billion in 1989. One Havana study of the Cuban economy said the island's gross domestic product fell 24% in 1991 and another 15% in 1992 . . .

In Havana, the electricity is usually off. Food, except at tourist hotels, is hard to find. Many of Havana's cats have been eaten. Meanwhile, prostitution, whose elimination was one of the Cuban government's proudest boasts, flourishes. A fixture of Havana life these days are the many young girls, known as jineteras, or "jockeys," who will accompany tourists for the privilege of a hotel meal.

Some 46,000 Cubans were affected by a mysterious nerve malady which could result in blindness. Malnutrition was believed to be the primary cause of the disease. The official newspaper *Granma* urged Cubans to eat seeds, leaves and flowers of vegetables in an effort to make up for the vitamins they lacked.

Compounding the economic troubles was a substantial decrease in Cuba's 1992-93 sugar crop due to a large storm and heavy rains that afflicted the island. The current crop amounted to 4.2 million metric tons; the previous year there were seven million metric tons. Because most of the sugar is exported, in barter or for hard currencies, the crop reduction damaged Cuba's trade capability. The bad weather also adversely affected the island's food and tobacco (another export crop) production.

At a U.S. Senate committee hearing on Cuba in July 1993 a senior Central Intelligence Agency official stated: "Castro's government is in acute distress. The impact of the economic crisis on the populace has been devastatiing".

A measure of the desperation of the situation was a cut in Cuba's armed forces, long the pride and a primary support of the Castro regime. Raúl Castro announced in April 1993 a "rationalization" of the military establishment. Not revealed was how large the reduction would be. Cuba was maintaining a huge force of about 6,000 Interior Ministry troops, 300,000 regular and reserve soldiers and paramilitary forces numbering some 1.3 million men and women. This was one of the largest military establishments in Latin America, ostensibly tasked with defending the country against a possible U.S. invasion but in actuality constituting a means of controlling a sizeable portion of the population through organizational discipline. And, of course, the forces are to be used to put down any major public manifestations of popular discontent. (Certainly Castro must wonder, in view of the failure of the Soviet and East European armies to suppress demonstrations against communist rule, whether the Cuban military would be any more dependable.)

There was little that was humorous in Cuba's ongoing tragedy, but the University of Miami's *North-South* magazine provided an ironic note in a brief news item on Cuba. The item: *"Private Enterprise. Shortages have reached the point where enterprising families fortunate enough to possess soap rent the bars for US$2.50 for a 'light' bath, or US$5.00 for a thorough cleaning."*

In addition to the armed forces cut, the Castro regime took other steps to try to alleviate the economic crisis. Most notable of these was granting permission to citizens to possess American dollars, ownership of which had been illegal. The move opened the way for exiles in the States and elsewhere to send dollars to needy relatives in Cuba — an influx which would surely amount to millions of dollars annually. But if this strengthened Cuba's hard-currency position, it also might have serious social ramifications. Castro was allowing creation of a two-sector society: people with dollars to spend, and people without any. It appeared that the latter group would consist mainly of pro-Castro persons none of whose relatives have fled. In effect, Castro was benefiting those persons less likely to be loyal to him.

Castro had lost the empire he was building, stretching form Angola to Nicaragua. He had lost the military assistance and subsidized trade he received from the Soviet Bloc. The economy was a shambles; Castro called off his annual July 26th anniversary celebration because of the economic crisis (and perhaps he didn't want to risk public displays of dissidence). The country's infrastructure was in terrible shape. People continued fleeing the island (1,131 on rafts during the first six months of 1993, almost double the number for the same period of the previous year).

Despite all this, there were, if not bright, at least positive spots for Castro. Efforts to open the country to foreign investments through joint ventures was showing some results. In July 1992 the National Assembly revised Cuba's constitution to permit foreign investment. Business enterprises could be established, regulated but not managed by the state. Exports and imports could be made without prior government clearance. Encouraged by the government, a French firm was planning to drill for oil, Spanish companies were helping to build new tourist hotels, a Canadian company was modernizing the island's mines.

Tourism was again — as it had been in pre-Castro days — a major asset to the economy. Nearly half a million tourists brought in $530 million in hard currency in 1992. Even more visitors were expected in 1993.

There were tentative moves toward a market economy. Correspondent Tim Golden reported in the *New York Times* (January 1993):

> *While the Government has sought repeatedly to crack down on what it considers "profiteers," it has quietly brought market forces to bear on some increasingly autonomous state*

enterprises in tourism, steel, textiles, cosmetics and furniture production. Producers who never before had to worry about sales, much less marketing, now buy their own supplies, develop their own products and invest their own earnings.

In September 1993 the government authorized private enterprise in more than 100 trades, crafts and services. These ranged from hair dressing to computer programming. Press reports said eager Cubans scrambled for copies of the newspaper to get details of the official move, and it was expected that private vendors would soon be on city streets. In the agricultural area, the government also slightly loosened its controls. It granted farm cooperatives more authority to handle their own affairs and it permitted private citizens to cultivate small parcels of government-owned land and to keep the produce.

Cuba has developed a biotechnology industry. Being produced are vaccines for treating cerebral meningitis and interferon for AIDS and cancer. Exports of the pharmaceutical brought in over $100 million in hard currency in 1991.

Cuba was no longer in hemispheric diplomatic limbo. Nations that had broken relations when Cuba was setting guerrilla fires all over Latin America in the '60s have restored diplomatic ties. Castro is routinely invited to meetings of Latin American heads of state, as one in Brazil in July 1993. Cuba remains suspended from the Organization of American States, but the General Assembly of the United Nations voted overwhelmingly in 1992 and 1993 to condemn the American embargo on trade with Cuba. (The embargo was instituted after Washington and Havana broke relations in January 1961).

Spain in May 1993 announced that it was giving Cuba a $40 million loan to alleviate the country's severe food shortage. It was the first Spanish credit to the island since 1986. Also in Europe, Cuba signed an accord with Germany under which the two countries would review 30 of the 90 treaties Cuba had with East Germany in order to ascertain which could be continued. Among the former treaties to be studied was one which provided Cuba with powdered milk, the loss of which caused an acute shortage on the island. In July 1993 the 13-nation Caribbean Community (Caricom) agreed to establish a joint commission with Cuba to seek ways to increase trade with the island and to foster cooperation in such areas of mutual interest as sugar, live-stock and fisheries.

Following the demise of the Soviet Union, assistance to Cuba virtually or completely disappeared and trade plummeted to minimal levels. Commerce between the two countries amounted to an estimated $13 billion in 1989. In 1992 it was estimated at $500 million. There existed, however, a stark reality that transcended ideology and politics: Russia has a great deal of petroleum and Cuba has a lot of sugar. And each country badly needs what the other has. In July 1993 Moscow announced that it was increasing from one million metric tons (7.3 million barrels) to 1.6 million metric tons (11.7 million barrels) the quantity of crude oil it would send to Cuba. Cuba would presumably increase the amount of sugar shipped to Russia, at least to the extent possible with a shrunken crop. Shortly after the petroleum announcement, the Russians reported that they were extending a $380 million credit to Cuba, mainly to support the sugar industry. A Russian official said this was "a normal commercial credit given to Cuba so that it can complete twelve projects that Russia has an interest in." This probably meant the funds would be used to improve the deteriorated infrastructure that produces Cuba's sugar.

Trade between Russia and Cuba was surely on a basis more equitable to Russia, unlike the former trade mixed with aid that resulted in the current Cuban debt to Russia of some $25 billion. The Russians and Cubans were also discussing setting up of joint ventures, including management of an oil refinery in Cienfuegos and a supertanker port in Matanzas. Apart from Russia, Cuba has also signed commercial agreements with at least six former Soviet republics.

Raúl Castro revealed in an interview published in a Mexican newspaper in April 1993 that he has been told in Moscow in 1980 that the Soviet Union would not defend Cuba if it were attacked by the United States. The Castros feared the newly-elected Reagan administration was planning to invade the island. Raúl quoted a Soviet official (probably Premier Leonid Brezhnev) as saying to him: "We can't fight in Cuba because you are 11,000 kilometers away form us. Are we going to go all the way just to have our faces smashed?" If the Soviet Union would not support Cuba in any showdown with the United States, the "new" Russia would certainly not do so. There was, however, the question of replacement parts. Cuba, all of whose tanks, warplanes and other material was provided by the Soviet Bloc, has been sorely in need of parts. Upon the withdrawal of the last Russian combat troops from Cuba, a Russian general referred to military cooperation between the two countries and said, "In comparison to the last three years, we are going to increase it." Probably this meant Russia would provide some parts and equipment that Cuba needed.

The other great power that has played a mighty role in Cuban affairs has been, of course, the United States. Cuba's geographical proximity has made the island of special interest to Americans since President James Madison sent an emissary in 1809 to the Spanish governor of Cuba to discuss possible annexation of the island. American trade, investments, tourist dollars and economic assistance (through sugar subsidies) helped make Cuba one of the most developed nations in Latin America by the 1950s. Castro ended all that and the Cuban economy ceased growing and began its three decades of degradation.

The issues between the United States and Cuba have spanned a wide range of problems, from immigration questions to the U.S. presence at the Guantánamo naval base, from the Bay of Pigs invasion to the attempted placement of Soviet medium-range missiles (900-1,080 miles) and intermediate-range ballistic missiles (2,100 miles). Over the years the fundamental troubles between the two nations have changed. At first there was Castro's seizure of American properties without compensation and his alliance with the communists. Castro and the communists consolidated their control over all sectors of Cuban life, all hope of a return to democracy disappeared, police repression and mobs in the streets reinforced the regime's grip on the populace.

When Castro perceived that the United States was trying to block his moves, he ordered the staff of the U.S. embassy drastically reduced. The United States responded by breaking diplomatic relations. There followed the Bay of Pigs and the missile crisis. After this, a problem which had already begun to evolve now moved to center stage. Castro's efforts to subvert other Latin American countries had reached hemispheric dimensions, with Cuba bringing in thousands of would-be guerrillas for training. The vast subversive program became the major issue between the United States and Cuba, as indeed it was between most of the Latin American countries and Cuba (only Mexico maintained diplomatic ties with Havana). Another continuing issue between the United States and Cuba was the conversion of the island into a military base for the Soviet Union. Soviet warships and aircraft visited the island, a Soviet command brigade was stationed there, all Cuban army, navy and air forces were equipped, trained and advised by Soviet military personnel.

Only during the Presidency of Jimmy Carter (1977-81) was there an easing of the tensions between Washington and Havana. A fishing accord was reached and also agreement to set up interests sections in each capital. Again, however, relations turned sour: Castro was expanding his military involvement in Angola. Now the major issues were Cuban subversion in the hemisphere, the Soviet military presence in Cuba and the Cuban military presence in Angola.

An element that Carter introduced into general U.S. foreign policy was the matter of human rights. With Cubans as a whole notably lacking in these rights, this too became a primary issue for the United States in looking at Cuba. And inextricably tied to rights was the issue of democracy: an essential human right is the right to have a say in who rules one's country. Cubans had no say.

The breakup of the Soviet empire in 1989 again altered the U.S.-Cuba picture. Moscow began pulling its military personnel out of Cuba, and the island no longer posed a threat as a Soviet base. (Castro still had the capability of making his own air strikes into other countries and of attacking shipping and transporting troops abroad.) The Russians lost interest in the Angolan adventure, and they helped broker agreements which led to the departure of all Cuban troops. Two successes, of sorts, of Castro's subversive efforts, the Sandinista victory and government in Nicaragua and the continuing leftist guerrilla campaign in El Salvador, came to an end when the Sandinistas were defeated at the polls in February 1990 and the Salvadoran rebels signed a peace agreement with the government in January 1992.

These developments removed some issues between Washington and Havana. Castro's long efforts to extend his influence and power to 2 continents had failed. The "new" Russia was no menace to the United States. Even the issue of Cuba being communist was perhaps largely academic (didn't the United States maintain trade and diplomatic relations with the major remaining communist-ruled country, the People's Republic of China?).

By the early 1990s Cuba was no longer a threat to the United States nor to Latin America. It was only a continuing threat to the well-being of its own people.

Castro's imperial designs in Africa had been terminated. His subversive schemes in Latin America, pursued since his first months in power, had had a final result of zero. His communization of Cuba, now confronted with harsh and urgent economic realities, was cracking as he permitted the hated dollar to circulate freely and the establishment of joint enterprises with foreign investment interests. And in February 1993 the first direct general elections were held under the Castro regime. The balloting was for seats in the 589-seat National Assembly (one of the candidates: Fidel Castro) and 1,190 seats in fourteen provincial assemblies. There was only one party — the Communist one —and one slate of candidates — the party's slate —but the ballot was secret and voters did have the opportunity of expressing aye or nay. According to the government 95% of the valid votes approved the official slate.

Press reports from Santiago de Cuba, where Castro cast his ballot, stated that he told reporters he would not run for reelection in five years, if the economy was improving. Castro reportedly indicated that it was time for younger persons to be taking over; his role would be to contribute ideas.

Castro willing to step aside? At minimal this was a shrewd propaganda ploy. It sent a signal to foreign countries that he did not intend to stay in power indefinitely. Some Latin American chiefs of state reportedly have quietly urged Castro to restore democratic processes. Castro's statement also might serve to deter future conspiracies within the military. Why risk a firing squad when the *jefe* might step aside in a few years?

On a broad level, what was Castro up to? Primarily, he was doing what he does best: survive. He was trying to alleviate the distress of the Cuban people, which otherwise might reach critical mass. He was also seeking to make his regime more acceptable to the United States, and specifically to the administration of Bill Clinton.

As of this writing Clinton was, in general, continuing the hard line towards Cuba of his Republican predecessors. At a White House reception for prominent Cuban-American Democrats on the anniversary of Cuba's independence, 20 May, Clinton stated, "Our administration seeks a rapid and peaceful transition to democracy so that all Cubans can enjoy the fruits of freedom as Cuban-Americans do today."

There were, however, tiny fissures in the United States' policy, or perhaps attitude, toward Cuba, much like the faults that sometimes appear in the wing of a plane. Clinton used the word "transition." The United States was not calling for the removal of the Castro brothers. Just over a fortnight earlier U.S. Deputy Secretary of State Clifton Wharton declared in regard to Cuba:

> Despite what the people of that nation have been told, the United States poses no military threat to their island..... We hope the Cuban people win their freedom through the kind of peaceful transition which has brought so many other nations into the democratic community. We oppose attempts to bring changes through violence.

In reporting Wharton's speech the *Washington Post's* veteran State Department reporter, John Goshko, noted that it "marked a big swing away from the Reagan administration's militant struggle against communism in Central America and Cuba."

Cuban officials were aware that several Clinton appointees to the State Department had been active in the Carter administration's abortive move toward detente with Cuba. Among them was the now-Secretary of State, Warren Christopher, who in 1977 declared that the United States and Cuba were moving toward normal relations. At his confirmation hearing in January 1993 Christopher said his 1977 comments were "overly hopeful, perhaps even naive." He told senators that it was "very hard to envisage normal relations with Cuba with Castro still in place." But he did not rule out future diplomatic relations with countries not "exactly like we are." All of which was a bit ambiguous, and this surely did not escape the attention of Cuban officials, either.

In fact, Cuban officials were clearly hopeful. Raúl Castro, in the aforementioned interview with a Mexican newspaper, stated, "What I can say is that there is less verbal aggression this year in the White House than in the last 12 years."

In a dispatch from Havana in the 31 July 1993 *Washington Post* correspondent Douglas Farah reported, "Relations between Cuba's Marxist government and Washington was less hostile than at any time in the past 15 years, with a sharp drop in the verbal feuding that characterized recent years." Farah mentioned steps taken by the Clinton administration, including Wharton's speech and the following:

> *Last week, the United States unveiled a proposal to normalize telecommunications. While Cubans said it was not all they hoped for, it was a much more generous offer than in the past. The move came after the Clinton administration allowed U.S. public health officials to travel to Cuba to help try to diagnose a rare eye disease afflicting tens of thousand of people here.*

A question that had not been fully addressed, at least not in many years, was now coming to the forefront: Was the American embargo punishing the Cuban people, but not Castro himself, and in fact providing him with an excuse to cover the inherent failures of communist management of a national economy? *The New York Times* reported in May 1993 that five dissident groups inside Cuba had written a joint letter to Clinton in which they insisted "that the Government of the United States must change its policy toward Cuba." The continued hostility by Washington, said the letter, resulting in "dangerous tensions and narrowing of space for diplomatic and political negotiations."

Pat Holt, former chief of staff of the U.S. Senate Foreign Relations Committee, writing in the *Christian Science Monitor* in February 1993, stated:

> *Except for Jimmy Carter, each of Clinton's predecessors.... tried to get rid of Castro in one way or another. Some ways were dangerous, some foolish; all were futile....*
>
> *The posture of the U.S. towards Cuba throughout the Castro regime has been that of an elephant terrified of a mouse. This is unbecoming in a great power.*

The *Washington Post*,in a lead editorial on 26 July 1993, the 40th anniversary of the Castro-led attack on Moncada barracks in Santiago de Cuba, called for a "New Look at the Cuba Embargo":

> .... *The embargo was meant to make it harder for the dictator to govern. But he has the police to tighten the screws, and he has used the embargo to burnish his nationalist credentials. The embargo has punished first the Cuban people.*
>
> *A further effect has been to build up tensions on the island and to heighten chances of an explosion — on throwing off large new waves of refugees. The United States should not be making such an explosion likelier or larger.... Lifting the embargo would make it clear that the misery is the responsibility of the regime.*

The counter arguments can be succinctly stated: To ease or remove the embargo would be to resolve Castro's biggest problem and relieve his regime of popular pressure brought by severe economic adversity. Rutgers University's Irving Louis Horowitz, a leading Cuba scholar, stated in a speech in Miami in March 1993:

> .... *[A] policy of accommodation to the Castro government is not consistent with United States policy toward tyrannies as such. For the United States to stand on moral principle when it come to "friendly tyrants" in the Middle East or Asia, but embrace Castro on pragmatic grounds would be a curious turn. It would grant Castro the fruits of his aggression, and provide him with diplomatic succor the United States has accorded neither to Kim Il Sung of North Korea nor Saddam Hussein of Iraq.*
>
> *Such a policy would also deny the realities of 34 years of implacable opposition by Castro to any and every democratic regime in the Western Hemisphere.... Such a policy would hold Castro blameless for adventures in Angola that did nothing to insure the democratization of that nation, and de facto legitimate his principle of military intervention by an armed praetorian force throughout the world*

What lies ahead for Castro and Cuba? In a study that this writer did for the Office of Cuban Broadcasting of the U.S. Information Agency, *The History and Role of the Armed Forces in Cuba*(1993), I set forth four possible scenarios. These were:

1. Castro continues in power indefinitely. A critical factor will be the economy. It has never been good since the revolution, and it deteriorated considerably more after the collapse of the Soviet empire. Nevertheless, the soil of Cuba is fertile and does produce food. Sugar, biotech products and tobacco (in that order) bring in foreign exchange and also can be used to barter in foreign trade. If Cuba is able increasingly to attract foreign tourists and investments, the economy is likely to improve.

2. Castro is assassinated, or is sidelined by illness. The question then would be, would Raúl his chosen successor, be able to maintain the regime in power? There would certainly be behind-the-scenes maneuvering. Even so, Raúl if he keeps the support of the army and secret police, might be able to hold on.

3. Popular discontent sparks and rapidly spreads into an uprising. Castro is fully aware of how this happened in East Europe and is determined not to let the same thing occur in Cuba. The handful of publicly-known dissidents is watched,

harassed and jailed. Reports of public disturbances have seeped out of Cuba, but so far these have been limited in scope. They are quickly squelched by the arrival of police and shouting, threatening pro-government mobs, the so-called *Brigadas de Accion Rapida* (Rapid Action Brigades). In every town, on every city block and in every factory there are members of the Committees for the Defense of the Revolution. Keeping an eye on everyone everywhere are agents of the Department of State Security. Nevertheless, spontaneous combustion is always a possibility. If a large and angry portion of the population takes to the streets, will the army fire on it? It is difficult to imagine the military, almost all of whose members come from the working classes, firing on "el pueblo"in the streets.

4. A military coup overthrows Castro. Historically, military dictatorships have not easily or frequently been destroyed by the military themselves. This writer, however, has long believed that if Castro is ever brought down by domestic action, it will be by the military. Only they have the muscle to do this. The execution of General Ochoa and his comrades was meant to deter any future thoughts of conspiracy among officers. Surely it has done so. That does not mean, however, that at some point a group of officers fed-up with the general situation and the rule of the Castros will not make another brave attempt to unseat them.

There may be another scenario, a variation of the first above. It is the one Castro himself hinted at in Santiago de Cuba. It is also the one that the Clinton administration favors. This would be a peaceful transition to democracy and a market economy. Castro and Washington probably would not, at least at present, be able to agree on the desirable time frame for and extent of changes. If a transition were proceeding, at what point would the Cuban government become acceptable to the United States? That would surely be a matter of heated debate.

As for Castro, he might leave and live abroad (unlikely, unless forced) or might take the role he evidently envisions for himself: influential senior statesman. Castro must face the inevitability of, in Horowitz's words, "the ravages of time and biological fate.... biology surely will not overlook him."

All scenarios finally point in one direction: the Castro regime, as it has existed, will come to an end. The questions are, When? and How? Castro will fall — will it be of old age?

This unique individual, who has often brought his small country into the focus of world attention, has also brought misery to millions of his countrymen and death and destruction to countries on two continents. At his trial in 1953 following the Moncada attack, Castro declared, "History will absolve me."

Wrong.

But covering this man for 35 years has been, in the vernacular, quite a trip.

editor's note

The articles in this book that comprise the first 13 chapters were written over a period of time for various publications each of which had their own editorial style. For the sake of readability, a single style has been used in this book. Similarly, to eliminate repetitious material, small excisions have been made. No substantive changes, however, have been made in the articles.

index